THE ROLLING ROAD

'The Bury Fly'—a coaching scene of 1775

THE ROLLING ROAD

*The Story of Travel on the Roads of Britain
and the Development of Public Passenger Transport*

by

L. A. G. STRONG

LONDON

HUTCHINSON

Hutchinson & Co. (Publishers) Ltd.
178-202 Great Portland Street, London, W.1

London   Melbourne   Sydney   Auckland
Bombay Johannesburg New York Toronto

First published 1956

Set in eleven point Monotype Baskerville,
one point leaded

Printed in Great Britain
by The Anchor Press, Ltd.,
Tiptree, Essex

Contents

Illustrations

7

8 ILLUSTRATIONS

With acknowledgment to the London Transport Executive

Foreword

THIS book is an attempt to describe in general outline the development of passenger road transport in Britain from the earliest times to 1948.

Most of the early history, and particularly the era of the stage-coach, has been covered in scores of books and is admirably documented. Certain of the more recent developments, particularly in the provinces, have hardly been documented at all, certainly not in any form accessible to the general reader: and some of the information in the later parts of the book is here collected for the first time.

The presentation of such a story offers a number of problems besides the major problem of compression. There are aspects of it so vivid and so wide in their appeal that only the most incurious reader could fail to take an interest in them. They illustrate human endeavour at its most versatile, and reveal in a comparatively small compass the working of powerful economic forces. Other aspects are so detailed, or so local, as to interest only people connected with the industry, or students of municipal history.

For example, the general reader will hardly thrill to the information that in nineteen-whatever-it-was Bugborough switched from trams to buses. This fact, while perhaps a source of civic pride to Bugburians, will leave the rest of England unmoved. We may derive sardonic pleasure from learning that in Rugborough a Mr. Smith started a bus service, and was crowded off the road by a wealthier rival, Mr. Jones, who in turn lost his interest to the municipality, which, scenting profit, put him out of business by the simple device of refusing him a licence: how the municipality in turn was wounded both in pride and pocket by the conduct of Slugborough, which insisted on running buses across Rugborough territory, until both went under to the enterprise of the giant undertaking at Plugborough, which was already running buses over five counties. Yet even this chronicle will only be justified in relation to the general growth of the industry; that is to say, in so far as it corresponds to what was happening elsewhere, or differs from it so markedly as to illustrate a special principle.

The subject, especially in the present century, is a very large

9

wood made up of a multitude of trees. I have tried to keep the wood in perspective, while loyalty to facts has obliged me to describe a great many individual trees. A London reader, even if he is interested in buses as such, may not particularly want to hear about buses in Manchester; but the book has to cover the whole country. On the other hand, it cannot possibly consider separately the history of every city. I have tried, with the advice of experts, to select a few cities and districts which can be regarded as typical of what was happening elsewhere.

A final word as to the standpoint from which the book is written. As far as I am concerned, politics have not entered into it at all. I have written about the industry itself, without regard to its ownership. I have written from the point of view of the ordinary, semi-reasonable, sometimes petulant user of public transport, who does not care what organisation runs his train or his bus as long as it is warm in winter and keeps to time. Obliged by my work to travel extensively both by road and rail, I am angry when, each winter, railway officials greet fog and snow with incredulous surprise, as if they had never seen either before; and when, having of their own free will proclaimed that a train should do a certain journey in a certain time, they explain reproachfully that this is impossible because of the state of the rolling stock or the track. I am indignant if bus companies appear to prefer their schedules to the comfort of the public they are supposed to serve, and when they allow women shoppers from a village five miles away, who have a two-hourly service, to be crowded off the bus by passengers going five hundred yards to a spot on the same route, which a choice of buses reaches every five minutes. I do not mind whether the service is nationalised or run by private enterprise, as long as it is run efficiently; and I know that no service can be run efficiently unless the employees are well treated and adequately paid.

In writing the book, therefore, I have had no axe to grind, unless it be that of the man or woman in the street whom all public utilities exist to serve.

One further general point I think I should make, in the interests of all concerned. The reader may think that in dealing with certain aspects of public transport which lie open to controversy the language I have used is cautious and lacks colour. If this is so, it is out of regard for the susceptibilities, sensitive on these points, of a number of excellent people who in fact need not shy from the bluntest comment. It is giving away no secret to say that the mere mention of the word monopoly sends a shudder through their frames. This, I conclude as a dispassionate observer, is not because the word is deserved, but because, used in a pejorative sense, it is the wrong word to apply. For example, the bus undertaking which serves the district where I live is sometimes spoken of by its patrons as a monopoly. True, it is the only form of transport linking certain villages and towns in the area—by services many of which incidentally are run at a loss. Yet it has built from its own funds a bus station at Guildford which seven different operators use in perfect amity, sending buses out to the tune of almost eight thousand departures per week, at the amazingly low cost of a penny-farthing per departure. A further result of this bus station is that, to the immense relief and comfort of police and public, no departures are made from the public street.

We have to remember, however, that buses are not the worst source of traffic congestion, even in market towns; and that any extra expenditure they may be obliged to incur may, in the long run, have to be passed on to the customers.

Furthermore, the company may not increase its fares without seeking a licence to do so, and must submit to a public court of enquiry, at which all objections can be aired and accounts are produced in support of the company's application.

I think that it will be apparent to any unbiassed reader of the chapters dealing with the development of the present systems of passenger road transport that the amalgamations to which exception is sometimes taken have almost always been made of sheer necessity, in the interest of economy and of more efficient running, and have ultimately been of benefit to the travelling public.

Needless to say, I could not have written this book without a great deal of help. In alphabetical order, my thanks are due to Mr. J. Amos, Chairman of the Scottish Omnibus Group; Mr. P. B. Dingle, the Town Clerk of Manchester; Mr. P. N. Gray, General Manager of the Aldershot & District Traction Co. Ltd.; Mr. J. Green, Traffic Manager of the North Western Road Car Co. Ltd.; Mr. R. E. Hyslop, General Secretary of the Municipal Passenger Transport Association; Mr. S. Kennedy, Chairman of the Tilling Group; Mr. C. F. Klapper, Editor of *Modern Transport*, who provided useful and original papers, most kindly read the script, and made many valuable corrections; Mr. Charles E. Lee; Mr. A. F. Neal, General Manager of Manchester Corporation Transport Department; Mr. H. E. Osborn, Chief of Accounts, Statistics and Funds with the British Transport Commission; Mr. Eden Phillpotts, who most kindly sent a document on early transport in Devon; Mr. T. G. Pruett of the Thames Valley Traction Co. Ltd.; Mr. R. M. Robbins, Secretary of the London Transport Executive; Mr. F. W. Robinson, Manager of London Coastal Coaches Ltd.; Mr. F. J. Speight, Deputy Chairman of the Passenger Vehicle Operators' Association; and the British Electric Traction Company Limited, but for whose encouragement and assistance this book would not have been possible. Their officers whom I have approached, particularly Mr. Raymond Birch and Sir Robert Gould, have given most kindly help and guidance throughout the project. Last, my greatest debt of all, to Mr. Michael Figgis, for invaluable help in research.

Where authorities differ, as they sometimes do, I have accepted the verdict of Mr. Klapper: but much of the comment is my unregenerate own. To minimise controversy, it seemed best to stop the story in the year when the policy of nationalisation was first tried. Otherwise, any comment was bound to offend somebody, and so make a scurvy return for help and co-operation generously given.

L. A. G. S.

CHAPTER I

The Green Ways

'The first step in civilisation is to make roads, the second to make more roads, and the third to make more roads still.'
Old saying quoted by W. H. K. WRIGHT
in *Locomotion, Past and Present.*

THE urge to find and establish the easiest way between two places is older than man. Hares and rabbits make their slender tracks in the grass and are snared because they keep to them. Sheep tread out their paths upon the mountains and the moors. Wild beasts of many kinds wear tracks to the drinking pool which even the lush growth of the jungle cannot cover. It has remained for man to transform an instinct, as in so many other fields, and travel not only of necessity but for his pleasure.

Anyone who cares to see the various stages illustrated in a microcosm may do so by exploring a rough ellipse drawn on the map of Devon, touching the Tamar on one side and Haytor on the other. On the moors he will find the myriad tracks of the rabbits, the narrow paths of the sheep, and, on the sheer sides of coombe and gulley, the paths of the moor ponies, whose hooves are sharp enough to wear through the grass and bare the soil below. On the high ridges northward wind the trackways trodden by Bronze Age man; and beside many of the stone rows and circles traces can still be seen where the granite fangs were dragged over peat and heather to be set up, no one can yet say how.

Next, he will find tracks that date from many centuries later, when paths marked parish boundaries, or the lands belonging to monasteries; for example, the path by the reeve wall that runs southward from Hessary, near Princetown, past a granite cross on which the words BOC LOND are deeply carved, claiming the land west of it for Buckland Abbey. Then, as at Eylesbarrow, he can trace the trackways of the mediaeval tin mines.

Hundreds of packhorse lanes, so narrow that even a small car will brush the hedges, thread the slopes and valleys. Some of these, till fifty years ago, were the only ways of reaching isolated villages. And, newest of all, wide shiny roads now span the distances, and along them coachloads of holiday-makers are smoothly borne to exclaim at the far-flung views and litter the valleys.

In the pages that follow we are concerned with man's travels on the roads he has built in Britain; but we must not forget the basic instinct which those roads and travels represent, or the link between the first rough faintly trodden path on plain or hillside and the parallel traffic ways of the Great North or the Great West Road.

II

We may not know what led the first men, at the end of the glacial epoch, to follow flowers and birds and animals northwards into Britain; but we can be sure of one thing. They were not travelling for pleasure. We have no evidence to show how these skin-clad hunters of the mammoth, the horse, and the reindeer made their journeys across the great land-bridge which then linked the cliffs of Calais and Dover, and allowed the Thames to join the Rhine in a marshy plain that is now the bed of the North Sea. The facts are sunk, like that plain, in the depths of pre-history. Intent upon their livelihood, these travellers would not have worried, even if they could have known, about the fact that erosion and subsidence were eventually to subdivide their hunting-ground into the collection of islands we now call Britain, smash the land-bridge behind them, and cut off their retreat. We know, however, that, once on what is now British soil, they had to keep to the high ground to avoid the marshy valleys and the vast forests full of wolves, bears, wild sheep, and cattle. In their need to save themselves these men, thousands of years before the Christian era, trod out routes that are still in use today.

As these hunters gathered themselves into tribes for their better protection, and became more proficient at cooking and at polishing their flint tools and weapons, what grew into the Old Stone Age faded imperceptibly into the New. The historian's dividing line, drawn at about 2400 B.C., is intended only to indicate the beginnings of a period in which these later Neolithic men started to live in pit-dwellings in the chalky uplands where flints abounded, in stone-built bee-hive huts or in wattle-and-daub villages beside the shores of lakes. For in this New Stone Age navigation and agriculture had begun, sheep and cattle had been tamed, corn was ground and made into a sort of bread, simple woollen garments were woven, and a system of trackways was established which allowed the communities

to barter their goods with one another and to reach the earliest
centres of industry. These centres grew around the flint mines at such
places as Cissbury in Sussex, where shafts were sunk as deep as forty
feet into the ground and the precious material was unearthed with
implements of horn and bone. Thus the earliest traders, possibly
with the help of pack-horses, marked out the beginnings of such roads
as the Salt Ways, Tin Ways, and Rush Ways that are shown on
modern Ordnance maps.

By the beginning of this New Stone Age, when the forests and
marshes in the low-lying parts of the island were still impassable,
the Ridgeways, or Greenways, as they are sometimes called, had
grown into a systematic arrangement of tracks, centred on Salisbury
Plain, which followed the line of the chalk downs into the southern
parts of the country, but made little impression on the mountainous
regions of Wales and the high plateaux to the north.

The Harrow Way extended from Dover to Cornwall, over some
of the earliest bridges, of which examples still stand in our Devon
microcosm, on Dartmoor; granite slabs supported by piers of small
stones. The Ridgeway proper, and the Icknield Way, as its extension
was later called, followed the Wiltshire and Berkshire downs to the
Chilterns and thence into Norfolk. What later became the Fosse
Way ran over the Dorset downs and, passing through the town we
now call Salisbury, crossed the Cotswolds in the direction of Lincoln
and the Humber.

Marking the course of these Greenways are round barrows or
tumuli. Some of them have been identified as burial grounds. All, we
can see from their regular disposal at roughly ten-mile intervals,
were designed to give protection for men and cattle at night. Distinct
from these, but often close to the early routes, are the long banks of
earth, also called barrows, many of which have been found to contain
burial chambers dating from the New Stone Age. Scholars have been
impressed by the alignment of some of these barrows, which suggest
that the Greenways for which they were landmarks were as straight
as the Roman roads that were later laid over them.

Though we may never know what rituals were practised in the
stone circles at Avebury and Stonehenge, there is no doubt that they
stood at the hub of the Greenways, in what was then the most densely
populated part of the country, and, maybe, the seat of its government.
These Neolithic sun-worshippers were not as ignorant as early
students supposed. Archaeologists have already discovered their feats
as engineers in bringing these stones astonishing distances by means
of rafts and primitive sledges; but there are huge gaps in our

knowledge. We can guess that great crowds travelled the Greenways to worship at these places, but can only imagine how they came. Perhaps the more important among them rode on horses or in some sort of chariot comparable to those used in Egypt, or the vehicles described in the Bible. Perhaps the dusty chalk tracks, lined with huge stones as they approached the temples, were only fit for men on foot. The methods by which these monoliths were hauled and erected suggest that some types of wheeled vehicles may have been in use. We do not know.

About 2000 B.C., the date given by scholars to the Bronze Age in Britain, metals were plentiful and there was abundant wood to smelt them. Copper was probably discovered first, but, since its cutting edge is little better than that of flint, the new age had to wait until tin—probably from the mines of Cornwall—was smelted with the copper and a fresh, revolutionary metal came into being.

This discovery could have brought about a great advance in the design of sledges and other early vehicles. Here again we have no certain knowledge. We do know, however, that as this new Bronze Age was developing, early townships appeared in such places as London, Winchester, Cirencester, and Canterbury, and that the Greenways, linking up these early centres of civilisation, led to the ports and thence to the great trade routes of Europe and Asia. The era of trade had begun, and the roads had to carry the regular traffic it entailed. The first pedlars, making their way from one cluster of square, windowless houses to another, began to hawk their wares among the women, who already wore linen, wool, and soft leather, and who adorned themselves with amber and jet, and, presently, with glass and silks brought in by Phœnician traders.

More and more evidence is forthcoming to show that Britain had a complex system of roads before the coming of the Romans. The road that ran from the Kentish ports through London and on towards Chester and the gold mines of Ireland may well have been as busy as the routes on which the Romans later laid the Fosse Way, the Icknield Way, and Ermine Street. On all of them we can legitimately picture groups of traders armed against marauding tribesmen, who would not need long to realise the opportunities for ambush given them by the roads. To the south, near the modern Dorchester, where the Fosse Way crosses the coastal track that runs east from the mines of Cornwall, a solid piece of evidence substantiates our imaginings. There stands the huge earth mound of Maiden Castle, the finest surviving example of the defended stronghold made by the trading communities of this period. Its massive ramparts are

The first London omnibus designed and operated by Shillibeer in 1829, it was heralded as 'a new carriage in the Parisian mode'

Below : Tottenham Court Road Turnpike, as seen by Rowlandson—*c.* 1800

Below : 'The Comet', a famous coach plying between London and Brighton—*c.* 1800

Sir Goldsworthy Gurney's two-ton steam coach of 1829, designed to carry 18 passengers

'The Enterprise', a steam omnibus built by Walter Hancock in 1833

two miles in circumference; and in the round barrows nearby have been found traces of the chariots which these people buried beside their warriors; contrivances which gave way to chariots even better than those of the Romans in the years to come.

From 800 B.C. and for about four centuries, successive waves of Celtic invaders poured into the country. By about 400 B.C. the Bronze Age had given way to the Iron, and there is clear evidence of the development in transport brought about by the Celts. When the Romans came, they found the tracks in the south of the island dusty from the packhorses of the traders. Coinage was in common use, houses had improved, and the razors, the mirrors and leather goods belonging to this period suggest that the Celts were a more sophisticated and artistic people than the Iberians whom they attacked.

The Celtic chiefs rode in simple horse-drawn chariots, oxen drew their ploughs, and three other types of vehicle with which they were familiar were later taken over by the Romans. But for the most part the tribes, whether conquering or conquered, were still at war with one another in 54 B.C., when the first Roman legions marched along the Greenways; and, when they moved at all, most of them moved on foot.

B

CHAPTER II

The Romans

'The Roman Road runs straight and bare
As the pale parting-line in hair
Across the heath. And thoughtful men
Contrast its days of Now and Then,
And delve, and measure, and compare;
Visioning on the vacant air
Helmed legionaries, who proudly rear
The Eagle, as they pass again.'

THOMAS HARDY: *The Roman Road.*

WHEN, early in the fifth century, the last of the legions withdrew
from Britain, the Romans left behind them one great legacy—
the roads. These roads literally laid down the lines along which the
country was to develop. For one thing, they decided the importance
of the new city sites, that of London among them. Although the
roads themselves slowly fell into decay, nothing to equal them was
built for fourteen hundred years; they are the basis on which were
founded our trunk roads of today.

We have to remember, however, that the lines of communication
which the Romans made in Britain add up to only a small part of
their total achievement as road-makers. Beyond Britain, their roads
stretched from the golden milestone set up in Rome by Augustus to
the chief cities in the Empire. They reached the Rhine and the
Danube in the north, Babylon and Nineveh in the east. They
spanned the coastal deserts of North Africa, and, overcoming the
Pyrenees, swooped into Spain. Even in Britain, where the roadmakers experienced peculiar difficulties, their success was such that
travel reached standards it did not touch again until what is, in our
history, no more than the day before yesterday.

The invasion of Britain, planned and reconnoitred by Julius
Caesar in 55 and 54 B.C., was not carried out until nearly a century
later. Then, in A.D. 43, four legions under the command of the
Emperor Claudius, marching with their auxiliaries by way of
Canterbury, Rochester, and the first miles of what was later to be
Ermine Street, struck hard at London.

The campaign developed fast in the south. To serve their needs,

18

the invaders took over the ancient trackways, improved them, and, wherever necessary, laid down new roads.

All these operations were governed by the geography of the country, which determined the strategy and procedure of the whole occupation. Thus, although the conquest of the southern plains and downlands took approximately four years, the tribes in the mountainous regions northward were unsubdued after forty. Caesar had conquered Gaul with four legions and auxiliaries in about eight years. Because of the nature of the country, the whole of Britain took roughly the same number of troops and all but ten times as long.

II

One great road, the Fosse Way, ran from Exeter to Lincoln, and divided the country into two main areas. To the south of it, where an orderly government was soon set up, securing what by the standards of the time were peaceful economic conditions, the roads were numerous and closely linked, like the Greenways before them. To the north and west of the Fosse Way, where the land was constantly disturbed by rebellion and where permanent garrisons had to be maintained, the vital task of road-making was interrupted by raids and by the need to keep the maximum number of troops available at the frontiers. And there were natural obstacles: the Pennines limited the number of new roads that could be made in this difficult terrain.

Thus, while the south-eastern part of the country was amply served by the better known Roman roads, radiating from the site of the present London Bridge, in the north there were only three. Two, on the east, ran from Lincoln towards Hadrian's Wall and thence into Scotland; the third ran west of the Pennines. So, apart from the northern garrison towns of York, Chester, and Caerleon-on-Usk, the famous Roman cities are all in the south: Bath, Dorchester, Canterbury, Exeter, Gloucester, Silchester, Winchester, St. Albans. Here the Romans had time to import and to indulge a manner of life that was not dictated by the island but reflected the luxury of cities in the southern shores of the Empire. These cities were laid out in rectangular design, surrounded by walls with massive, arched gateways; and their numerous public rooms, baths, and villas were adorned with frescoes and mosaics. Very different, though characteristically elaborate, were the stations of the fighting legionaries in the north.

The straightness of the Roman roads is proverbial. They were so built, not simply because they had to be defended, or because, as ingenious scholars have suggested, Roman vehicles lacked articulation and were difficult to turn. The builders worked upon a sound Euclidian principle. Their roads were straight because the primary purpose was to carry troops and baggage wagons from the ports to the inland garrisons in the shortest possible time.

Moreover, the proverb, like most proverbs, is not literally true. A glance at an ordnance map will show that most of the Roman roads which still survive do not in fact run straight throughout their course. The gradual curve of Watling Street, between London and Wroxeter, is composed of nine distinct straight links between the military stations on the route. The road-builders did not make a fetish of their principles. They were always ready to alter their course if serious obstacles stood in the way. Wherever possible they avoided marshes and valleys, and in southern downland often changed the direction of a road in order to take advantage of an easy gradient. They also made their river crossings at the highest point to which cargoes could be brought, so that waterways supplemented road transport. Gloucester on the Severn and Arundel on the Arun are examples of the many towns which sprang up as a result of the trade brought by a bridge. (A bridge can take away trade, too; witness the opposition in Dartmouth today to the proposal to build a bridge which would carry traffic above the shops now reached by a ferry.)

III

The average Roman road in Britain was between sixteen and twenty-four feet wide. This was adequate for the transport of the time, and allowed troops to march six abreast. Each legion was responsible for making its own roads and carried technical experts for that purpose. The methods of paying for upkeep foreshadowed systems used in later centuries, and varied with the type of road. Imperial or State roads were maintained by the government, lesser roads by Roman officials put in charge of the rural authorities, and a considerable number by voluntary contributions. The streets running through the gates of cities to the main points of the compass were maintained by the householders who owned frontages along them.

Pioneer or campaigning roads, which had to be improvised rapidly, were usually made with one or two layers of logs laid close together. Such roads often peter out at the foot of hills, but they were strong enough to carry cavalry and baggage wagons over marshy ground or other difficult country. The *viae publicae*, however, were more elaborately made.

First the width of the road was marked out by two furrows and the loose soil excavated to a solid foundation—which might, in some instances, be the sub-soil of a Greenway. On this the road was built up, usually in four layers. The solid foundation of earth tightly rammed down was built up into an embankment called the *agger*. The next layer, the *statumen*, consisted of small, squared stones, sometimes left dry, sometimes set with mortar. This supported the *rudus*, a mass of small stones or heavy ballast mixed with lime.

Next came a bed formed of a mixture of lime, chalk, broken tiles, or earth, well beaten together. Variants were possible here, according to the nature of the country and the materials readiest to hand. Sometimes the roadmakers used gravel, sometimes sand and lime mixed with clay. This bed was termed the *nucleus*, and it carried the top surface of the road. For highways carrying heavy traffic, this consisted of irregular flagstones, or, often, a firm layer of gravel and lime. The finished road formed a causeway six to seven feet high which drained into marginal ditches and gave a commanding view of the countryside. This is the type of causeway construction that gave rise to the terms 'Highway' or 'High-road'.

Bridges were constructed with similar thoroughness. The legions were skilled at making improvised river crossings, carrying with them planks and small boats which they put down somewhat after the manner of a modern Bailey bridge: but their more permanent constructions were made of timber resting on stone pillars, and carried a central road for horse traffic and raised side-walks. These bridges had most of them disintegrated by the time of the Norman Conquest, though the foundations of a few stone arched bridges, in which cement was used, still survive.

IV

During the four years needed for the conquest of the south, the fatigue work of road-making must have advanced at remarkable speed, for the legions depended on their lines of communication, and, by A.D. 47, the boundaries of Roman Britain are given by Tacitus as the Severn and the Trent. There was, however, continual trouble with the rebellious tribes in the north and on the boundaries of

Wales; and in A.D. 61 the Iceni of what is now Norfolk and Suffolk (after whom, according to some authorities, the Icknield Way was named) expressed their resentment of the severity of Roman rule in the most celebrated of the rebellions.

Perhaps, as Professor G. M. Trevelyan has suggested, this tribe had been treated much as Englishmen treated Bengal after Plassey, before Clive and Hastings had undertaken the organisation of the British raj. In any event, although the King of the Iceni had attempted to placate the Romans by naming the Emperor Nero as one of his heirs, his family was so badly treated after his death that his Queen, Boadicea or Boudicca, set forth in her scythe-wheeled chariot and led her tribesmen in revolt. Marching on Verulamium (St. Albans) and London while the nearest legions were committed on the Welsh border, the tribesmen killed thousands of Romans and Roman-minded Britons, and laid waste the towns. But the odds were far too heavy, and the returning legions massacred the rebels.

This was the only large-scale revolt during the early part of the conquest. By the time Agricola arrived as governor in A.D. 78, these devastated towns had been restored and, as far as the Romans were concerned, the only remaining problem was the North-West frontier.

The Welsh tribes had been subdued, after thirty-five years, by a system of roads and forts: a task which took the castle-building Normans several centuries. But the Northern tribes, the Picts, the Brigantes, and the Caledonians, who were of partly Celtic origin, were not completely checked until, in A.D. 210, the Emperor Severus renovated the wall which Hadrian had built from Solway to Tyne in A.D. 123.

On this astonishing structure were sited fifteen permanent stations, each with massive gates, barracks, granaries, and baths; and the whole length of it was permanently patrolled by mail-clad infantry. Although in the intervening centuries, Hadrian's Wall has been constantly plundered in order to build dykes, farms, and roads, it still runs shoulder high across the seventy-three miles of moor that separate Solway from Tyne, and remains the most impressive Roman memorial in the country.

If this outpost of the Northern Empire and the other garrisons were to be administered efficiently, postal services and vast quantities of transport were essential. Thus, throughout the state roads, a day's journey apart, Augustus had set up government posting stations, where light carriages, post horses, and postillions were kept for the conveyance of government dispatches and for the use of travellers on state business, who were required to carry *diplomata*, or passports.

At the roadside stood inns where travellers could get food and lodging, though many seem to have preferred to make their own encampments, leaving the inns for those of lower rank. The vehicles which were used bring us to the heart of our subject, and so must be considered in some detail.

V

Of the different types of vehicle used in Roman Britain, some were taken over from the Celts and Britons. Cicero had written to a friend, "I hear that in Britain are most excellent chariots; bring me one of them for a pattern." The *Cisium* and *Essedum* were light, two-wheeled carriages, designed to carry two passengers, and were used at the posting stations. The chief difference between them was that the *Essedum* was drawn by two horses instead of one. It developed undoubtedly from the heavier type of British war-chariot, which had had a stout pole between the horses, so that the warriors could run forward to throw their missiles. The charioteers who drove these vehicles seem originally to have ranked high in the British tribal armies. When captured, they were sometimes exhibited at the gladiatorial shows in Rome, where their skill as drivers was much admired. Perhaps the Roman drivers of the *Essedum* tried to imitate them; at any rate, severe penalties against careless driving were imposed in Roman Britain.

It is interesting to note that this type of vehicle, as used at the posting stations, may have stretched its influence across the centuries and determined the gauge of the modern railway track, for when these were first laid down the lines were placed the same distance apart as the wheels of the stage-coach; and the track of the coach has been found to be the same as that of the light Roman gig, or *Cisium*.

The *Covinus* was another popular type of carriage, designed for light travel and built to hold only the driver. It was developed from the celebrated British war-chariot with scythe blades attached to the spokes of its wheels, the pattern in which Boadicea is said to have driven.

The *Carpenta*, a four-wheeled baggage wagon which was sometimes covered in, was taken in the same way and used for general purposes. Cæsar is said to have found such vehicles among the Gauls, who used them for a circular defence around their encampments. Richly ornamented, seating two or three besides the driver and drawn by a pair of mules, horses, or oxen, the *Carpenta* was the type of vehicle used on ceremonial occasions: for example, women of the imperial family were allowed to attend festival processions in them. Later, they were used as private carriages. Not unlike them in design was the *Rheda*, but larger. This the Romans are thought to have found in Britain on their arrival; it was adapted to carry several people and their baggage.

A number of vehicles, in common use throughout the Empire, were brought to Britain by the Romans, and some of them were probably adopted by Romanised Britons. The *Carucca*, a four-wheeled carriage plated with bronze, silver, and sometimes even with gold, and drawn by horses with gold embossed harness, was the type of carriage used by Romans and nobility. The *Pilentum*, another richly ornamented four-wheeled vehicle, was usually furnished with cushions. It had open sides, so that the Roman matrons and maids, when they used it for driving to sacred processions and the games, could readily see and be seen. At the games, in the arena of many amphitheatres in the cities of Roman Britain, they could watch races between skilled drivers of the *Currus*—the fastest vehicle of them all.

The *Currus* had two wheels, with a single pole and a yoke attached to the horses' necks, and was closed in front only. It was raced with two, three, or four horses. If four were used, the second pair was attached by traces. The charioteer and his companion had to stand. In these and similar, larger chariots, magnificently decorated, victorious generals made their triumphal entries into Rome.

Compared to the *Currus* and the occasions which it calls to one's mind, the *Plaustrum*, a flat dray with four wheels, built wide so as to do as little damage as possible to the roads, sounds cumbersome and dull. Yet the *Plaustrum* was the regulation carriage of the times. In these vehicles, heavy and hard to turn as they were, goods and undistinguished travellers were slowly drawn by oxen over the roads of Britain; and the descendants of the *Plaustrum* are in service to this day.

Surprising as it may seem, these means of transport made travel easier in Roman Britain than did the transport at the close of the seventeenth century. Then—thirteen hundred years later—a cross-country journey could be a hazardous undertaking. The roads were incomparably worse, and there were then no imperial troops to guard them and keep robbers under control. But travel under Roman rule was comparatively safe. Throughout the Empire, and to a slightly smaller degree in Britain, we have reason to believe that the *viae publicae* were in constant use. Along them went the marching legions, and the government officials driving in their *Cisia* and averaging a good five miles an hour; the merchants with their pack-horses, their wagons, and, sometimes, their slaves. Now and then the countryman would see a Governor driving in state to inspect some outlying part of his domain, or a group of athletes, pedlars, and musicians travelling to one of the fairs or festivals. Here and there would be wealthy citizens riding to their country villas in *Carucae* or *Rhedae*, followed by their attendants; but most of the daily traffic was made up of the slow-moving supply vehicles on their way to the garrison towns.

In the cities, where traffic was often restricted by law, wealthy nobles might be seen reclining in the simpler kind of conveyance so popular in the south, roofed litters of various designs, carried by long poles that rested on the shoulders of slaves. Rome was the power in the land: the Roman enjoyed comfort, and he liked travelling too. The essence of this characteristic is caught in the word *viaticum*, meaning everything that a person would require for a journey.

Presently, however, the *pax romana* was broken. Civil war broke out in the Empire. The garrisons had to be reduced, and the northern tribes, seizing their advantage, crossed the wall. Fresh invaders poured in to sack the towns and villas in the south. The fall of Rome was coming, but throughout the Empire great things had been achieved. The Romans, withdrawing, left the foundation of British travel behind them. They left new cities, new lines of communication, and a standard of efficiency in transport and methods of travelling which, we must emphasise once again, were not to be equalled for fourteen perilous centuries.

CHAPTER III

The Saxon Roads

'London Bridge is broken down—
Gold is won, and bright renown.
Shields resounding,
War-horns sounding,
Hildur shouting in the din!
Arrows singing,
Mail-coats ringing—
Odin makes our Olaf win!'
SNORRE STURLASON: *Saga of King Olaf the Saint.*

OVER many aspects of the Dark Ages historians are still in dispute, but they agree on the one point that concerns us here— that there is a sudden break in the story of travel. Travel, as the Romans understood it, was soon not even a memory.

During the five centuries that separate the break-up of Roman Britain from the time when the country was united under one king, these noble roads, receiving no care or attention, slowly decayed. In some places they disappeared altogether. The bridges crumbled, and such peaceful travellers as there were had to make use of the paved fords, or, in times of flood, to stay at home. But the Romans had built on strong foundations. Enough remained of their great roads to help speed the Saxon, Danish, and Norman conquests; yet for several centuries they traversed a land that had relapsed into barbarism. The first invaders who trod them and made new names for the chief of them—Watling, Ermine, and Fosse—knew nothing of Caesar, their creditor, but gave thanks to Woden and Thor. To regain something of their former glory, the roads had to wait until after the Norman conquest, when a colourful array of horse and foot travellers set out, in greater numbers than ever before, to use them for peaceful purposes.

Before we can take a reasonable view of travellers, and understand what they came to be doing in England at that time, we must consider briefly the boisterous centuries in which the racial basis of the country was established.

II

The Roman attempt to civilise Britain failed for several reasons, of which the chief was that there were too few Romans. When the legions who defended them had been withdrawn, the untrained people were quite unable to deal with the rush of invaders. The Picts were pouring over the wall in the north, other enemies were attacking the south and east coasts, and the situation soon became desperate. Appeal after appeal was sent, but the Roman commander in Gaul had no troops to spare for a lost cause, and by the middle of the fifth century the Romanised Britons were left to shift for themselves.

The news spread fast. The Teutonic tribes from the mouths of the Elbe and the Rhine increased their raids, and presently shipped their families into these new defenceless lands, so rich in cornfields and well-watered pasture. The Anglo-Saxons had come to stay.

The Jutes occupied the whole of Kent. The Saxons took parts of Hampshire and Sussex and extended their holdings eastwards to Essex, where their boundary met that of the Angles, who had occupied the eastern part of the country as far north as the Humber. The invaders pushed inland, using the rivers, and, according to some authorities, the Saxons journeyed from their eastern landing-places towards Wessex by such a route as the Icknield Way.

The Britons could make no reply. In spite of the ancient earthworks and the new cities, walled in stone, which the Romans had left them, they withdrew helplessly before their hated foes towards the fastnesses of Wales and Cornwall.

In 577, after the battle of Deorham, the Saxons captured the entire Severn valley, which gave them command of such centres as Gloucester, Cirencester, and Bath, and so cut off the Britons in Devon and Cornwall from those in Wales. In 613 the King of Northumbria captured the valley of the Dee. Thus, by the close of the seventh century, the Britons were penned into the western mountains.

It is uncertain whether the final work of destruction was carried out by a single army or by a series of marauding bands which devastated the greater part of the buildings the Romans had made. In any event, when the initial fighting was over, these Teutonic invaders, being farmers as well as pirates, settled down to build their wooden 'townships' in clearings which they made in the forests. For the most part they avoided the cities which they had wrecked, and left the ruined villas among their thickets as places for birds to nest in. Furthermore, because of the danger of plundering bands from neighbouring areas, they kept well away from the roads.

The dwellings and farmsteads which they set up became the sites of hundreds of villages of today, and explain why these so often lie in out-of-the-way places and, until the coming of modern transport, were so hard to get at. A comment on the wisdom of avoiding the main thoroughfares is suggested by the laws of Kent and Wessex which read:

> If a man from afar or a foreigner fares through a wood off the highway and neither hollas nor blows a horn, he shall be counted a thief and may be slain or put to ransom.

By the time the worst of the bloodshed and savagery was over, the western part of the country was in the hands of the vanquished Britons, and a group of separate Anglo-Saxon kingdoms had come into being. The shifting frontiers and fortunes of these kingdoms of the Heptarchy make the central theme of the period which precedes the coming of the Danes. First Kent claimed supremacy over Northumbria, over the central kingdom of Mercia, over the southern kingdoms of Wessex and Sussex, and the eastern kingdoms of Essex and East Anglia. Then Northumbria took control: then Mercia: until finally Egbert, King of Wessex, brought the country under some semblance of unity, just before the terrifying Scandinavian sailors set out in their long-boats to reconnoitre its eastern shores.

III

A journey through Anglo-Saxon England must have been a harassing experience. A traveller who wandered down an earth track from one of the Roman highways would soon find a forest clearing with a village, roughly circular in form, enclosed in most cases by a wooden palisade. Many a village of today, with a place-name ending in the Saxon syllables 'ing', or 'ham', or 'tun', derives from such beginnings, and, for some, the parish boundary is at some point defined by a Roman road.

The Saxon tribesmen lived in simple log huts, supported at the ends by split tree-trunks to form the gavel or gable, and fitted with stalls for horses and cattle, and lofts where servants slept and corn was stored. At one end of the main floor was a fire on an open hearthstone, the smoke from which had to find its way out through a hole in the roof. Near by, in a room boarded off from the rest, slept the family of the Saxon farmer, whose animals and possessions were thus closely guarded at night.

The log hall of the lord or thane, around which the huts of the community were gathered, was appropriately larger. It had often some attempt at decoration, being painted, and adorned inside with

burnished armour hanging on the walls. Here the people gathered
to receive rough justice at the hands of their lord and to hear orders
for their protection. Here they paid tribute according to the land
they held, and celebrated with the mead cup the harvest that had
been gathered for their master from the strips of land surrounding
the village. For while the lord was obliged to lead his retainers into
the local wars against the neighbouring kingdom, the greater part of
such a community must have been kept busy in the forest with the
wolves, and the foxes that attacked their livestock, the deer and the
rabbits that raided their crops, with the making of new tracks, and
with the work of their eight-ox ploughs in the virgin fields.

And when some special occasion brought them together on what
was the forerunner of the village green, the scene must have been full
of colour. All wore gaily coloured mantles, fastened at the shoulder.
The legs of the men were elaborately protected by leather or cloth
cross-gartering and their hair hung to their shoulders. The women,
on the other hand, were never to be seen without their headdresses of
twisted cloth, secured by a circlet, and there is plenty of evidence
that their gowns and jewellery were rich and gay.

IV

These Saxon farmers were not travellers in any modern sense of
the word. Except in times of war, there was little upon the roads but
local traffic and the wagons and pack-horses of merchants bound for
the market town. From the seventh century onwards, however, a new
class of traveller began to make regular use of the roads. After St.
Augustine's Church had been founded at Canterbury, the monks
moved northwards towards the followers of St. Columba, preservers
of the Celtic form of Christianity which had lived on in Ireland,
Scotland, and Wales. Along roads which the legions had trod came
this second Roman conquest, its celebrants singing canticles, preach-
ing, administering to the sick, and building wooden churches with
their own hands. Here and there they founded schools, as in Jarrow,
where the monk Bede, the first and one of the greatest of English
historians, was born in the year 672.

The advance of Christianity into this almost pagan country was
attended with considerable success, and, among other changes, gave
a new interest for men's minds. While the balance of power in the
Heptarchy swung from one kingdom to another, the British or Celtic
church was soon arguing with the Roman about the date of Easter

and various points of ritual: issues which, after the Synod of Whitby
convened by Oswy, King of Northumbria, were decided in favour of
Rome.

But life was by no means settled. Danes and Norwegians were
setting out in their long black ships in search of lands to plunder.
It is not difficult to understand the terror which must have been
struck into the heart of the Saxon farmers when they saw the dipping
oars, the dragon-headed prows, and the overlapping shields of these
Viking pirates who, each spring, crept up the North Sea on their
way to raid the coasts of Ireland and Scotland. Soon, terrifyingly
soon, these Northmen, with their ring shirts, their yellow hair, and
their incredible courage, were to be anchoring their boats in the
estuaries of East Anglia, stealing horses to carry them on their quick,
savage raids, and plundering England itself.

In the eighth century, finding a weakened Northumbria easy
prey, they raided towns and monasteries from Edinburgh to the
Humber. In the ninth century, as soon as King Egbert of Wessex
had finished his successful battles against the other kingdoms of the
Heptarchy, and had brought some semblance of unity into the
country, the dare-devil raids were over and worse was to come. The
Danes, intent now upon the actual settlement of the country, began
the full terror of their invasions. Winters of preparation had been
spent in the ship-building towns along the fjords, and instead of the
small flotillas that had come raiding, the fleets of the Danes had
grown to two and three hundred ships, each ship holding about a
hundred men.

v

It was left to Alfred the Great to save Wessex and, some maintain, our English civilisation. Not only did he organise an army of
mounted thanes and their vassals, but he equipped a navy with
longer and swifter ships than those of the Danes. He restored churches
and monasteries. A scholar himself, he did much to improve educa-
tion, especially that of the clergy. By translating Latin works into
English, and by starting the first year-to-year record in the language,
known as the Anglo-Saxon Chronicle, this all-round king also made a
contribution to English literature.

Certainly England fell under Danish rule, but not until these
invaders were Christians and ready, in some degree, to carry on the
work that Alfred had begun. Before this point was reached, however,

he had forced them, after the Treaty of Wedmore, to retire from Wessex into Mercia and Northumbria—an area which became known as the Danelaw, and was bounded on the west by Watling Street—and to accept Christian baptism. Thus when they presently attacked again, and, with no Alfred to oppose them, captured the whole country, it was as Christians, or at least as a people with different ideas from the original relentless invaders.

But the enmity between Saxons and Danes could hardly be forgotten. With London locked and defended against them, they had built up boroughs and trading centres within the Danelaw. Little had been done to the roads, but rivers were abundant, and a mercantile people found it simple to use them for commercial purposes. Hence it came about that during the disastrous reign of King Ethelred, the Danes under King Sweyn and his son Canute so fought and bargained and made such progress that, in 1017, Canute became King of all England. Wisely, he made haste to decentralise his power, entrusting the rule of the kingdom to his earls, and exerted himself to unite England and Denmark.

Later, while Godwin, Earl of Wessex, and his son Harold were watching and hoping for the throne of Edward the Confessor, the half Norman king, another power began to arise. It resembled the Danish power in its scope, but, unlike theirs, it was expressed in grandeur, knightly splendour, and ideas of 'chivalry'. This new power was growing up in Normandy, under William, who had some claim to the Confessor's throne. Indeed, it might be said that Edward was preparing the way for the Normans.

The story is known everywhere. Harold, as soon as he had been crowned king on Edward's death in 1066, hurried to Stamford Bridge, near York, to defeat an invading army under the Norwegian King. There the news reached him that Duke William was landing at Pevensey. Down the Roman road marched the brave Harold, determined to meet the Norman invaders at the first possible moment. He himself covered the two hundred miles to London in four days: his army marched it in nine.

The battle of Hastings soon began, and was soon over. By pretending defeat, William managed to turn his forces and to catch his enemies in the open plain; and after a battle in which the English infantry, faced with bowmen and mounted knights, showed rare courage and tenacity, William the Norman was William, King of England.

The Saxons who fled headlong across the downs by the Greenways cared little who he was.

CHAPTER IV

The Middle Ages

'Whan that Aprille with his shoures sote,
The droghte of Marche hath perced to the rote,
And bathed every veyne in swich licour,
Of which vertu engendred is the flour;
Whan Zephirus eek with his swete breeth
Inspired hath in every holt and heeth
The tendre croppes, and the yonge sonne
Hath in the Ram his halfe cours yronne,
And smale fowlës maken melodye,
That slepen all the nyght with open eyë,
(So priketh hem nature in hir corages):
Then longen folk to goon on pilgrimages. . . .'
GEOFFREY CHAUCER: *Prologue to the Canterbury Tales.*

THE imaginative writer usually makes the best historian, because he realises the human value of what he sees. In this business of our English roads we have to wait a long time for his help. Between the events at the end of the last chapter and the time pilgrims were able to set out for Canterbury in the manner made famous by Chaucer, some three centuries had gone by. The whole of the period known as the Middle Ages divides the companionable jogging of that animated cavalcade from the journeys of the Saxons who fled from Hastings. The Church had now taken on responsibility for the safety of travellers, and life on the roads of England was changed out of recognition.

What is more, we get, at last, vital information about it. Instead of the bare facts and vague impressions which are the best that the early state records have to offer, we have living, eye-witness accounts of travel in all its aspects. All life needs the writer's eye, if it is to be real for a later age. Luckily, the fourteenth century gave us flowers of our early literature, blossoming in the language that was soon to become Modern English; and, quite suddenly, the story of travel is animated before our eyes.

For this happy change two writers bear the credit. Each drew from life, with a strong creative imagination to give the pictures warmth and colour. To Chaucer and to Langland we owe much of our knowledge of how the people of those days lived and went about their business. From Chaucer in particular we learn how the social

32

'The Automaton', a steam omnibus which ran in London in 1836. Built by Walter Hancock

London's first horse-drawn trams— Marble Arch

A Scottish development of steam propulsion, 1870. This 'handsome and commodious vehicle' could carry 65 passengers

An L.G.O.C. horse-bus of the knife-board type common in the 1870s

The horse-bus in its heyday—1900—and a traffic jam at Charing Cross?

standing and the motives of the travellers were reflected in their
different ways of travel. In action before us, pausing at ale-houses,
arguing, laughing, singing, go the Innkeeper, the Knight, the Mer-
chant, the Man of Law, the Miller, the Reeve or Bailiff, the Prioress,
the Pardoner, giving us a conspectus of the range of English social
life at the close of the Middle Ages, as exhibited on a journey characteristic of the time.

Other writings give us detailed descriptions of royal processions,
made up of countless knights, marshals, bowmen, and lackeys. We
read of the equipage of lords with two or three hundred retainers in
their train as they rode about the country on visits to their estates,
while their massive baggage wagons lumbered behind them. Judges,
booted and spurred, travelled richly on circuit; Norman officials
rode Saxon serfs into the ditch. We have contemporary accounts of
the host of foot travellers—the pedlars, minstrels, monks, and farmers, the beggars and messengers who dragged from inn to inn on
muddy roads in winter, or plodded through the summer dust on
their way to the many famous fairs.

Even a superficial glance at fourteenth-century literature makes
plain that, though the vehicles were still primitive, travel had
developed a long way since the days when King Harold raced southward to join battle with William the Norman. In spite of many
dangers, all except the serfs made greater use of the roads than did
their successors in the early nineteenth century. What was left of the
Roman system of roads had come into its own again, and travel, in
the Roman sense, was once more an integral part of people's lives.

Before we can fully understand this development, we must consider, very briefly, the social changes that had helped to bring it
about.

II

In the three hundred years these changes had been slow, but far-
reaching. Saxon resistance to the Normans soon slackened, and most
of southern England was quickly seized from the men who had
opposed William at Hastings. The new king, confirmed in his office
by the central council known as the Witan, ruthlessly put down
isolated risings in the north.

Once this was done, he was in a position to institute his own
version of the Feudal System. This is best represented by a target of
concentric circles, the bull'seye being the King. All land belonged to

the King, and, in return for military service, he parcelled it out to the next circle, the greater barons. The greater barons let it out to the lesser barons, and they, in turn, sub-let to other tenants.

All such tenants were freemen, but below them was the great crowd of serfs, Saxons, Danes, Britons, and Celts. These, the lowest members of the community, were tied to their land. Like the inhabitants of an occupied country in time of war, they had to jump out of the way when Norman nobles and their retinues went riding by. Their strips of land, as well as the scattered estates of their overlords, were recorded to the minutest detail in the famous Domesday survey: and their lot was hard.

Until the time of Magna Carta, the serfs might not so much as kill themselves a dinner in the enormous hunting forests of the King; and, for a long time to come, lest they should wander in hope of better conditions, they had no right to travel further than the village tracks that led them from their huts to the fields. For the rest of the community, things were very different.

The Church, having inherited money and land throughout the country, was no longer what it had been when celibate monks first preached the gospel along the dusty Saxon roads. Worldliness, avarice, and slackness were bringing about the corruption that in the later Middle Ages so discredited it. The Norman barons, whose consciences must often have been uneasy, subsidised monasteries, endowed chapels, and paid for the beginnings of some of the country's great cathedrals.

More and more roads were needed so that the monks might travel to collect their rents. Road repair and maintenance, and the building of a great many bridges, thus became the responsibility of some of the richer monasteries. Religious guilds were formed to undertake such work, and bishops granted indulgences to those who contributed money and labour. Hermitages and small priories were founded—'St. Bartholomew of the Causeway' at Arundel is a good example—tolls were collected from passers-by, and, in order to make it clear that it was the Church that protected wayfarers, it became a common practice to build chapels upon bridges.

In some places fortified towers were built, to defend the bridge and the town to which it led. The most famous example is London Bridge, begun by Peter of Colechurch in 1176. This had a chapel, a tower, and two lines of houses that overhung the Thames and from time to time toppled into it. Thus the haphazard system of road and bridge maintenance became a religious observance, and the Church, having strong practical motives, held itself responsible.

The work was opportune, for the country roads of the Saxons had become little more than muddy rivers in winter and, in summer, dusty tracks over which the heavy farm carts lumbered with their wide, nail-studded wheels. Where the Church failed to attend to main roads, having no need for them in a particular district, no one else did much about them. The lord of the manor would fill in a few pot-holes in his own tracks, but very often he left the highway to care for itself. If a local farmer needed stone, he knew where to find it; and sections of the old Roman routes became impassable.

When bridges collapsed, trees fell, and dead cattle blocked the way, neither law nor custom made it anybody's business to clear the way; and the accidents that occurred when folk attempted their own river crossings are recorded as commonplace events, the sort of thing any traveller might expect. It is not surprising, therefore, that on one occasion in the middle of the fifteenth century the summoning of Parliament had to be postponed because the 'jeopardous' condition of the roads prevented country members from reaching London in time.

III

Travel had other hazards. Throughout the Middle Ages, the disrepair of the roads was only one form of danger to travellers. There was a more cogent reason for a pilgrim to pray when he entered a wayside church and knelt beneath a mural of St. Christopher. A special clause had been included in the Litany for the safety of travellers, since bands of robbers often lurked in the undergrowth at the roadside. As late as 1281, wolves and outlaws were coupled as vermin sheltering in woods which the Abbot of Gloucester had to have cut down. Even barons were not above the sending out of bands to waylay merchants and private travellers, and the 'robbers of Alton' are but one example of the gangs who beset the roads. This particular crowd preyed on the Winchester Road until they were imprudent enough to seize the King's wine.

Against such dangers the Statute of Winchester was passed in 1285. Highways leading from one market town to another were to be enlarged, bushes, woods, hedges were to be cut, and dykes filled, 'so that there be neither Dyke, Underwood or Bush whereby a man may lurk to do hurt within two hundred foot of the one side and two hundred foot of the other side of the way.'

No statute, however, could put an end to roadside robbery.

Outlaws such as Robin Hood, who killed the King's deer in the forests and, according to the ballad makers, plundered the rich to help the poor, expressed the attitude of the common people to the Forest Laws.

We may doubt if such outlaws were as altruistic as tradition suggests. In any case, there is evidence that, however much the people might like the idea of them, once the 'hue and cry' was raised and the outlaw made for sanctuary in one of the many churches that could grant him that privilege, a great many joined in the chase. This was understandable. The law made it clear that anyone who refused to help in the chase risked being taken for a robber himself.

In effect, the roads of mediaeval England made it unlikely that anyone should travel purely for pleasure. All, except perhaps the monks, travelled in groups for their better protection, and everyone was anxious to reach his destination before nightfall, for curfews were then rung in towns to show that the gates were closing, the cresset pots on church towers were lit to guide belated travellers, and those that were stranded had only an open fire with which to comfort themselves.

Still, there appear to have been many who thought little of such conditions. Apart from the richly dressed trains in royal processions, the judges travelling on circuit, the sheriffs riding from hundred to hundred, and the messengers of the Courts, the Church, and the great lords, the bulk of the traffic was made up of the wagons and pack-horses of merchants and traders, and was especially heavy at the times of fairs, which were held in almost every town in the country. There cattle were bought and sold, stocks of clothing and household goods were laid up for the winter, and, at every corner of the market, the quacks, the pedlars, and the sellers of knick-knacks carried on their unchanging trade.

Langland's Prologue to *The Vision of Piers the Plowman* (Skeat's edition) mentions such everyday figures on the mediaeval road:

> Some choose to be chapmen, to chaffer for gain;
> And it seems to our sight, such surely succeed.
> And some to make merry, as minstrels are wont,
> Getting gold with their glee, yet guiltless, I trust.
> As for jugglers and jesters, all Judas' children,
> That feign silly faces, apparelled as fools,
> Having wit, if they willed it, to work as they ought—
> I pass o'er what Paul would have preached to these sinners.

Next beggars and bedesmen were hustling about
Their bags and their bellies with bread were well cramm'd,
By falsehood they fed them, and fought o'er their ale,
As greedy as gluttons they go to their beds,
And rise up as ribalds, these robber-like knaves . . .

Next pilgrims and palmers would plight them together
To seek out Saint James and saints known in Rome;
They went on their way with many wise tales,
And had leave to tell lies all their lifetime after . . .
Of hermits a huge heap, with hooks to their staves,
To Walsingham went; and their wenches went after;
Great lubbers and long, that to labour were loath . . .

IV

The instinct which today leads people to get into their cars and
visit the houses of famous men was strong in the Middle Ages, but
had a religious bias: and religion, it must be remembered, was
sometimes hard to distinguish from superstition. Admiration for
holy men and women developed the wish to visit the places with
which they were associated, and to inspect the shoes, girdles,
clothing, even the bones that these saintly people had left behind
them. There was a popular belief that such articles retained the
virtues of their owners and could bring about miraculous
cures.

Some pilgrims were anxious to win the cure of spiritual benefit
promised to those who worshipped at a particular shrine, and paid
money for a badge that showed they had done so. Others were little
more than sight-seers, concerned mainly with the adventures which
might come from a journey in pleasant company and with adding a
fresh badge to their collection.

These and other motives for going on a pilgrimage are exemplified
in the people Chaucer describes. The Knight, lately returned from a
Crusade, the Monk and the Friar, lightly satirized for their worldly
habits, the scarlet-stockinged Wife of Bath who was proud, amongst
other things, of the number of shrines she had visited—all had
different reasons for their journey. Not all the motives were exalted.
Chaucer neatly pricks the Pardoner, whose bag was crammed with
bogus relics that he hoped to sell at exorbitant prices, as Langland

did the worldly-minded clergy who liked to disguise themselves in
fashionable clothes upon such journeys.

Except for the poor who went on foot, journeys of this kind were
usually made on horses. The women rode either astride or pillion
behind a servant, until, towards the end of the fourteenth century,
the side-saddle was introduced. A few of the nobility and anyone who
was sick sometimes made use of a horse-litter, resembling a sedan-
chair supported on long poles between two horses that were driven
in tandem. It was by such means that Edward I made his last
journey to Scotland.

The rich, if they did not ride, travelled in sturdy, four-wheeled
springless carriages, little better as vehicles than the two-wheeled
box-like carts, drawn by horses, oxen, or mules, which carried
baggage or were used by farm workers for carrying roots or dung.
These simple wagons and carts could be hired in large numbers in
order to make up a nobleman's train, and the usual commercial rate
for carrying a ton of goods was twopence per mile.

Jusserand's *Wayfaring Life in the Middle Ages* makes it clear that
some carriages were rather more elaborate. The best of them, he
tells us, had four wheels, and were drawn by three or four horses, one
behind the other, one of them mounted by a postillion provided with
a short-handled whip of many thongs. The framework was made of
solid beams, which rested on the axles, and above it rose an archway
rounded like a tunnel.

But, even though the whole was ungainly, the details were
elegant. The wheels were carved, and their spokes decoratively
shaped: the beams were painted and gilded, and the inside of the
carriage was hung with tapestries. Embroidered cushions lay on the
seats.

> A lady might stretch out there, half sitting, half lying; pillows were
> placed in the corners as if to invite sleep or meditation, square windows
> opened on the sides and were hung with silk curtains.

Jusserand goes on to describe the dress and appearance of such a
lady, her dress clinging closely to her body, her forehead artificially
lengthened by the plucking of eyebrows or even of some of her hair.
Her knight, if he shared the carriage with her, was as tightly clad:
but any possible dalliance must have been restricted by the noise and
the outrageous bumping of the vehicle, as it jolted from one pot-hole
to another, stuck, and, at an extra effort from the horses, leaped
forward with a violent jerk and all but overturned.

V

To such journeys, and in particular to the journeys of the pilgrims, we owe some of our oldest surviving inns. The George at Glastonbury, the Pilgrims Hostel at Battle, and the Hostel of Godbegot at Winchester are but three examples of well-known stopping points on mediaeval roads. For while the monasteries acted as hostels for the wealthy, the inns on the main routes provided food, drink, and a reasonable bed—if one did not mind fleas—for such intermediate classes as merchants, scholars, and husbandmen. Although he was writing two centuries later, it was such an inn that Thomas Deloney had in mind when he wrote his description of a meeting between three merchants in London:

> ... and being once entered into their inn, according to old custom, good cheer was provided for them; for these clothiers were the chiefest guests that travelled along the way; and this was as sure as an Act of Parliament that Tom Dove could not digest his meat without music, nor drink wine without women, so that his hostess being a merrie wench would oftentimes call in two or three of her neighbours wives to keep him company; where, ere they parted, they were made as pleasant as Pies ... Tom Dove called for music, William of Worcester for Wine, Sutton set his delight in hearing merry tales, Simon of Southampton got him into the kitchen, and to the pottage pot he goes, for he esteemed more a messe of pottage than of a venison pastie. Now sir, Cuthbert of Kendal was of another mind, for no meat pleased him so well as mutton, such as was laced in a red petticoat.

These inns had two or three rooms strewn with rushes on which, at bedtime, the pallets were laid. More primitive still were the ale stakes that were dotted along the main roads. The only sign to distinguish them from simple cottages was their long poles bearing a few leafy boughs. However, they provided sufficient warmth and comfort to content the poorer and hardier traveller of these times.

The owners of some of the inns seem to have realised what they could contribute to the development of travel, and improved their standards very quickly, if we may judge by William Harrison's picture in his sixteenth-century *Description of Britain*:

> ... Our innes are (also) veric well furnished with naperie: bedding and tapesterie especiallie with naperie: for besides the linnen used at the tables, which is commonlie washed dailie, is such and so much as

belongeth unto the estate and calling of the ghest. Ech comer is sure to lie in cleane sheets, wherein no man hath beene lodged since they came from the landresse. . . . It is a world to see how ech owner contendeth with other for goodnesse of interteinement of their ghests, as about finesse and change of linnen, furniture of bedding, beautie of roomes, service at table, costliness of plate, strengthe of drinke, varietie of wines, or well using of horses.

VI

The roads themselves, poor as they were, slowly improved, and during the Middle Ages there came into being a popular standard of width for any road of importance that fell within the King's protection. It had to be wide enough for two wagons to pass; for two oxherds, standing on either side, to be able to touch the points of their goads; and for sixteen armed knights to ride side by side.

Nevertheless, in spite of improvements and the maintenance work done largely by the Church, the Highway was still not so much an actual strip of land as an abstract right of passage for the King and his subjects. This, however, did mean a good passage; and where the way was 'foundrous', everyone had the right to diverge from it on to neighbouring farmlands.

So began, no doubt, some of those bends in our roads today which seem so arbitrary and unnecessary. And the compulsory clearing of space at the roadside, in order to protect wayfarers from ambush, was responsible for the wide borders that are the charm of some of our country roads, as well as the narrow fields, enclosed in the eighteenth century, on which the mediaeval traveller used to graze his horses and cattle.

By the close of the Middle Ages the administration of justice and finance was drawing men of all classes except the serfs to London. Travel, still primitive, was becoming more and more important.

CHAPTER V

Tudor Roads

'Now to speake generallie of our common high waies through the English part of the Ile ... you shall vnderstand that in the claie or cledgie soile they are often verie deepe and troublesome in the winter halfe.'

WILLIAM HARRISON: *Description of Britain* (1586).

IN Tudor England, despite the roads which William Harrison described, people had begun to travel for much the same reasons as they do today. Young men journeyed to Oxford and Cambridge, sometimes on foot; lawyers followed the judges on circuit; the King's Council and his courtiers were often on the move; the sick travelled in carriages and litters to well-known watering-places, such as Bath; merchants with their wares rode in and out of every market town in the country.

The Dissolution of the Monasteries, however, put an end to one of the principal landowners in the country and, by so doing, destroyed the one haphazard system of road maintenance that existed, and removed one of the chief classes of traveller. After the Reformation pilgrims no longer journeyed to the holy shrines at Canterbury, Walsingham, and Glastonbury; and travel, like so much in this age of scientific and material development, moved away from the influence of the Church.

The most frequented highways continued to be impassable in bad weather, not only because of wear and tear but because no one looked after them; and those connecting the smaller towns were still nothing more than country tracks. Presently, under pressure of public opinion, Parliament made a move. The Highways Act of 1555, having pointed out that 'highways are now both noisome and tedious to travel in, and dangerous to all passengers and carriages', put responsibility for their maintenance on the parishes through which the roads ran. A surveyor, elected by each parish, was obliged to see that all parishioners contributed (free) the necessary horses, carts, tools, and labour. Moreover, in addition to supervising the repair and use of his roads, he had to extract the necessary fines for the many offences created by the statute.

It is one thing to legislate, and another to see that legislation produces the desired effect. Things, as Kipling once remarked, are only done by means of people: and the English have a peculiar genius for nullifying laws they do not like. Thus it is no surprise to learn that the duties of this unpopular (and unpaid) office were widely and massively shirked. Meanwhile, wheeled traffic remorselessly increased; one ineffective Highway Act followed another; and all the time roads continued to deteriorate, a regress which continued, as we shall see, until the eighteenth century.

In 1600 one William Kemp embarked upon a morris-dance from London to Norwich. However odd the enterprise, his experience was typical. Having made various aspersions in his journal on the 'foul way', he reaches a climax:

> At length coming to a broad plash of water and mud, which could not be avoided, I fetched a rise, yet fell in over the ankles at the further end. My youth that followed me took his jump, and stuck fast in the midst.

II

Although our first concern is with these and other hazards which befell the traveller on the roads, it would be misleading not to mention an alternative method of transport which, especially in the neighbourhood of London, was freely used throughout the fifteenth, sixteenth, and seventeenth centuries. This was the variety of boats and barges that sailed upon the great highway of the Thames. As long as the roads around the capital continued to be so bad, it was both cleaner and cheaper to travel by boat. The result was that a steady traffic of barges and boats carried the King, his nobles, and the common people up and down the river from Windsor and the new palace built by Wolsey at Hampton Court to the Tower and on to Greenwich. Throughout the Middle Ages wool and fuel had been carried by boat to the London Markets, and throughout the Tudor period Kings and Queens were brought in state barges to Westminster for coronation and for burial.

A contemporary account of the coronation of Elizabeth of York, Henry VII's Queen, suggests the kind of river scene that was part of such an occasion. The Queen was attended by the Lord Mayor, the the sheriffs and aldermen of the city.

'There was attending upon her there the maior, shrives and aldermen.' . . . 'Divers and manie worshipful commoners', members of the city companies, each in his livery, came in barges newly equipped, 'everie craft in their liverages, in barges freshly furnished', with banners and decorated with streamers of silk, 'the arms and banners of their craftes'. Conspicuous among them, and 'passing all other', was a barge called 'the batchelors', adorned with a great red dragon which opened and spouted fireworks into the river: and there were many other features in what made a splendid and costly pageant.

III

But to come back to the roads. Towards the end of the sixteenth century, one important aspect of road travel was being given belated attention. Maps and itineraries were put upon the market. John Leland's Itinerary, made between 1533 and 1539, was the work of the King's Antiquary, and it covered most of England. During the fifteen-seventies, under the auspices of the Privy Council, Christopher Caxton surveyed all the counties of England and Wales.

What we may call the first 'road book' was the work of William Harrison, one of the earliest of countless men to make detailed studies of both the people and the natural products of the country. His 'Description of England', issued in 1577, included in its extensive information a list of the 'common ways' and indicated the distances between towns, and was thus of practical use to the traveller.

The fashion caught on; Harrison's book paved the way for the countless guides and road-books that followed. With the help of such books a number of foreign visitors to the country in Shakespeare's day overcame the many difficulties that still opposed the wayfarer, and travelled remarkable distances. Some even included Scotland in their tours.

The fastest method of travel was by means of post-horses. These were to be had at fixed stages, usually in inn-yards: and from 1572, when Thomas Randolph became Postmaster, a postal system for carrying official persons and letters between a prescribed list of places became a permanent institution. There was still no official method for sending private correspondence, but private travellers could hire post-horses for threepence per mile or, if they so required, for the whole day. These horses were usually made to travel at about ten miles an hour, so that journeys of seventy to a hundred and fifty miles could be accomplished between sunrise and sunset.

Guides were often necessary, an additional expense, for no stranger could hope to distinguish the highways from the local roads, and signposts had not yet appeared. A further difficulty was that one could not always get horses at every stage of the journey. This was met by a device more satisfying to officials than to the public at large. When there was a shortage at a posting station, officials were entitled to seize the mounts of private travellers in the King's name. Bureaucratic encroachment on the rights of the civilian is no new thing. Not surprisingly, many officials abused their privilege, and the less scrupulous of the public took advantage of it. The whole business became such a nuisance that, in 1603, a law was passed to prevent postmasters from supplying horses to men who claimed to be on government business, unless they could produce some document signed by a State official.

In spite of this law, and in spite of the fact that the animals were often branded, and that death was the penalty for stealing them, inn-keepers continued to lose their horses. Royal persons were among the worst offenders, for they could commandeer horses and defer payment wherever they went. The warning given to the Host in the *Merry Wives of Windsor* refers to this practice.

> Have a care of your entertainments: there is a friend of mine come to town, tells me there is three cozen-germans that has cozened all the hosts of Reading, of Maidenhead, of Colebrook, of horses and money . . .

IV

Posting horses were normally used for urgent business, so that the term 'posting' came to be an image of speed. Shakespeare calls on it often. Kent tells of King Lear:

> There came a reeking post,
> Stew'd in his haste, half breathless, panting forth
> From Goneril his mistress salutations;
> Deliver'd letters,—

Hamlet cries out on his mother's marriage

> O most wicked haste, to post
> With such dexterity to incestuous sheets.

Since it was possible to change horses about every ten miles, many who travelled by this means set up record rides. Perhaps the

most famous is that of Sir Robert Cary who, on Queen Elizabeth's
death, carried the news from London to King James in Edinburgh.
Some time between nine and ten in the morning he set off along the
Great North Road—Ermine Street, as it still was—and covered the
hundred and sixty-two miles to Doncaster before nightfall. On the
following day he rode a further hundred and thirty-six miles to his
own home in Northumberland. By noon on the third day he had
reached the Border; and, had he then not suffered a serious fall
which made it necessary for him to ride 'softly', he might well have
reached the King that afternoon instead of at bedtime. As it was, he
had covered in three days a distance that thirteenth-century heralds
used to cover in forty, and set up a record which stood until William
Nevinson, the seventeenth-century highwayman, rode the two hundred and twenty miles from Rochester to York in a single day.

The means of travel most in vogue were riding and walking.
Riding was for the rich man, walking for the poor. Great distances
were covered on foot; Ben Jonson appears to have thought little of
walking from London to Edinburgh. All the time wheeled vehicles,
though they never replaced riding on horseback, were developing
slowly in comfort and performance. Horse-litters, crude carriages,
and primitive carts, similar to those of the Middle Ages, were still in
use; but improved carts were gradually taking the place of pack-
horses for transporting goods, and coaches a little less cumbersome
than their predecessors were beginning to be popular amongst the
rich in Elizabethan England.

The Queen, who sometimes travelled through London in a
sedan-chair carried by her courtiers, was presented by a Dutchman
with one of the earliest coaches of this period, and although she
complained vividly of the 'aching pains' she suffered through riding
in it, this vehicle must have helped to set a fashion. The caroche, for
town use, was a smaller version of the leading type of Tudor coach.
Both could sport carved roofs, sometimes adorned with plumes of
feathers, and upholstery of velvet or scarlet cloth, lace-trimmed.

They were capacious, too. According to one eye-witness, a
nobleman's lady found it possible to carry with her 'her gentle-
woman, maid, children and what necessaries as they or any of them
are to use'. Though windowless, springless, and uncomfortable as
Queen Elizabeth found them, these vehicles seem to have been
thought more suitable than a horse's back for women who liked to
wear farthingales and gowns and bodices stiff with jewels and gold
embroidery.

Although some of the roads, especially in the north, remained impossible for wheeled vehicles, the principal towns had carriers who travelled at regular intervals to and from London. The carriers took their commissions in the London inns : commissions which sometimes included the delivery of private letters, and, though their 'long covered wagons' were slow and hideously uncomfortable, the carrying of a few passengers. Little more attractive were the lumbering, springless stage-wagons, drawn by six horses, which were introduced during the later years of the century. For the Elizabethan who was no horseman, travel was a slow and arduous enterprise.

v

The dangers of the roads continued as bad as ever, and, though the gallows waited for every captured thief, the plundering of travellers, both rich and poor, was a calling which attracted many daring and lawless spirits. Organised gangs operated in lonely areas such as Shooters Hill near Blackheath, Salisbury Plain, and Gadshill near Rochester. The exploits of Falstaff and Prince Hal, as Shakespeare described them, rang plausibly to contemporary ears. As in that immortal exploit, chamberlains, ostlers, and tapsters were in a good position to find out what a traveller carried in his purse and saddlebags and where he meant to go next day. Once they had found out, they had only to pass the word to thieves who depended on such information and would give them their cut of the takings.

Nor were professional robbers the only danger. Amateurs took part in the game, armed with staves twelve feet long and carrying a twelve-inch pike, with which to threaten a peaceful traveller. It was therefore necessary for everyone making a journey to be armed.

'No man,' William Harrison points out, 'travelleth by the way without his sword, or some such weapon, with us, except the minister, who commonly weareth none at all, unless it be a dagger or hanger at his side.'

But travel had its joys, chief of them the inns that welcomed one when each stage of the journey was accomplished. As suggested in the last chapter, these improved rapidly after the fourteenth century. In Tudor England some towns had several, for derelict monasteries and houses had been turned into inns and posting houses. Marked by the most elaborate and expensive signs, these competed keenly over the food, the drink, the music, and the hospitality with which they regaled their guests. Fynes Moryson, who was acquainted with the inns of many European countries, was enthusiastic about the public hospitality of Tudor England.

> The world affords not such Inns as England hath, either for good and cheap entertainments at the guests own pleasure, or for humble attendance on passengers. . . . For as soon as a passenger comes to an Inn the servants run to him, and one takes his horse and walks him till he be cold, then rubs him and takes him meat, yet I must say they are not much to be trusted in this last point without the eye of the master or his servant to oversee them. Another servant gives the passenger his private chamber and kindles his fire, the third pulls off his boots and makes them clean. The Host or Hostess visits him, and if he will eat with the Host, or at a common table with others, his meal will cost him sixpence, or in some places but fourpence (yet this course is less honourable, and not used by gentlemen): but if he will eat in his chamber, he commands what meat he will according to his appetite, and as much as he thinks fit for him and his company, yea, the kitchen is open to him to command the meat to be dressed as he best likes: and when he sits at table, the Host or Hostess will accompany him, or if they have many guests will at least visit him, taking it for courtesy to be bid to sit down: while he eats, if he have company especially, he shall be offered music, which he may freely take or refuse, and if he be solitary, the Musicians will give him the good day with music in the morning.[1]

In view of the dynamic developments in the arts, in science, and in politics which gave energy to life in Tudor England, we may be surprised that travel made poor progress; but one achievement must be written in the credit column. The English inn was established as a permanent comfort and a centre for the new trade that the roads were slowly enabling.

[1] *Shakespeare's England*, Vol. I.

CHAPTER VI

Travel Under the Stuarts

'I returned to Chatham, my chariot overturning on the steep of Bexley-Hill, wounded me in two places on the head; my son Jack being with me, was like to have been worse cut by the glass; but I thank God we both escaped without much hurt, though not without exceeding danger.'

JOHN EVELYN: Diary.

THROUGHOUT the seventeenth century the state of the roads grew steadily worse. There was still no system of repair, and no recognised authority responsible for seeing to them: and wheeled traffic was increasing every year. As a result, the roads became even more forbidding than they had been in Tudor times.

True, life itself was less in danger than it is today, when speeds rise and roads are overcrowded; but the discomforts the seventeenth-century traveller had to endure were remarkable. It was possible for a horseman to lose his way on the Great North Road. The legislation about the width of the roads and the clear space on either side had lapsed, so that, on sections of such highways as the Canterbury Road, it was difficult for two mounted men to pass. Pepys tells us that the road between Finchley and Barnet was 'torn, plowed and digged up', and on another occasion he speaks of having his horse 'almost sink to the belly'.

The private coaches which, as we shall see, became increasingly popular in the latter part of the century, were often confined to the stables in the winter. After heavy rain London could be cut off from the Midlands, and miles of all but impassable clay made it hazardous, at best, to journey into Sussex. And, of course, there were still highwaymen and robbers, making it unwise for a man to travel unaccompanied in deserted places, or, as Sir John Evelyn points out in the following extract from his diary, to ride too close to a hedge.

The weather being hot, and having sent my man on before, I rode negligently under favour of the shade, till, within three miles of Bromley, at a place called the Procession Oak, two cut-throats started out, and striking with long staves at the horse, and taking hold of the reins, threw me down, took my sword, and hauled me into a deep thicket some quarter of a mile from the highway, where they

Above: An early single-deck horse-bus operated by 'Thomas Tilling—Job-Master' in 1900

Centre: This horse-bus, preserved in the British Transport Commission's museum, shows a remarkable display of advertisements

Below: Omnibus in Trafalgar Square, 1895. Operated by W. S. Birch & Son in the Atlas Association's livery

Early single-deck horse-drawn tram with covered driver's seat—Leeds, 1873

Two-horse tram with front stairs and knife-board seating on the upper deck—Edinburgh, 1890

Three-horse double-deck bus run by Glasgow Tramways before 1900

Single-deck horse-bus—Leeds City Transport, 1896

might surely rob me, as they soon did. What they got of money was not considerable, but they took two rings, the one an emerald with diamonds, the other an onyx, and a pair of buckles set with rubies and diamonds, which were of value, and after all bound my hands behind me, and my feet, having before pulled off my boots; they then set me up against an oak, with most bloody threats to cut my throat if I offered to cry out, or make any noise for they should be within hearing, I not being the person they looked for. I told them that if they had not basely surprised me they would not have had so easy a prize, and that it would teach me never to ride near a hedge, since, had I been in the mid-way, they durst not have adventured on me; at which they cocked their pistols, and told me they had long guns, too, and were fourteen companions . . .

Evelyn managed to escape and to raise the hue and cry, but many travellers were less fortunate. The most impressive feature of his experience, from our point of view, is the matter-of-fact way in which he relates it, much as we should describe our sufferings in an unheated train, or when we were held up at an airport by fog; showing that perils of this kind were all in the day's work, things which any traveller might expect.

The state of the roads grew to be a scandal, and sporadic attempts were made to better it, ranging from inventions for road maintenance to attempts to restrict the traffic. None of them, however, did much to improve the lamentable condition of the roads. There was no central authority, no co-ordination. When we realise that legislation under Charles II permitted carts and wagons with four wheels and drawn by ten or more horses to carry loads of sixty to seventy hundredweight, we are no longer surprised to learn that it was a common experience to be caught fast in a quagmire. We understand too why the timings of stage-coaches were qualified with the phrase 'if God permits'.

II

Yet, for a variety of reasons, reform was resisted. It was so often the wrong reform. When the first Turnpike Act of 1663 authorised gates on the Great North Road, so that tolls might be collected for the repair of roads in Hertfordshire, Cambridgeshire and Huntingdonshire, there arose such an outcry from the public that this system was crippled for the rest of the century, and the battle of the Turnpike Trusts was begun.

D

A more promising approach was through the passing of legislation which revised the taxes imposed on the various types of vehicle,
and authorised surveyors to find local labour for the repair of
particular roads; but even these measures were little more effective
than the attempts to bring the roads up to date, made under the
Tudors.

We might well suppose, therefore, that in this troubled century,
with all its political and social convulsions and the hideous burden
of Civil War, road conditions alone would have reduced travel to a
minimum. But the behaviour of the English has always been unpredictable. Travel flourished. In addition to those who continued to
make journeys for trade and private business, more and more took to
the roads, not simply for pleasure, but, with guide-book and map in
hand, to see and learn about their country. After the Restoration,
amongst the well-to-do, tours of Britain grew to be almost a fashion.

This important change in attitude, this wish to make journeys
voluntarily rather than from necessity, can be clearly seen in the
journals and letters of the times. Pepys, Evelyn, Sir William Dugdale,
Ralph Thoresby, and Celia Fiennes are amongst the many who
travelled with a new motive.

Celia Fiennes started to make journeys in order to regain her
health through variety, change of air, and exercise. In a preface to
her account of long and hazardous expeditions on horseback, she
considers that more people would be well advised to 'spend some of
their tyme in Journeys to visit their native Land, and be curious to
inform themselves and make observations of the pleasant prospects,
good buildings, different produces and manufactures of each place,
with the variety of sports and recreations they are adapt to. . . .' This,
she considers, 'would be a souveraign remedy to cure or preserve
from these epidemick diseases of vapours, should I add Laziness?'

Thus, while the country squires, the doctors, and the lawyers
continued to go about their affairs on horseback, while the couriers
rode post-haste with His Majesty's Mails, and while the poor, receiving the same treatment as the merchandise beside them, were
bumped over pot-holes in the long, covered wagons, the well-to-do,
passing stocks and pillories that marked the Puritan attitude to
vagrancy, set out on their tours of exploration, or drove in coaches
about the fashionable parts of the towns.

The diaries and letters of the Restoration period exult in this new
pleasure. Evelyn made a seven-hundred-mile tour in his own coach
and took his wife, newly arrived from France, on long journeys to
visit friends deep in the country. Celia Fiennes, more concerned to

travel than to arrive, ambled through county after county, noting their characteristics with careful eye. Pepys, more and more the man of fashion as his career developed, shared the pleasures and pride of the beaux who could afford to spurn public vehicles.

'To the Park,' he records in April, 1669, 'my wife and I: and here Sir W. Coventry did first see me and my wife in a coach of our own; and so did also this night the Duke of York, who did eye my wife mightily. But I begin to doubt that my being so much seen in my own coach at this time, may observe to my prejudice, but I must venture it now.'

III

Yet, in spite of the popularity of the private coach in the latter part of the century, improvements in the design of all vehicles came very slowly. Like the Elizabethan coach which preceded it, the heavy family coach that was used in the reign of Charles I was still windowless and almost enclosed. It had uncovered 'boots' projecting at the sides, and was wide enough for three people to sit abreast. When an owner could afford it four or six horses were used; it was customary to have postillions; and, on longer journeys, the nobility usually travelled with outriders whose horses could at need replace those of the team, or help to pull the coach when the going was bad.

The first 'glass coach' was made for the Duke of York in 1661, but the coach-builders went on fitting the vehicles of lesser folk with shutters or leather curtains until the century was out.

Improvements to the suspension were equally slow to come. These heavy vehicles were low hung, and the body was supported by large leather braces in such a way that, on rough roads, the superstructure could swing clear of the chassis like a pendulum. Coaching, therefore, meant getting used to a motion which the stomach must have strongly resented. Moreover, these pleasures were expensive. Pepys was obliged to pay his coach-builder the princely sum of fifty-three pounds for a pair of fine black horses.

Experiments with various types of light two-wheeled vehicle, drawn by one horse, which were called 'Chariots', went forward faster. These had been tested on the Continent, where they soon became popular. Their development in England was largely the result of private enterprise, encouraged by the Royal Society.

After dinner comes Colonel Blount, (wrote Pepys,) in his new chariot made with springs; as that was of wicker, where in a while since we rode at his house. And he hath rode, he says, now his journey, many miles in it with one horse, and out-drives any coach, and out-goes any horse, and so easy he says. So for curiosity, I went into it to try it, and up the hill (Shooter's Hill) to the heath (Blackheath), and over the cart ruts, and found it pretty well, but not so easy as he pretends.

Evelyn was less impressed with the account of a two-wheeled gig that was tried out in Dublin in 1685.

Sir Richard Bulkeley described to us a model of a chariot he had invented which it was not possible to overthrow in whatever uneven way it was drawn, giving us a wonderful relation of what it had performed in that kind, for ease, expedition, and safety; there were some inconveniences yet to be remedied—it would not contain more than one person; was ready to take fire every few miles; and being placed and playing on no fewer than ten rollers, it made a prodigious noise, almost intolerable.

IV

The hackney-coaches which filled the streets of London by the middle of the century offered keen competition to the owners of sedan-chairs and to the Thames watermen. The sedan-chairs were introduced to England from France by Sir Saunders Duncombe. They became fashionable round about 1634, and were used generally by the middle of the century. The Duke of Buckingham, the first to ride abroad in one, incurred censure on the ground that he was degrading human beings by making them perform the office of a beast.

This prejudice soon disappeared, and the chairs became the private conveyances of the well-to-do. They were used for shopping, for paying calls, for going to the theatre, the assembly, or the ball. They could be hired, though it was better esteemed to have one's own. The drawback was that they carried only one passenger; and, as a link-boy with a torch was needed at night, that meant a team of three to transport him or her.

There was thus a ready market for the hackneys. Most of them had started life as private carriages of the nobility, and many bore noble arms, a tradition which survived into the nineteenth century, when broken-down hansoms and four-wheeled cabs had often some sort of a coronet on their panels. At first, however, these hackneys did not 'crawl' or ply for hire, but waited until sent for in their owner's yard.

In 1633 a Captain Bailey became a pioneer in this new and important business. He chose the Strand as the first regular stand for such vehicles, put his men into livery, and gave them instructions 'at what rate to carry men into several parts of the town'. Other owners followed his lead, and within two years the trade grew to such an extent that the streets of London and Westminster became 'pestered with the unnecessary multitude of coaches therein used'.

The result, one of the earliest enactments for traffic control, has its echoes today. In 1635 a proclamation of Charles I forbade their use unless the passenger was travelling at least three miles out of town, and the owner of the coach was able to maintain four good horses for the King's use. One contemporary account suggests that this reduced the number of hackneys within London and the suburbs from six thousand to sixty.

Soon after the Restoration, however, the number of hackneys plying for hire had again reached the level of a nuisance, and a further proclamation appointed Commissioners with a charge to restrict the total to four hundred and to issue licences to their owners. The chief result was vigorous and wholesale bribery: licences changed hands for huge sums.

The fact was that the public liked the coaches and meant to have them. By 1677, when the Worshipful Company of Coach and Harness Makers was established, the Thames watermen and the owners of sedan-chairs had already lost their battle against the competitors they had long opposed. The usefulness of the hackney-coach was obvious to all, and the age of public vehicles had begun.

v

Throughout the first half of the seventeenth century the heavy stage-wagons drawn by six horses continued to make long journeys as slow and uncomfortable as possible. But a change was on the way. A new vehicle, the first example of what can properly be called the stage-coach, had made its *début*. By 1640, two years before the King's standard was raised at Nottingham, two types of stage-coach service had already been tried.

The first, using a vehicle similar in design to the heavy private coach and travelling at about four miles to the hour, joined London to all the main towns within a thirty or forty miles radius. The coachman sat on a bar between the two forward posts from which the body was suspended; the body of the coach carried six to eight passengers inside. Behind, over the axle, there was a large basket for baggage and such additional passengers as could contrive to make themselves comfortable in the straw provided. In those days, when road conditions and the design of coaches made it impossible for anyone to remain on the roof, unless lashed on with ropes, this was the first attempt to carry passengers 'outside'; and loud was the outcry raised by horse-copers and by inn-keepers at posting stations, who thought that this new form of transport was going to ruin their business.

Here again public demand settled the controversy. The coach service developed rapidly and, by the sixteen-eighties, a town in the Home Counties, such as Windsor, had at least six coaches in and out every day. The advantages to trade were obvious. Town Councils up and down the country did all they could to improve communications by similar means.

VI

It is interesting to trace, in these early days of travel, a line of development similar to that which in living memory happened to the internal-combustion engine. Two main themes arose, speed and comfort. Speed came first. Distinct from the stage-coaches, though the first examples resembled them in design, were the flying coaches. These, by using additional horses, began to travel longer distances, and at a speed no one had imagined. The epithet 'flying', apart from its dramatic value, was probably intended to distinguish these new vehicles from the cumbersome stage-wagons which had been making such journeys for many years, and charged a halfpenny or a penny a mile instead of the threepence demanded by the coach.

The new speedy service—which usually had to be suspended in winter—could cover the hundred and seventy-five miles from London to Exeter in ten days. By 1673, the time had been reduced to eight. The state of the roads and, of course, the hills, caused wild variations in over-all speed. In contrast to the Exeter journey, the hundred miles to Bath was covered in three days. Chester was reached in six, Oxford in two—though there was one reckless service that covered this journey in a single day.

This was all right for the main routes. A cross-country journey could be haphazard. In 1684 a traveller from Lyme Regis who wanted to reach London had to take post-horses to Salisbury, where he picked up the stage. He then paid a fare of thirty shillings for himself and servant, and four-and-sixpence 'at several stages to gratify coachmen'.

These journeys were still subject to the perils and discomforts that had beset earlier travellers. One of the first opponents of the stage-coach, John Cressel, makes this abundantly clear:

> Is it for a man's health to be laid fast in foul ways and forced to wade up to the knees in mire; and afterwards sit in the cold till fresh teams of horses can be procured to drag the coach out of foul ways? Is it for his health to travel in rotten coaches and have their tackle, or perch, or axletree broken, and then to wait half the day before making good their stage?

Cressel had an axe to grind, as had many who feared that the saddle would become obsolete: but he had plenty of disinterested support. The letter of a man who travelled by stage-coach from Preston in Lancashire to London in 1662 makes it clear that the ordinary passenger was not always enthusiastic:

> I got to London on Saturday last; my journey was noe way pleasant, being forced to ride in the boote all the waye. The company y^t came up with mee were persons of greate qualitie, as knightes and ladyes. My journey's expense was 30s. This travell hath soe indisposed mee, y^t I am resolved never to ride againe in ye coache. I am extremely hott and feverish. What this may tend to I know not. I have not as yet advised my doctor.

I find this excerpt very disquieting. It is to be hoped that he took a well-laced posset, went to bed, sweated out his chill, and woke up his own man again.

VII

The haphazard method of sending private correspondence by carrier's cart was not improved until 1635, when Thomas Witherings was appointed Master of the Posts. The year was momentous, for with that appointment the modern Post Office began. Though, because of the difficulty of communications and the restricted chances of meeting anyone who lived far off, few had reason to correspond with people outside their parish, a private letter could at this time be sent eighty miles for twopence. The postmasters along the highways, who were still paid a retaining fee for supplying horses for the King's messengers, took on, in embryonic form, the responsibility for delivering it which they assume today. In 1657 the Master of the Posts became Post Master General, the first of a long line of officials whose duties were to supervise the carrying of letters and to furnish post-horses.

The volume of correspondence was small, and news sheets were not regularly published until the censorship of the press was abolished at the end of the century, but the first of these duties quickly became the more important. As the number of stage-coaches increased, 'travelling post' became less necessary, and in 1780 the Post Office relinquished its monopoly in post-horses.

After this, in return for a five-shilling licence, inn-keepers were again free to hire post-horses at the authorised rate of a penny a mile. If the inn-keeper could not supply them, the traveller who was not on a recognised stage-coach route was free to get them wherever he could.

So, by the end of the seventeenth century, the term postage had begun to refer to the conveyance of letters, and no longer to a method of travel.

CHAPTER VII

Coaching

'You will say and think with me, I dare say, that in spite of wet
and cold, frost and snow, and all the variations of temperature that
one used to go through on a coach, they were jolly times.'

BIRCH-REYNARDSON: *Down the Road.*

THE literature of coaching is so profuse and generous that a large
volume would be needed even to represent it. Many large
volumes have been written, and there will always be room for more.
Like hunting, cricket, and Christmas, coaching has somehow got
itself embedded in the history of the English spirit, and has come to
be an exemplar of our old-fashioned virtues. The difficulty, in a
quick survey such as this, is to make a selection which will give a hint
of this abundant chapter in our history, and to keep one's enthusiasm for it within bounds. After centuries for which the material is
short and sparse, it is hard not to lose one's head and grab with both
hands from such a heap of riches. But, if only to keep a sense of proportion, the temptation must be crushed.

One luxury we may allow ourselves, the joy of quotation; and
indulge it not from laziness, but because the writing of the time gives
the real flavour of the coaching era far better than any summary or
paraphrase. Even though the quotations are well known, something
true results from assembling them close together.

II

It has been obvious, almost from the start, that the evolution of
transport was controlled by the roads more than by any other factor,
or set of factors. Throughout the greater part of the eighteenth
century they improved very little. The road from London to York
seems to have been passable, judged by the poor standard of the
times, for a handbill dated 1706 advertises the journey as taking
four days, and restricts the weight of luggage to fourteen pounds for
each passenger, with threepence a pound excess. But the general
level remained very bad. In 1722 Defoe used the words 'deepest' and
'dirtiest' when describing the route from Tunbridge to Lewes, on

57

which he saw a lady 'of very good quality . . . drawn to church in her coach with six oxen'. He adds: 'nor was it done in frolic or humour, but meer necessity, the way being so stiff and deep that no horses could go in it.'

Even between Kensington and London, coaches were often bogged, and of the two roads through the Park, one—Lord Hervey observed in 1743—was 'so convex and the old one so concave, that by this extreme of faults they agree in the common one of being, like the highroad, impassable'.

As late as 1770, when the Turnpike system was firmly established, Arthur Young, the agriculturalist, considered that the roads in Lancashire were fit only for horsemen.

> I know not in the whole range of language, terms sufficiently expressive to describe this infernal road. Let me most seriously caution all travellers who may accidentally propose to travel this terrible country to avoid it as they would the devil; for a thousand to one they break their necks or their limbs by overthrows or breakings down. They will here meet with ruts which I actually measured, four feet deep, and floating with mud only from a wet summer. What, therefore, must it be after a winter? The only mending it receives is tumbling in some loose stones which serve no other purpose than jolting the carriage in the most intolerable manner. These are not only opinions, but facts; for I actually passed three carts broken down in these eighteen miles of execrable memory.

There is no lack of corroboration, right up to the end of the century. Sydney Smith, hymning the invention of steam, records that it took him nine hours to go by coach from Taunton to Bath, and that on the journey he suffered 'between ten thousand and twelve thousand severe contusions.'

Along such roads, carried by long lines of pack-horses with pannier baskets, came the clay and china from Staffordshire and the cloth from the Yorkshire mills. Along them, too, moving even more slowly than the heavy stage-wagons, came the herds and flocks for Smithfield, and the pigs, geese, and turkeys that were driven to the markets in the capital. There, butchers and poulterers had to wait for supplies; and the supplies, impeding every vehicle that tried to make time, shuffled towards them at the sauntering pace of the herdsman.

If these conditions had not improved, we could have had neither the industrial nor the agricultural revolution. The improvement, as generally happens in this country, came only when conditions had

These two advertisements are taken from a copy of the first edition of the Liverpool Courier *dated 6th January, 1808. In both cases the advertiser appears to seek to establish a personal relationship which no doubt reflected the friendly intimacy of coach travel in those days*

FLEECE INN, DALE STREET.

T. WARD and Co. under a sincere impression of gratitude for past favours, and more especially for the great patronage and liberal encouragement their Coaches have met with, since they commenced running from the above Inn, to Manchester, beg leave to return their sincere thanks to their friends in particular, and the public in general; at the same time take this opportunity of informing Travellers and others, that they have started a new Coach, called the TRAFALGAR, from Liverpool, through Warrington, Manchester, Halifax, Leeds, York, Beverley, and Hull: and it is (as it always was) their determination to provide careful drivers and good horses; proper attention to the accommodation of passengers; and punctual care in the carriage and delivery of parcels, by which alone they expect a continuance of that patronage they have already experienced.

N. B. The above Coach not more than five hours going from Liverpool to Manchester; breakfasts at half past eight o'clock at Rainhill. The only Coach that breakfasts on the road.

SUPERIOR TRAVELLING,
From the SADDLE INN, VERNON-STREET,

A Light Post COACH, the ROYAL LIVERPOOL to London in 36 hours, every Tuesday, Thursday, and Sunday Mornings, at seven o'clock.

This is the only Coach between London and Liverpool, whose Proprietors have kept their word to the Public in only being one Night on the Road, at the following reduced Fares. To London inside, £2. 12s. 6d. ditto outside, £1. 6s. Small Parcels 2s. each, and Luggage 2d. per lb. Also, Northampton, Welford, Lutterworth, Lichfield, and Newcastle Coaches, performed by NEWBY, VARTY, DUCKWORTH & CO. who return their sincere thanks to their Friends and the Public for the unprecedented Encouragement they have met with and hope by a strict attention and regularity, to continue to have that preference which they have uniformly received.

N. B. The Proprietors will not be accountable for any Parcels or Packages above the value of £5. unless entered and paid for accordingly.

grown intolerable. The worst burdens resulted from the measures aimed at bettering the roads. At one time some two thousand Road Acts instituted the Turnpike Trusts and tried to govern them: until the outcry against this whole system, which had begun in the seventeenth century, rose to a fierce crescendo.

When the revolt started, toll-gates were smashed and their keepers attacked and even murdered in their cottages. The law's reply was to extend the death penalty to all such crimes; and, by slow degrees, countrymen began to realise that there was something to be said for having their local roads maintained at the expense of the stage-coach and the rich man's carriage.

Thus, as the century continued, sections of the main roads were slightly improved by the Turnpike Trusts; although the parishes, with a sort of Statute Labour, were still responsible for the by-ways. This liability was seldom fairly discharged, since the Statute Trusts often delegated their maintenance work to farmers who were apt to pocket the proceeds without doing the work. Also, those contracts were valuable, and there was a good deal of bribery and corruption in order to get them. The course of many Turnpike roads was presently affected. Towns that were not on them when they were planned saw to it that they were put on in fact; and those that were not in league with the administrators could find the road zigzagging past them.

Still, the system slowly developed and improved. By the nineteenth century there were some twenty thousand miles of Turnpike, accounting for eight thousand toll-gates, and many of them had been surveyed to the extent of having posts and stones that showed the distance between the towns.

Thirty years earlier, Arthur Young had not been impressed by this progress. What was he to say of the roads in the West Country, he asked himself: what was he to say of

> '. . . the turnpikes' as they have the assurance to call them and the hardiness to make one pay for? From Chepstow to the halfway house between Newport and Cardiff they continue mere rocky lanes full of hugeous stones as big as one's horse, and abominable holes. The first six miles from Newport they were so detestable, and without either direction posts or milestones, that I could not well persuade myself that I was on the turnpike, but had mistook the road, and therefore asked everyone I met, who answered me, to my astonishment, 'Ya-as'.

In conditions like these, the 'flying' coaches continued to creak and rumble over their twenty leagues a day; and although some forty years still separated the country from the roads that permitted the Golden Age of coaching, pioneers such as John Metcalf were already aware that a foundation of stones bound by dirt was the essential basis for any good road. Metcalf, though a blind man, remade hundreds of miles of turnpikes and highways, and his work was to lead to the revolutionary roads of Telford and McAdam.

These two, honoured always in the history of road travel, in the second decade of the nineteenth century were remaking smooth-surfaced roads throughout the length and breadth of the country. Telford believed in properly excavated foundations: McAdam held that a road, if properly drained and correctly built, could be laid on the subsoil and surfaced with stones 'smooth, solid, and so flat that a carriage may stand upright'.

Miles of such roads, permitting coaching speeds that will be described presently, were put down by capitalist companies, and through them the macadam of the modern motor road recalls the Scottish pioneer.

III

Thirty years earlier, while towns like Manchester and Liverpool were vying with one another over the speed of the 'flying coaches', one John Palmer of Bath had conceived the idea of a specially built mail coach, to be supplied with good horses at frequent stages, which could supersede the carrying of mails by men on horseback. This service had fallen into disrepute. Inn-keepers, having been given more scope in arranging the supply of horses, had taken the chances offered and started to reserve their best mounts for the rich. The post-boys had to make do with what was left over. Thus the postal service had become slow, and badly organised, and the mail was plundered by highwaymen with monotonous regularity.

Once Palmer had overcome the natural opposition to his revolutionary scheme, the first mail coach ran from London to Bath in 1784, taking fourteen hours for the journey. This was not bad. In 1836, after McAdam, the coach succeeded in cutting only three hours from the time. Palmer's coach carried a limited number of passengers, and the mail. It travelled twice as fast as the post-boys and, with the extra advantage of a guard to protect it, scored an immediate success. As a result, Palmer was appointed Controller General of the Post Office.

By 1792, sixteen similar coaches, each bearing the Royal arms and carrying a scarlet-coated guard with a blunderbuss, served London daily. The coaches and horses were often provided by contractors who owned stage-coaches, but the guard was a government servant whose duty, whatever accident befell the coach, was to go forward at all costs with the mail.

In order to pay for a service of such speed, punctuality, and comparative safety, postage rates were increased by approximately a penny a stage. This did not include the delivery of letters to places off the route.

IV

It calls for a real effort of imagination for us to realise the extent to which our forbears depended on the mail coaches. They were, like the telegraph today, an image of sudden and dramatic news, of joy or disaster. They carried from the city to the remote villages along their route news of peace and war, casualty lists, promotions, great events abroad, the rise and fall of human fortune. As de Quincey shows, the very moment of their departure was dramatic:

> From eight-fifteen or twenty minutes later, imagine the mails assembled on parade in Lombard Street, where, at that time and not in St. Martins-le-Grand, was seated the General Post Office. On any night the spectacle was beautiful. The absolute perfection of all the appointments about the carriages and the harness; their strength, their brilliant cleanliness, their beautiful simplicity but more than all, the royal magnificence of the horses—were what might first have fixed the attention. Every carriage, on every morning of the year, was taken down to an official inspector for examination—wheels, axles, linch-pins, pole, glasses, lamps, were all critically probed and tested. Every part of every carriage had been cleaned, every horse had been groomed, with as much vigour as if they belonged to a private gentle-man. But the night before us is a night of victory; and behold, to the ordinary display what a heart-shaking addition—horses, men, carriages are all dressed in laurels and flowers, oak leaves and ribbons. . . . The spectators, who are numerous beyond precedent, express their sympathy with those fervent feelings by continual hurrahs. Every moment are shouted aloud by the post-office servants, and summoned to draw up, the great ancestral names of cities known to history through a thousand years—Lincoln, Winchester, Portsmouth, Gloucester, Oxford, Bristol, Manchester, York, Newcastle, Edinburgh, Glasgow, Perth, Stirling, Aberdeen. . . . Every moment you hear the thunder of lids locked down upon the mail-bags.

Since the speed of the Mails attracted travellers who had pre-viously made their journeys by stage-coach, the stage-coach pro-prietors were obliged to improve both their vehicles and their time-tables if they were to hold their own. They did their best to meet the challenge. The basket of rumble-tumble in the rear was replaced by boots fore and aft. For those who preferred to save money by travelling outside, less perilous seats were provided. Six 'inside' passengers were carried at first, and because these, the first-class passengers, often complained of the rowdy travellers who shouted and clamoured overhead, a number of enterprising proprietors started to introduce faster and more expensive Post coaches, which had nothing to do with the Mails, for carrying 'inside' passengers only.

In his book, *Stage-Coach and Mail*, C. G. Harper quotes the advertisement of such a coach.

For Portsmouth

A new Carriage on Sprints
called
THE LAND FRIGATE.

Sets out from the Bell Savage Ludgate Hill, to the Red Lyon at Portsmouth, every Tuesday and Saturday, at 6 a.m. Fare 15*s*. each passenger. Ladies and Gentlemen are requested to observe that the Frigate is elegantly sashed all round, and that in order to preserve the respectability of the vehicle no outside passengers are carried.

V

With these developments came another, freeing travel. Faster vehicles and the armed guards of the Mails were driving highwaymen from the roads. This, however, took time. Until the end of the eighteenth century highwaymen continued to haunt the celebrated covers on the roads to Dover and Bath, and to frequent the commons around London. According to the *Gentleman's Magazine*, the Bristol mail in 1740 was robbed a little beyond Knightsbridge by a man who mounted the post-boy's horse and made off with the mail bags. Horace Walpole had occasion to write that, unless country squires would take time off from shooting partridges and shoot highwaymen instead, society would be dissolved. He was speaking from personal experience. On an evening in 1781,

Lady Browne and I were, as usual, going to the Duchess of Montrose at seven o'clock. The evening was very dark. In the close land under her park-pale and within two yards of the gate, a black figure on horseback pushed by between the chaise and the hedge on my side. I suspected it was a highwayman, and so, I found, did Lady Browne . . . I heard a voice cry 'Stop!' and the figure came back to the chaise. I had the presence of mind, before I let down the glass to take out my watch and stuff it within my waistcoat, under my arm. He said, 'Your purses and watches.' I replied, 'I have no watch.' 'Then your purse.' I gave it him; it had nine guineas. It was so dark

I could not see his head but I felt him take it. He then asked for Lady
Browne's purse, and said 'Don't be frightened; I will not hurt you.'
I said 'No; you won't frighten the lady?' He replied, 'No; I give you
my word I will do you no hurt.' Lady Browne gave him her purse
and was going to add her watch, but he said, 'I am much obliged to
you, I wish you good night,' pulled off his hat and rode away.
'Well,' said I, 'Lady Browne, you will not be afraid of being robbed
another time, for you see there is nothing in it.' 'Oh, but I am,' she
said, 'and now I am in terror lest he should return, for I have given
him a purse with only bad money that I carry on purpose.' 'He
certainly will not open it directly,' said I, 'and at worst he can only
await for us at our return; but I will send my servant back for a horse
and a blunderbus.' Which I did.

Time and the literature beloved by small boys have thrown rain-
bow legends of courtesy and romance and general Robin Hoodery
across the exploits of such 'gentlemen of the road' as Claude Duval,
Tom King, Dick Turpin, and their many competitors. When I was
a small boy, whole libraries were devoted to their doings. The *Dick
Turpin* series consisted of four twenty-thousand word stories a month,
each complete with coloured frontispiece, at a penny. The *Claude
Duval* library was nearing its close, but many copies were still to be
had: and, such was the vogue, a *Jack Sheppard* library promoted this
burglar to highwayman status.

All three, like Robin Hood in the similar series devoted to him,
were persons of heroic courage with a penchant for rescuing distressed
damsels from villainous males or guardians, and robbed the rich
only to help the poor.

The facts were less pleasing. Masked men, usually coarse and
abusive, were at best a nuisance and at worst a menace to life on the
roads. Tyburn continued to take toll of them and wayside gibbets to
creak with their carcases on windy nights. But the real end to the
danger came not through the blunderbuss, the speed of the coaches,
or the fear of being pressed to death, which was the fate of any who,
after capture, refused to give a full account of themselves. The real
end came from an economic blow, the Act for the Limitations of
Cash Payments, passed in 1797. After this, travellers began to carry
less money on their journeys, and the game to lose its point. Though
serious robberies continued into the nineteenth century, the footpad
and the common thief had replaced the well-horsed highwaymen of
Georgian days.

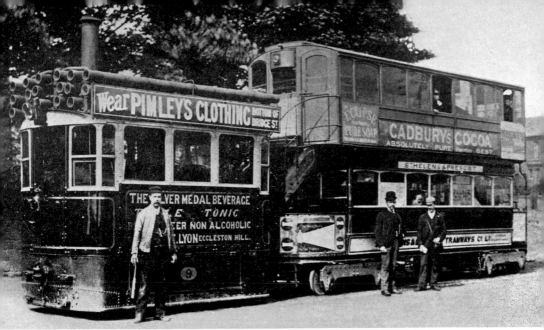

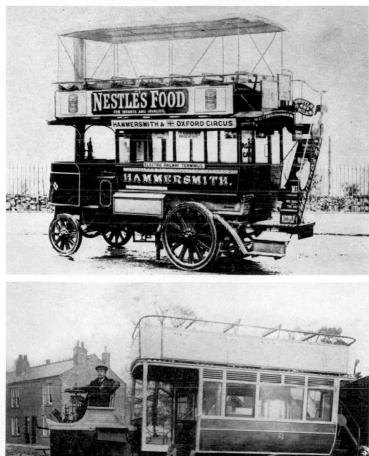

Steam tram unit of St. Helens Tramways, 1897

Steam bus built by Thorneycrofts used in London by the Road Car Company, 1902

Barton Transport steam bus, Clarkson type. One of the first to be operated in the provinces

Early Daimler waggonette—Barton Transport Company, 1898

Milnes-Daimler motor-buses—Eastbourne Corporation, 1903. The first to be run by a municipa

G.W.R. Milnes-Daimler bus on the Helston-Lizard service, 1903.
First to be operated by a railway company

VI

In the opening years of the new century rivalry between the Mail and the stage-coach was fierce, and drew impassioned partisanship. Many writers of the period, from Hazlitt and Dickens to Borrow and Thomas Hughes, were as strongly excited by coaching and all that went with it as men of today are stirred by the performance of a streamlined gleaming car. Among the scores of eulogies that could be quoted, the following by Cobbett has the extra merit that fewer people know it:

> Next to a fox-hunt the finest sight in England is a stage-coach just ready to start. A great sheep or cattle fair is a beautiful sight; but in a stage-coach you see more of what man is capable of performing. The vehicle itself; the harness, all so complete and so neatly arranged, so strong and clean and good; the beautiful horses, impatient to be off; the inside full and the outside covered, in every part, with men, women, and children, boxes, bags, bundles; the coachman, taking his reins in one hand and the whip in the other, gives a signal with his foot and away they go, at the rate of seven miles an hour—the population and the property of a hamlet. One of these coaches coming in after a long journey, is a sight not less interesting. The horses are now all sweat and foam, the reek from their bodies ascending like a cloud. The whole equipage is covered perhaps with dust and dirt. But still, on it comes, as steady as the hand of a clock.

The coachmen of the Royal Mails were important men, and to sit on the box beside one and offer a cigar—the latest novelty of the age —was a privilege coveted by the enthusiast. Compared with the fit, sinewy youthfulness of these aristocrats of the road, the coachmen of the stages were plump, noisy, and ostentatious. That, at least, is the impression we get from many early Victorian prints. Washington Irving supports it. This is how he described the type:

> He has commonly a broad, full face, curiously mottled with red as if the blood had been forced by hard feeling into every vessel of the skin; he is swelled into jolly dimensions by frequent potations of malt liquors, and his bulk is still further increased by a multiplicity of coats, in which he is buried like a cauliflower. . . . He wears a broad-brimmed, low-crowned hat; a huge roll of coloured handkerchief about his neck, knowingly knotted and tucked in at the bosom; and has in summer-time a large bouquet of flowers in his button-hole; the present, most probably, of some enamoured country lass. His waistcoat is commonly

E

of some bright colour, striped, and his small-clothes extend far below the knees, to meet a pair of jockey-boots which reach about half way up his legs . . .

He enjoys great consequence and consideration along the road. . . . When off the box, his hands are thrust into the pockets of his great-coat, and he rolls about the inn yard with an air of the most absolute lordliness. Here he is generally surrounded by an admiring throng of ostlers, stable-boys, shoeblacks, and those nameless hangers-on that infest inns and taverns. . . . These all look up to him as to an oracle; treasure up his cant phrases; echo his opinions about horses and other topics of jockey-lore; and, above all, endeavour to imitate his air and carriage.

Such was the man who, on arrival at an inn, jumped down from his box and, growling 'Twenty minutes gen'l'men. Not a second more,' watched over the ostlers as they replaced the steaming team with four fresh, stamping horses. Since the passengers had scarcely time to snatch a meal, travel in this respect was still absurdly uncomfortable. Both Mail and Stage stopped for breakfast and dinner, but seldom for longer than this specified time. The menu might offer for half-a-crown 'boiled beef, roast pork, a roast aitchbone of beef, a boiled hand of pork, roast goose and a boiled leg of mutton'; but the first course would scarcely have begun when the guard started to blow his horn and the coachman remounted his box. In such conditions the inn-keeper could make his food go a long way, and coachman and guard were doubtless rewarded for the robbery they were able to encourage.

Surtees thus suggests the inn which took advantage of its passengers in this way:

Our passengers had been driven through the passage into a little, dark dingy room at the back of the house, with a dirty, rain-bespattered window, looking against a whitewashed wall. The table, which was covered with a thrice-used cloth, was set out with lumps of bread, knives, and two and three pronged forks laid alternately. Altogether it was anything but inviting, but the coach passengers are very complacent; and on the Dover road it matters little if they are or not. Coats No. 1, No. 2, and No. 3 are taken off in succession, for some people wear top-coats to keep out the heat; chins are released from their silken jeopardy, hats are hid in corners. Inside passengers eye outside ones with suspicion. . . . Presently the two dishes of pork, a couple of ducks, and a lump of half-raw, sadly mangled cold roast beef, with waxy potatoes and overgrown cabbages were scattered along the table. 'What a beastly dinner!' exclaims an inside dandy in a sable-collared frock; 'the whole place reeks with onions and vulgarity.' 'Now, harkee, waiter, there's the guard blowing his horn, and we have scarcely had a bite apiece,' cries Mr. Jorrocks, as that functionary sounded his instrument most energetically in the passage; 'blow me tight if I stir.'

Once in a way the passenger managed to finish his meal. W. H. K. Wright passes on a story he was told of a man who, when all the other passengers had hurried out cursing and grumbling and taken their places, remained quietly at the table.

'Coach starting, sir!' cried the landlord.

'Is it? But I shan't, till I have eaten my egg. And I can't do that till I find a spoon.'

'A spoon? There are a dozen here.'

In alarm the landlord scanned the breakfast table. Not a spoon was to be seen.

'My silver! My silver! Hi! hi!'

He rushed out, stopped the coach, and insisted that every passenger be searched. The man who had started all this took advantage of the delay and the uproar to eat a thorough breakfast. When he had finished he offered to be searched, then went and took his seat.

The coach started, the baffled landlord glowering in the doorway, bearing as best he might the abuse of coachman and passengers. As soon as he was safe, the well-fed traveller called out, 'Have a look inside the teapot.'

The landlord rushed in to the table, and there, sure enough, were his dozen silver spoons.

VII

By 1819 some seventy stage-coaches a day were covering the improved road between London and the fishing village of Brighton, which the patronage of the Prince Regent had turned into a fashionable resort. By 1836, the year in which McAdam died, coaching had reached its peak with some seven hundred mails and three thousand stage-coaches which ran, at about ten miles an hour, the length and breadth of the country. About a hundred and fifty thousand horses were being used by the coach proprietors; the biggest had over a thousand; and close on thirty thousand men were employed as coachmen, guards, horse-keepers, and yard-hands. The taxes from all this raised for the Revenue almost five hundred thousand pounds a year.

The journey from London to Edinburgh cost an inside passenger eleven and a half guineas. An outside traveller, who was prepared to face the weather and several days of hard jolting, had to pay seven and a half, together with the cost of his meals and the tips which the coachmen demanded. Brighton could be reached in five hours fifteen minutes; the hundred and seventy-one miles between London and Exeter were covered in seventeen hours. On the two hundred and sixty-one miles run to Holyhead, which took five minutes under twenty-seven hours, many stretches must have been covered at a pace well above the standard rate of ten miles an hour.

Journeys by long-distance coach, like many of those by modern aircraft, demanded an early start. Dickens described the bleak prospect at six o'clock on a dark, cold morning when the passenger reached his point of departure:

> The coach is out, the horses are in and the guard and two or three porters are stowing the luggage away, and running up the steps of the booking-office and down the steps of the booking-office with breathless rapidity. The place which a few minutes ago was so still and quiet is now all bustle, and early vendors of the morning papers have arrived and you are assailed on all sides with shouts of 'Times, gen'l'men, Times. Here's Chron-Chron-Chron. Herald, ma'am . . .'
>
> 'Take off the cloths, Bob,' says the coachman, who now appears for the first time, in a rough blue greatcoat, of which the buttons behind are so far apart that you can't see them both at the same time . . .
>
> 'Now, gen'l'men,' cries the guard, with his waybill in his hand. 'Five minutes behind time already!' Up jump the passengers—the two young men smoking like lime-kilns and the old gentleman grumbling audibly. The thin young woman is got upon the roof by dint of a great deal of pulling and pushing and helping and trouble and repays it by expressing her solemn conviction that she will never be able to get down again.
>
> 'All right,' sings out the guard at last.
>
> 'Let 'em go, Harry; give 'em their heads!' cries the coachman, and off we start as briskly as if the morning were all right as well as the coach.

Later in the day, the traveller, as Dickens well knew, might have to cover some of the journey on his own feet. The following passage from *The Tale of Two Cities* refers to the Dover Mail as it lumbered up Shooters Hill:

> He walked up hill in the mire by the side of the mail, as the rest of the passengers did; not because they had the least relish for walking

exercise, under the circumstances, but because the hill, and the harness, and the mud, and the mail, were all so heavy, that the horses had three times already come to a stop, besides once drawing the coach across the road, with the mutinous intent of taking it back to Blackheath. Reins and whip and coachman and guard, however, in combination, had read that article of war which forbad a purpose otherwise strongly in favour of the argument, that some brute animals are endued with Reason; and the team had capitulated and returned to their duty.

With drooping heads and tremulous tails, they mashed their way through the thick mud, floundering and stumbling between whiles, as if they were falling to pieces at the larger joints. . . . As often as the driver rested them and brought them to a stand, with a wary 'Wo-ho! so-ho, then!' the leader violently shook his head and everything on it—like an unusually emphatic horse, denying that the coach could be got up the hill . . .

VIII

And so, with a programme that ranged from slow journeys in bad weather to lightning dashes in the sunshine of new roads, the first three decades of the nineteenth century became the glorious age of coaching. The wealthy used their own britskas, barouches, and other light carriages that the London coach-builders had developed, but other classes shared in the advantages of the new age: hired post-chaises made fast travel possible for anyone at the moderate rate of a shilling a mile. These postchaises were light, four-wheeled vehicles, drawn by a pair of horses with a postillion, and they became extremely popular. The rivalry between the mails and the stage-coaches brought the changing of horses to a fine art, and inn-keepers, with their retinues of ostlers, porters, waiters, and stable-boys, were able to smile at the prosperity the roads had brought them.

It is not surprising that few paid serious attention to the strange-looking steam carriages which began their experimental journeys in the eighteen-thirties. They looked dirty, their boilers seemed likely to burst at any moment, and they were so heavily taxed at the toll-gates that the coaching world decided they were of no more consequence than the 'hobby-horse'—a primitive type of cycle which the rider propelled by swinging his feet along the road. The steam-carriage, it was prophesied, would soon die out.

Yet, although the people whose business and pleasure depended on horses shouted derisively at the triumph of George Stephenson's 'locomotive', short local lines were laid down in the Midlands, and coal was hauled along them by steam power. And when the mails themselves were carried by rail from Liverpool to Manchester in 1830, it was clear that a revolution in transport was on the way. The coaches, in fact, were doomed. What Sir James McAdam called 'the calamity of railways' had arrived.

CHAPTER VIII

The Railways and the Motor Car

'Soon shall thy arm, Unconquer'd Steam, afar
Drag the slow barge, or drive the rapid car.'
ERASMUS DARWIN: *Steam Power* (1792).

ALTHOUGH its sudden application to the problems of transport brought about one of the greatest changes in the social and
economic life of the country, there was nothing new about steam. Its
power had been known for a long time. There was nothing new,
either, about the idea of permanent ways: ever since the seventeenth
century, wooden and metal rails had been laid down to lighten the
load of horses drawing coal. What was new was the fusion of these
principles, the way in which steam power was harnessed to new iron
roads, creating, in three decades, a system of travel that for a while
threatened to displace the roads of England altogether.

In this book we are not concerned with railways, but we cannot
understand the way in which road travel was presently to develop
and expand if we do not for a time consider the evolution of the train.
For a while the railways were supreme. All other forms of transport
had to give them best.

In 1801 Parliament authorised the first public horse-drawn
railway, which carried coal, corn, and merchandise from Wandsworth to Croydon. The Mumbles Railway, the first passenger railway
in the world, was opened six years later, and for a long time remained
horse-drawn. A source of great local pride, it is still working.

Again in 1801, a Cornishman called Trevithick, with Boulton and
Watt's experiments to support him, produced the first locomotive to
carry passengers by steam power. With a bellows to blow up the fire
it climbed a hill a quarter of a mile long, as one eye-witness put it,
'faster than I could walk'.

Though this type of locomotive was a failure on smooth rails, and
the early colliery locomotives used the rack and pinion principle of
Swiss funiculars, Trevithick's engine was a forerunner of the steam-
carriages that struggled their way along the roads in the eighteen-
twenties. By that time George Stephenson's engine had shown that
smooth wheels need be no disadvantage on rails, and primitive
steam locomotives began to replace horses for the transport of goods
in various parts of the country.

71

In 1827, two years before Shillibeer's first public horse-bus carried twenty-two passengers between Marylebone and the Bank, Gurney's steam-coach travelled between London and Bath. This formidable contraption was designed more or less like a stage-coach, and equipped with cumbersome boilers and smoke stacks behind the passengers.

Next came one Walter Hancock, who brought out a number of these road-steamers. His 'Infant', which ran from London to Stratford in 1831, to the amazement of all who saw it, was the first mechanically propelled vehicle to carry paying passengers.

A service of steam buses between Paddington and the City followed in 1833, and although it was claimed that these vehicles had the superiority over horses in speed, climbing-power, safety, and economy, vested interests strongly opposed them. Moreover the public obstinately believed that the boilers were likely to burst at any point in the journey, and there was evidence to support their mistrust.

Such prejudice might have been overcome, however, if the Road Commissioners had not succeeded in making out that steam-carriages would endanger both horses and highways. The Turnpike Trusts therefore raised the tolls until a steam-carriage had to pay three pounds where a coach paid three shillings, and legislation imposed serious penalties for locomotives that travelled on the highway at more than four miles an hour. No novelty could stand up to such punishment, and, after a short experimental life, steam-coaches were driven off the roads. But the proprietors of the stage-coaches did not long enjoy their triumph. The men who were laying down railways for goods, and enjoying success beyond all hope, renewed their bid for passengers.

II

The turning point came in 1821 with the decision to cover the distance between Stockton and Darlington by railway. These towns are twelve miles apart, but the railway, which came down from the Shildon area, ran for twice that distance. At first there was some doubt whether the motive power was to be the horse, a stationary engine using ropes, or one of the locomotives which Stephenson had working in the colliery at Killingworth. This had, to support its claim, the performance of drawing forty-eight tons at six miles an hour on level ground. Edward Pease, one of the principal supporters of the project, arranged for Stephenson to survey the line and make arrangements for his locomotive to run, aided by stationary engines on the gradients. Amid loud prophecy of failure one of the most valuable enterprises in the story of travel had begun.

The formal opening of the railway took place on September 27th, 1825. Stephenson's engine pulled its tender, six wagons of coals and merchandise, a coach containing the proprietors of the railway, six wagons reserved for guests, and fourteen others for the workmen who were to ride proudly through the flag-waving, incredulous crowds. The weight of the train thus loaded came to fourteen tons; and, to the amazement of those who knew nothing of Stephenson's work, the locomotive, with its tall, frilled chimney and vertical, hissing pistons, managed to draw its load most nobly over the twenty-six miles.

Although this Stockton to Darlington line was partly worked by horses, the possibilities of a steam passenger service had been demonstrated. As a result, and after trials in 1829, the Liverpool to Manchester Railway, which involved the building of several bridges and the crossing of Chat Moss, was designed for a steam-hauled passenger service. In 1830 about 700 people attended the opening ceremony. This, with six processional trains including Stephenson's *Rocket* and a band that played 'See the Conquering Hero Comes', was an even greater triumph. The cost of the journey and the time had been reduced by half. Travel had entered a new era.

From that moment, engineers confidently settled down to the technical problems of track laying and bridge building which were ahead of them. Railway supporters pondered the prophetic book by Thomas Gray. Its title was long and explicit: *Observations on a General Iron Railway, or Land Steam Conveyance; to supercede the Necessity of Horses in all Public Vehicles; showing its vast superiority in every respect, over the present Pitiful Methods of Conveyance by Turnpike Roads, Canals, and Coasting-Traders. Containing every species of Information relative to Railroads and Locomotive Engines.* The book ran to two editions and Gray became the first exponent of Railway Nationalisation. The centre was to be London, with trunk lines to Edinburgh and the west. From these, Gray maintained, branch lines could run to all places of importance in the country.

III

Needless to say, these grand ideas aroused vehement opposition. Prejudice and protest were loudly voiced. Even the achievements of the engines were decried. It was said that 'iron-hearted speculators' were ruthlessly promoting railways that would cut the farms into fragments, spoil the hunting, and ruin the nation's livestock. Medical propaganda reached unusual heights of absurdity. There was the customary outcry about tampering with the laws of nature. It was suggested that tunnels would produce colds and consumption, and that the noise and the glare of the engine's fire would be devastating to the nerves of the travellers. These unheard-of speeds would be dangerous for the lungs. The motion of the train would produce a variety of disorders, ranging from apoplexy to blindness. While fanatics wrote in such vein to editors, entreating them to oppose the evil of these impious pioneers, more matter-of-fact critics said simply that the railways would not pay.

The opposition was not wholly based on theory. In the 'thirties, when the railway companies were beginning the long argument about the gauges, and when one Railway Act rapidly followed another, the Trusts and the coach proprietors realised that their business would soon be overthrown. A few famous coaches, driven further and further into the provinces, continued to compete with the railways, or at least to supplement them; but although they had plenty of propaganda in their support, they were fast losing ground.

In 1841, when Thomas Cook made his first Conducted Tour from Leicester, the mails had been given to the railways, and the London to York Mail made its last run. The Midland Railway Company was formed in 1844 from an amalgamation of smaller companies, the main areas for the 'big' companies were being defined by statute, plans for new lines were being issued by the dozen, and the public were scrambling to buy the latest stocks and shares. Already it was clear that the railways were going to pay.

Long before the last mail-coach ran between Thurso and Wick, in 1874, a great many turnpikes had been removed, and countless coachmen, ostlers, and stable-boys had had to find other jobs. In *The Uncommercial Traveller*, Dickens speaks of an abandoned turnpike:

> I came to the Turnpike, and found it, in its silent way, eloquent respecting the change which had fallen on the road. The Turnpike-house was all overgrown with ivy; and the Turnpike-keeper, unable to get a living out of the tolls, plied the trade of a cobbler. Not only that, but his wife sold ginger-beer, and, in the very window of espial through which the Toll-takers of old times used with awe to behold the grand London coaches coming on at a gallop, exhibited for sale little barber's-poles of sweetstuff in a sticky lantern.

The political economy of the master of the turnpike thus expressed itself.

'How goes the business, master?' said I to him, as he sat in his little porch repairing his shoe.

'It don't go at all, master,' said he to me. 'It's stopped.'

'That's bad,' said I.

'Bad?' he repeated. And he pointed to one of his sunburnt dusty children who was climbing the turnpike-gate, and said, extending his open right hand in remonstrance with Universal Nature. 'Five on 'em!'

'But how to improve Turnpike business?' said I.

'There's a way, master,' said he, with the air of one who had thought deeply on the subject.

'I should like to know it.'

'Lay a toll on everything as comes through; lay a toll on walkers. Lay another toll on everything as don't come through; lay a toll on them as stops at home.'

'Would the last remedy be fair?'

'Fair? Them as stops at home could come through if they liked; couldn't they?'

'Say they could.'

'Toll 'em. If they don't come through, it's *their* look out. Always—toll 'em."

Finding it was as impossible to argue with this financial genius as if he had been Chancellor of the Exchequer, and consequently the right man in the right place, I passed on meekly.

IV

Kill a road, kill the businesses that had relied on it for custom. Villages that had been prosperous two decades before were by-passed by the railways; coaches stood idle in the yards of their inns; the doors of empty stables banged in the wind. In his *Down the Road*, Birch-Reynardson laments the decay of the once-famous inns:

> . . . the great rambling, half-aired, half-appointed inn; waiter acting boots, boots acting post-boy, or maybe all three; and cook acting chambermaid, barmaid and all.

In such places men cursed bitterly the success of the railways that sent their clanking sounds echoing across the fields. And by the time the soldiers returned from the Crimea to be stared and laughed at for a new toy, the cigarette, that dangled from their lips—by the year 1856—the railways had triumphed.

But there was still a long way to go. Speeds were good, as we

shall see in a minute. Amenities were bad. Although Queen Victoria
was said to have been delighted by her train journey from Windsor to
London in 1842, travel by rail in the middle of the century was nearly
as uncomfortable as it had been in the worst of the coaches.

The first-class carriages, the only kind to have sides, had indiffer-
ently cushioned seats. The second class had bare boards. Passengers
in the third class rode 'like cattle in open trucks', with no seats at all.
Some of the early carriages copied the stage-coaches by having
additional seats on the roof. These were soon discontinued, because
of accidents to passengers who stood up when the train was passing
under a bridge. More serious accidents often happened, through
burst boilers, blocked tunnels, and defective lines. There were hardly
any palliatives or facilities to lighten the tedium of travelling. The
refreshment-rooms were a disgrace. On this point Dickens, once
again, scores a bullseye:

> What with skimming over the open landscape, what with mining
> in the damp bowels of the earth, what with banging, booming and
> shrieking the scores of miles away, I am hungry when I arrive at the
> 'refreshment' station where I am expected. Please to observe—
> expected. . . . The apartment that is to restore me is a wind-trap
> cunningly set to inveigle all the draughts in that countryside, and to
> communicate special intensity to them as they rotate in two hurri-
> canes; one about my wretched head, one about my wretched legs.
> The training of the young ladies behind the counter has been directed
> on the assumption of a defiant dramatic show that I am *not* expected. . . .
> Chilling fast, and subdued by the disadvantage at which I stand,
> I turn my disconsolate eyes on the refreshments that are to restore me.
> I find that I must either scald my throat by insanely ladling into it,
> against time and for no wager, brown hot water stiffened with flour;
> or I must make myself flaky and sick with Banbury cake; or I must
> stuff into my delicate organisation a currant pin-cushion which I know
> will swell.

Nevertheless, in spite of these discomforts and in spite of wet, cold,
smoke, and panic—passengers were apt to dramatise their experience, and referred to their journeys of thirty miles an hour as
'flights'—trains were already carrying as many passengers as thirty
coaches, and five times as fast. In 1849 the Bristol express reached
fifty miles an hour. In the 'fifties a speed of over fifty miles an hour
is recorded. As time went on, the coaches were better built, guards'
vans and refreshment cars were added to the trains, electric signals
and automatic brakes made the journey less hazardous.

And, although rugs were an important part of every passenger's equipment, travel by rail had become less uncomfortable. One could change from the train of one company to that of another without more than the conventional wait on a draughty platform. York could be reached from London in four hours. In 1868 ordinary third-class travel on the London, Brighton and South Coast Railway was a penny a mile, and it cost twopence three-farthings a mile to travel first on an express. Speed was slowly increasing. Twenty years later, the Great Northern and the London and North Western were in fierce competition to reduce the standard ten hours of the journey to Edinburgh. Minute by minute this was brought down to six hours, so that the trains of the 'eighties were averaging sixty to seventy miles an hour. Nevertheless an American, writing to the *New York Tribune* in 1879, had to point out that in all this progress England did not stand alone:

> I have travelled in England and Scotland both faster and slower than ever I did in America, but I am not, for that reason, sure that any of the 'flying' English trains can beat the fastest trains between New York and Philadelphia. . . .

V

During the 'sixties, the scene on the broken-down, overgrown roads was pitiful—little better than it had been in the early eighteenth century. A few coaches still ran in those parts of Cornwall and Yorkshire that the trains had not reached, and the carriers' carts, turning to avoid the toll-gates, rumbled along the by-ways: but for the most part the country roads carried little more than farm carts and the carriages of the squire.

After the violent objections raised at the first appearance of steam-coaches, a law was passed in 1865 whereby no mechanically propelled vehicle should travel at more than four miles an hour. Worse, it might not appear at all unless a man carrying a red flag walked in front of it. Thus the roads had almost returned to the stagnation of the early Middle Ages: everyone who had any real distance to travel went by train.

Throughout the 'sixties and 'seventies it certainly seemed as though the supremacy of the railways could never again be challenged. Public road transport over long distances had ceased. True, there were plenty of little local buses, carriers' gigs, and wagonettes, and many a gentleman still took the road in his private carriage; but the

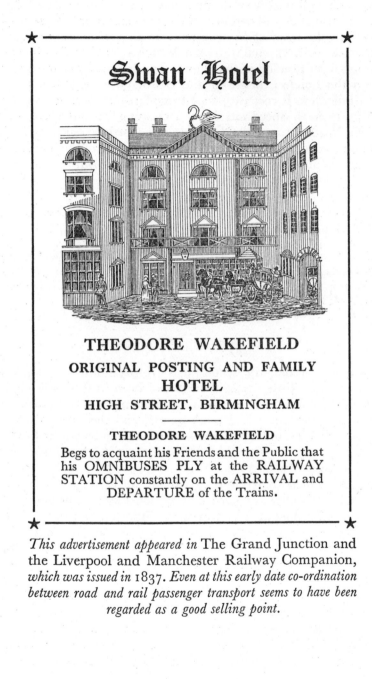

This advertisement appeared in The Grand Junction and the Liverpool and Manchester Railway Companion, which was issued in 1837. Even at this early date co-ordination between road and rail passenger transport seems to have been regarded as a good selling point.

glory had departed. By the side of the once great highways one unemployed coachman after another must have hoped, as he glanced up from his pint-pot—on the rare days when he could afford one—and saw a solitary dog-cart or a gig go trotting by, that, surely, the fun and excitement and hard-earned money of the coaching days could not have gone for ever. Such life, such skill, such organisation; there must be a place for it all in any decently ordered world. A more sophisticated mind might have reflected that the whole course of transport, from the Roman Wagon to the national Mails, could not finally have come to nothing. Surely, one day, road travel must be restored?

Slowly, very slowly, it was, and by mechanical means.

The first agent of revival was the cycle, a perilous form of conveyance that was regarded as fit only for hardy young men with more energy than sense, and a menace to everyone else. By 1869, the 'hobby-horse' had developed into a crank-driven 'bone-shaker' which had wooden wheels with iron rims. The demand for safety and greater comfort led to the tricycle, a less hazardous mount for cautious persons; the demand for speed made the 'bone-shaker' give way to the famous 'penny-farthing'. This perilous bicycle had a front wheel with a diameter of four or five feet, which carried pedals on the hub and provided the rider with spectacular falls.

In the 'eighties a machine known as the Safety bicycle appeared, recognisable in terms of the push-bikes of today. By the 'nineties, when the pneumatic tyre could be had, cycling clubs were urging enthusiasts to train themselves for long tours, and the cyclist, known at first as the 'cad on castors', was seen everywhere. With speed races, marathons, and Touring Clubs to popularise it, and rivalry among manufacturers to bring down the cost of machines, cycling became 'the thing'. Women took to the sport, amid outraged protests, and expensive, gaily coloured cycles became so popular that Hyde Park had to be placed out of bounds to cyclists during the day.

Jane Oliver in *The Ancient Roads of England* quotes a contemporary description of the female enthusiast:

> . . . and I can well recollect seeing quite a little crowd collected at her door in Great Cumberland Place to see her start upon her ride, when, regardless of her admiring audience, she jumped lightly on to her machine, and, ringing her bell smartly once or twice as a warning, wheeled away with her dogs frisking and barking behind her. She knows nothing whatever of fear, and with quite unruffled countenance will cross that dangerous wide space between Constitution Hill and Piccadilly and turn up the hill of Hamilton Place. . . . She is always

very neatly dressed, generally in dark blue, with white revers on her
coat and a natty sailor hat; but I have seen her very smartly clad with
fluttering silk blouse and flowered hat, if always the same neat and
perfectly cut skirt.

These cycling tours along the quiet roads of the 'nineties seem to
have encouraged other forms of travel, for we hear of the well-to-do
beginning to drive longer distances in their gigs, their phaetons, and
their dog-carts, and even a few 'butterfly coaches', as they were
called, made excursions during the summer to beauty-spots within
easy reach of London. The inn-keepers who remained in business
began once more to brighten their dilapidated houses, and to smile
at the trade that was returning to the roads. They little realised
that the pneumatic tyres of the cycles propped against their walls
were soon to encourage a far more impressive form of transport.

VI

The motor-car, that strangest of contraptions to every eye that
beheld it, came very suddenly. It was not born in England. Like the
sedan-chair, the omnibus, and the cycle before it, the motor-car was
imported. As the names of the early manufacturers show, the first
cars were German or French: Benz, Panhard, Mercedes, Daimler,
Lutzmann, De Dion, Renault, Peugeot.

Although Daimler had produced his first motor-cycle in 1885,
and test races for steam, electric, and petrol-driven cars were held
in France in 1894 and 1895, the first car to be seen in England—with
the exception of Volk's electric dog-cart in 1888—did not appear until
this last year. It was a Daimler. Perhaps this prototype and its
successors were less impressive than they might have been, for they
met even greater ridicule than the early railways. The clause in the
1865 law which made it necessary for all road vehicles to be preceded
by a man with a red flag, a regulation which would make any
conveyance look absurd, was repeated in 1878. A genuine impulse
in human development cannot be halted. The will-power of a determined body of people is irresistible, especially when the young are
on their side.

By 1896 the protests of motor enthusiasts had caused the red-flag
law to be repealed, and the first drive of automobiles from London
to Brighton in that year celebrated Emancipation Day.

Spectators on these pioneer occasions are apt to play a base part.
They applaud success and revile failure. To the delight of the gaping,

Omnibus with all-metal
body and front stairs.
Chassis built by Brush
Company, 1904

Early Thomas Tilling
motor-bus, with Till-
ing-Stevens petrol-
electric engine

Leyland-Crossley
omnibus plying
between Chalk
Farm and Char-
ing Cross, 1906,
belonging to
Birch Bros.

Right : Bolton Corporation tram decorated for the Coronation of King George V

Below: Six-wheeled trolleybus—Bradford, 1922. Forbear of modern trolleybus fleet now running in that city

Above : Railless car—Leeds City Transport, 1911.

Below : Experimental coupled tramcars—Potteries Electric Tramways Company, 1924

jeering crowds, many of the cars broke down, but the passengers in
and on them were men of mettle, enthusiasts who lived for their cars,
and knew they had something worth living for. They believed in the
future. In spite of noise, dust, discomfort, and cold, unperturbed by
the fact that more time was spent in tinkering than in driving, the
motorists persevered.

VII

Perseverance called for all their courage and resolve. Carburet-
tors were of the most primitive type, using wicks or cotton-wool
soaked in petrol, with hot tube ignition, and they frequently choked.
The steering gear gave way, gaskets blew out of the exhaust, ignition
was precarious. Cars were difficult to start, and, once started, by no
means easy to stop. But the growing corps of drivers was not daunted.
By 1903 a Mors car had exceeded sixty miles an hour, and an impos-
ing Daimler limousine with a flat roof had been built for King
Edward. Although they cost about two hundred and fifty pounds,
cars were becoming so popular that new legislation was necessary.

The Motor Car Act of 1903 imposed a general speed limit of
twenty miles an hour on the roads, required all cars to be registered,
licensed, and illuminated at night, and made compulsory the display
of number plates and some means of giving an audible warning of
approach. The money from licenses was paid into the Road Fund for
the repair of the roads.

This was of the first importance, for, as motorists quickly found
out, the roads were quite unsuitable for cars. Dust, the bane of early
motoring, was not only annoying but dangerous; it could temporarily
blind the driver. Thus the early motorists, protected by helmets,
goggles and leather coats, sat perched like mountaineers beside
hardy female companions whose hats were lashed on with enormous
veils.

All manner of sprays were tried in order to lay the dust, including
sea water, but by 1907 a decision was given in favour of tar. This was
first laid by hand, but progress came fast, and by the end of 1908 a
thousand miles of road had been sprayed. Before the first decade of
the twentieth century was out, the motor vehicle had established
itself not only as a private conveyance, but as a means of public
transport, in the forms of motor bus, motor-lorry, and motor char-à-
banc.

F

CHAPTER IX

Cabs

'In days of old when folks got tired
A hackney coach or a chariot was hired;
But now along the streets they roll ye
In a shay with a cover called a cabrioly.'
                                   Victorian Popular Song.

THERE flourished some thirty years ago and more a music-hall artist called The Great Wieland. His act consisted in spinning plates on a long trestle table. Starting with three or four, he would soon have a dozen spinning, and be obliged to run from one end of the table to the other in order to give a reviving twist of the fingers to one that was on the point of collapse. As his act proceeded, the number of plates grew and grew, and the audience would cry out with excitement and call to him when some moribund plate seemed past aid. I saw him several times, and he never let a single plate wobble to a stop.

Everyone who attempts to write an account of a complex period or undertaking sooner or later finds himself in The Great Wieland's position, though not always equipped with the same skill. The story has so many aspects, all of which have to be kept alive in the reader's mind. Concentrate on one and the others will fall. Keep to a strict chronological sequence, and you will fail to trace the growth of individual elements. Attend to the elements, and you will have to dodge about in time, running like Wieland from one century back into the one before to keep an interest alive.

On the whole, it seems better to follow Wieland's method, and, at all costs, try to keep the plates spinning.

II

The railways and the motor trade are so closely linked that they have had to be considered together, with the result that we have run ahead of our story, and must hurry back for some account of all that had to happen before a motor vehicle could be hired privately, or picked up by the roadside in the form of a taxi.

We have seen already how the narrow two-horsed hackney-coach of the seventeenth century overcame or evaded the proclamations issued against it. The cost of licences was raised to fifty pounds, and a five pound tax was levied because of the damage hackneys were said to do to paving-stones. Nevertheless, the hackney carried on. In the middle of the eighteenth century a thousand of them were licensed to stand for hire in the streets of London, and to charge fares which, though they varied from time to time, averaged about a shilling for a mile-and-a-half and eighteenpence for two. 'Caddies' or 'cads' were licensed to water horses on the stands while the coachman drank or slept in the nearest tavern, and for this service a halfpenny was supposed to change hands every time a hackney drove off the rank. Though some of them had come to be relatively luxurious, these vehicles were obliged to know their place on the road, for a hackney-coachman was liable to a penalty of five pounds for 'not giving way to persons of quality and gentlemen's coaches'.

At the beginning of the nineteenth century more lightly built and faster vehicles came into vogue. The fashion spread to the hackneys, and emerged in the so-called 'chariots', which could carry two inside passengers and a third on the box. Some drivers continued to ride the nearside horse, others drove from the box. They were dashing, reckless types, the heroes of many young bloods; for the hackney-coachman himself was not licensed, and the proprietor was responsible for the conduct of his drivers. It was not uncommon for proprietors to be blackmailed by men who turned common informer over breaches of the numerous cab regulations.

About the time that Shillibeer's bus was being hailed with enthusiasm, a correspondent wrote the following description of a hackney-coach in the *London Magazine*:

A hackney-coach—fogh! Who can be a gentleman and visit in a hackney-coach? Who can, indeed? to predicate nothing of stinking wet straw and broken windows, and cushions on which the last dandy has cleaned his shoes, and of the last fever it has carried to Guy's, or the last load of convicts transported to the hulks.

Once again it is Dickens, this time in *Sketches by Boz*, who gives the most vivid account and shows what radical improvements were needed if the hackney was to survive:

There is a hackney-coach stand under the very window at which we are writing; there is only one coach on it now, but it is a fair specimen of the class of vehicles to which we have alluded—a great, lumbering, square concern of a dingy yellow colour (like a bilious brunette), with very small glasses but very large frames; the panels are ornamented with a faded coat of arms, in shape something like a dissected bat, the axle-tree is red, and the majority of the wheels are green. The box is partially covered by an old great-coat, with a multiplicity of capes, and some extraordinary-looking clothes; and the straw with which the canvas cushion is stuffed, is sticking up in several places, as if in rivalry with the hay which is peering through the chinks in the boot. The horses, with drooping heads, and each with a mane and tail as scanty and straggling as those of a worn-out rocking horse, are standing patiently on some damp straw, occasionally wincing and rattling the harness; and, now and then, one of them lifts his mouth to the ear of his companion, as if he were saying, in a whisper, that he should like to assassinate the coachman. The coach-man himself is in the watering-house; and the water-man, with his hands forced into his pockets as far as they can possibly go, is dancing the 'double-shuffle' in front of the pump, to keep his feet warm.

Even if we allow for a little graphic exaggeration, it is not surprising that the more well-to-do Londoner wanted to see a lighter and more efficient vehicle, such as the *cabriolet de place* that had been running in Paris for some years. So, although they at first had to work in a limited part of the city, there appeared in the 1820s a number of light two-wheeled gigs, suitable for two passengers, with the driver's seat at the side, between the body and the wheel. Though the shape of the hood earned these vehicles the name of 'coffin-cabs', their quicker and cheaper journeys soon made them popular.

Fares had risen by this time, but these vehicles charged only eighteen pence a mile and fourpence for every additional half mile. They came into their own just as competition between the horse-buses was increasing, and the cab-drivers, proud of their ability to cut in and out between hackneys and slow-moving traffic, added greatly to the excitement of the streets. Riding in them became a recognised form of sport, and many of the young men who patronised cabs would boast of the number of times they had been thrown. 'Cabs', Dickens observed, 'are all very well in cases of expedition, when it's a matter of neck or nothing, life or death, your temporary home or your long one.'

Many hackney-coachmen naturally wanted to change to these light, fast 'cabs', but there was at first a firm monopoly among the well-to-do owners, and licences were hard to come by. In 1831, when there were over two thousand cabs in Paris, London had only a hundred and fifty. Next year the monopoly ended, and hundreds more cabs took to the streets. By the time of the Great Exhibition in

1851, a great many proprietors had sold their hackneys and gone over to cabs.

III

A disadvantage of the 'back-door cab' or 'omnibus slice', which also appeared in the 'thirties, was that the driver, who sat precariously on top of it, could be bilked of his fare. For wagers, devilment, or the obvious motive, there were people who would disappear through the back door of these vehicles and leave the driver unpaid.

Some improvement in design was urgently necessary, and in 1834, Mr. Joseph Aloysius Hansom, an architect, patented a huge, square vehicle which had wheels seven and a half feet high, and the driver's seat above the two doors in the front. Like George Shillibeer before him, Hansom received little financial benefit for his ingenuity; the vehicle which carried his name into the twentieth century was a modified design by a Mr. John Chapman.

Chapman's was a more compact version, and better balanced, because the driver's seat was set further back, and so relieved the weight on the horse. As the ubiquitous 'Hansom', the 'Gondola of London', it kept its popularity for more than sixty years. At first the company that held the patent tried to prevent imitations, but prosecutions against impecunious cab-owners recoiled on those who brought them, and the vehicles multiplied steadily.

An improved kind of covered four-wheeler, which carried two people inside and one on the box, was introduced in the 'thirties by the General Cabriolet Conveyance Company. This, the 'Clarence' or 'growler', attracted the attention of Lord Brougham, and a superior version of it, called after him, became the elegant one-horse family carriage of Victorian England.

There was nothing to compare with it among the numerous private carriages of the day, until, in the 'seventies, the Prince of Wales imported a cab-phaeton from Paris. This, distinguished by a low-hung, curving body and a folding hood that was adequate to ward off showers, became known as the 'Victoria' and was highly popular among ladies.

IV

At the time of the Great Exhibition the cabmen reaped as good a harvest as the horse-buses, and legislation tried once again to make the cabs treat their patrons fairly. The cabmen themselves were made to take out licences, fares were reduced to about sixpence a mile, and a table of them had to be displayed in the vehicle.

No law, however, could put an end to the cabby's traditional behaviour, which the very nature of his trade encouraged. He had no profit until he had earned enough to pay his proprietor, and he might expect any call from the rank to be his last for the day, so that he was always under the temptation to demand an excessive fare, and to sharpen his tongue at the passenger's expense if he did not get it. How long could he be made to wait? How much could he charge for waiting? Was it part of his duty to knock at the house to which his fare was travelling? These and many other questions were argued continually.

For a time the cabby was a sort of humorous public enemy, a nuisance: and although the 1853 Act placed the licensing and inspection of cabs under the Commissioner of Police, strikes and disputes between driver and owner held up the development of the service. Even so, by the 'seventies there were over seven thousand cabs (including over three thousand hansoms) on the London streets, and by 1900 the vehicles licensed totalled eleven thousand.

Dickens' *Dictionary of London* summarises the problems that faced the average cab-user in 1879:

> The cab laws of London are now, except with regard to the distinctions drawn somewhat arbitrarily here and there between four-wheelers and hansoms, very simple and easy to be remembered. The main points to bear in mind are: that luggage carried outside is always to be paid for; that hansoms, though charged at the same rate as 'growlers' when hired by distance—which is almost the only time when there is any particular gain in hiring them—cost sixpence an hour more when hired by time, and eightpence an hour more when standing still; and that you cannot make a man drive you about by the hour for more than one hour at a time. As for the calculation of fares, that must depend entirely on your own power of judging distance. Some people when in doubt take the driver's ticket, and tell him to name his own fare; and when he is satisfied that he will be summoned if he be found to have overcharged, the plan is no doubt efficacious. The difficulty is to impress that conviction on his mind. A better plan is to judge by the time occupied, and it will be found that about a penny per minute is fair to both parties. For fifteen minutes one and sixpence should be paid, and fourteen minutes may be taken to be within the shilling. This is not an official rate but will save trouble and generally prove right. It is as well to start with the clear understanding that, doubtful character as cabbie too often is,

he is really by no means so black a sheep as he is sometimes painted. A hirer should always observe the number of a cab. If he leaves any property in the cab he will possibly find it next day at the Lost Property Office, Great Scotland Yard, when, on payment of a per centage on the estimated value as a reward to the cabman for his honesty, he can obtain it back again.

When this side of Victorian transport is looked at in detail, it is not difficult to see why the cabby had often as much cause for complaint as the public. Too many drivers were provided with indifferent vehicles, unlikely to collect the more attractive fares. The hire-purchase agreements by which some bought their cabs were unfair and gave rise to disputes. The cabby's livelihood, at all times, was precarious. Until the 'seventies, there were no shelters in which cabmen could eat and rest. There were no provident funds to look after the aged, to provide for the cabby who found himself out of business through accident to horse or vehicle, or to deal with the legal difficulties in which he might be involved.

A very common cause of dispute arose when the railway stations gave to 'privileged' cabs the right to use their private property. (It can still arise today.) By the beginning of this century, however, these grievances and hardships had been largely overcome, and the cab service entered the more recent part of its development, which must be considered later.

CHAPTER X

The Rise of Public Transport in Victorian England

'I have had much experience in cheapening vehicular transit,
having originated and established the omnibus in England.'
SHILLIBEER: Evidence before the Annual
Board of Health Committee, 1849.

WE have already seen that, for a period, the success of the railways hit other forms of transport so hard that the country
roads were almost deserted. Steam coaches had left the highway by
the middle of the century, vanquished by heavy tolls; and once the
Mails had been handed over to the railway, such inter-town communication as existed was provided by the train. Stage-wagons had
given up passengers and started to specialise in carrying goods: the
progressive firm of Pickfords had announced 'fast caravans' between
Manchester and London as early as 1817.

The stage coach—to be exact, the short-stage coach—survived
in an attenuated form, in and close to cities and towns, by turning
into the small horse-bus. In the middle of the century their range of
operation was sharply limited. Many of them did little more than
provide fitful services between the town on which they were based
and a few of the villages near by; but there were brilliant exceptions,
such as the network of short-stage coaches between Hull and the
surrounding villages.

London was never without a supply of these short-stage vehicles.
In the 1820s, for instance, there were some fourteen journeys a day
to Uxbridge. But a plentiful supply does not always imply a superiority of organisation. It would be a mistake to think that London
led the way in the development of urban services during the second
half of the century, and that other cities and towns followed a similar
pattern. London's variegated history is peculiarly her own. From the
time of Shillibeer's first omnibus in 1829, she has a unique story of
competition varied by voluntary co-ordination between the members
of various 'associations' and the larger omnibus companies. We
shall be examining this history in the next chapter: for the
moment, let us be content to say that the process of co-ordination

in London's omnibus transport continued until the revolution brought about by motor-buses at the turn of the century.

In Chapter XII we shall outline the development of London Tramways. These, though slower to develop than the tramways in many provincial towns, became a supplementary part of the capital's transport system. London's trams did not eclipse the horse-buses, as did those in other towns and cities. Their rôle has been largely suburban; they have never reached the heart of the city. The bus reigns in London, because her narrow streets have always made dense traffic undesirable.

This consideration, plus the enormous expense that would have been involved, explains why the railways have penetrated little further than the trams. The big termini are scattered in a loose oval ring: only a couple of small ones can be called central. As a result, buses have played a vital part in linking and serving the termini, and in providing a network of communication between the surface and underground railway stations in the suburbs. Buses are more mobile, and far more easily diverted to suit emergencies. They have had the further advantage of being less hedged about by regulations. As long as their vehicles have been correctly licensed, the operators of buses have enjoyed a great measure of freedom in running their services. Tramways, on the other hand, provoked elaborate legislation, which hampered their progress.

II

The development of transport in provincial towns, which will next be outlined, went more by way of tramways than of buses. First horse trams, in the last years of the old century, then electric trams, triumphed over all other forms of transport.

This was because provincial roads and streets in the middle of the last century were thought to be less suitable for buses, and because the railway took over the inter-town communication which had previously happened by road. For a period the bus seemed redundant, and, convinced that its day was done, a number of private undertakings pioneered horse, steam, and finally electric tramways. The Tramways Act of 1870 gave to a local authority the right to acquire these services after a period of twenty-one years; and the exercise of this option started many of the ninety-seven municipal undertakings which operate their own town and city services to this day. By 1924, fourteen thousand electric trams were running in the whole of the country. On the outbreak of war in 1939, the figure had fallen to nine thousand; motor buses, on the other hand, had increased steadily, both in number and efficiency.

During the early years of this century the development of motor transport in the provinces so increased that road communication between towns once again became possible. By the time war broke out in 1914, new motor omnibus companies were beginning to compete with the tramways, and both to challenge the prosperity of the railways. All three advertised the cheapness of their fares. Long-sighted folk, trying from various motives to judge the situation, decided that the railway was clearly established for all time, but the motor bus would prove a deadly rival to the tram. It turned out, however, that the two could complement each other, and in many cases did. The way in which these two services, which at first were so highly competitive, slowly struggled to co-ordination, will be described in later chapters.

Even so, it is misleading to generalise. The development of transport in the provinces varied from one town to another. One of the many problems of a short survey such as this is that it is hard, if indeed possible, to take any single story as typical. Things are done by means of people. The way the things went in each instance depended first of all on the personalities of the men who pioneered the service, then on the needs and behaviour of the public, on the attitude of the local authority, and on the precise conditions that stimulated competition. In each instance the vehicles, the facilities they provided, the new projects that were mooted, the fist-shaking that greeted them in the council-chamber, the response of the public when this or that so-called improvement was tried, and the eventual co-ordination of services, if it was accomplished—all these formed a pattern peculiar to the town.

III

Under the heading of personality, there was a further, corporate problem. Provincial cities and towns are nests of local patriotism, which is often expressed in the negative form of resistance to any idea or suggestion from outside. The North of England is not always disposed to welcome promptings from London and the South. One county will automatically decide against what has been adopted by its neighbour. At a Cornish music festival where I was judging, I heard with some perplexity the chairman refer to a number of entries from foreigners. It transpired that he meant entries from beyond the Tamar.

Thus from the point of view of that dynamic pioneer the British Electric Traction Company, an organisation which promoted the development of tramways, and later of buses, in various parts of the country, the greatest problem they had to face was the unprogressive and unco-operative attitude of many municipal authorities. We must remember, too, when we look at the story that follows, that the right of towns to run their own transport, and the right of private enterprise to run it for them, made one of the bitterest political issues of the opening years of this century.

IV

A hundred years earlier, many of the roads, bridges, and other utilities had been managed by public bodies. Then, as public opinion hardened and officialdom came under attack, numbers of them fell into the hands of private enterprise. But the public, unlike the King in *Princess Ida*, can always find something to grumble at: and, as time went on, there came a reaction against *laissez-faire* and outcries against the powerful monopolists—a view that was reflected to some degree in the Tramways Act. This Act, as we shall see, left the last word on this part of the industry with the local authorities, and gave them even larger powers of veto than had originally been intended. Thus, as always, the pioneers, the men of enterprise, and in this particular context the promoters of tramways most of all, had serious obstacles to overcome before they won their way.

The Times, alive to such injustice, attacked it in 1906 with a leading article.

> At every stage promoters are thwarted by Parliament, by municipalities, by chaotic survivals from legislation passed before electric power was heard of, and by an equally chaotic overlapping of different jurisdictions.

Anyone who knows the English scene will not need to be told that these adventurous undertakings, the British Electric Traction Company in particular, became the target of much political abuse. We are all of us sensitive to the cry of 'monopolies', and the company was execrated by the popular press under the name of 'Octopus'. Public opinion was stirred, as if one stirred a swarm of bees with a broom-handle, and the furious political buzzing which resulted did much to impede the co-ordination of transport until after the First World War. As we have already suggested, the details of the struggle vary from place to place. We will therefore use the next two chapters to discuss a few cases in detail. First, however, we will pay our respects to the capital, and consider the development of transport in London. Back, therefore, like the Great Wieland, to the other end of the table—in this case, to the early eighteen-hundreds.

CHAPTER XI

The London Bus in the Nineteenth Century

'Every driver or conductor of an omnibus who refuses to admit
or carry at the lawful fare any passenger for whom there is room,
and to whose admission no reasonable objection is made, or who
demands more than the legal fare for a passenger, is liable, for every
such offence, to a fine of twenty shillings.'

From: *The Law of London Cabs and Omnibuses, 1867.*

ALTHOUGH a regular omnibus service with a uniform fare had
been established in Paris in the seventeenth century, the word
'omnibus' was not applied to a public carriage until 1827, when a
retired French Army officer started a service in the city of Nantes.
This was about the same time as Gurney's steam-carriage was
pioneering its way along the Bath Road, initiating an enterprise that
was not fulfilled until the arrival of the motor car. It was also the
time when George Shillibeer, having retired from the Royal Navy
and learnt the trade of coach-building in London, was establishing
a coach business of his own in Paris. Commissioned to build some
vehicles for service there, Shillibeer saw that the same type would
be suitable to London where, in the eighteen-twenties, the slow
and expensive short-stage carriages were the only comparable vehicles
which the public could use.

Shillibeer therefore sold his Paris business and, as recorded
in Chapter VIII, introduced a long-bodied coach, with the word
'Omnibus' painted on its side, which made its first journey between
Paddington and the Bank on July 4th, 1829. Drawn by three horses
abreast, carrying a uniformed conductor and driver and with room
for eighteen 'inside' passengers, this vehicle appears to have impressed all who saw it. The *Morning Post* was enthusiastic and, in view
of the cost of hackney-coaches, and their usual condition, one shilling
for the full distance was not thought exorbitant. More vehicles of
the same kind followed, and, when the Stage Coach Act of 1832
made it legal for passengers to be picked up and set down at any
point on the route, more stages could be introduced, and smaller
fares. The omnibus service was an established fact; an institution.
Shillibeer, its begetter, deserved a more successful career than he was
allowed. Driven off this, his original route, by lighter and better
buses, he started another service, between the West End and
Greenwich, only to find that competition from the London and

93

Greenwich Railway, the first in London, was too much for him. The 'express carriage' which he ran between London and Brighton was a failure. He then introduced a patent hearse, but this had little better success, and he was obliged to abandon his high ambitions and spent the rest of his days as a disgruntled undertaker. One major victory did come his way, and was suitably recognised. He succeeded in bringing about the repeal of the post-horse duties and the tax on postmasters' carriages; and in gratitude for this benefit the post-masters of Great Britain feasted him and gave him a substantial purse.

The success of the service Shillibeer had introduced, with its strict adherence to route and time-table, brought a large number of bus proprietors into the business. It was every man for himself, and the wild rivalry between one bus and the next made riding in them a sport almost as dangerous as big-game hunting. Most of the early drivers did all they knew to promote the spirit of the game. To quote the Edinburgh Journal of 1845, many of them were 'coarse fellows who used the foulest language and performed the most reckless feats in driving and racing'.

The object was twofold; to collect the maximum number of fares, and to see to it that a rival did not get them. If a 'pirate' came on to a route, he was 'nursed': in other words, the buses of an established proprietor ran immediately in front of and behind him. Drama began when the leader had to stop, and the 'pirate' took his chance and made a determined effort to get in front. The races that developed between vehicles with three horses abreast, bouncing and jolting along rough, muddy streets, can be imagined. They often led to serious accidents and to police prosecutions.

When we consider the co-ordinated system of transport that eventually developed in London, from the ferocious rivalry and free-for-all scrapping of this early period, we should take off our hats to one of the greatest victories of good sense and goodwill which local history can show. Many of the civilised institutions which we enjoy and take for granted have been newly won for us, and hard won at that.

Certain minds in the industry had always envisaged and hoped for the kind of co-ordination we now enjoy. There were associations of proprietors even in 1832, the time of the Stage Carriage Act. But the competition in these days told hard against the little men, who learned the need of forming more and larger associations to protect themselves and the routes they were trying to serve. They realised that it would pay better to co-operate rather than to compete.

There is some conflict of authorities as to where the credit for these moves towards co-operation belongs. Some give it to the small owners, others to the big. Without concerning ourselves, we can simply record that the associations grew by degrees until they were more powerful than any single large proprietor. Misfortunes united them. When, for instance, a newcomer on the Paddington-City route successfully indicted his rivals for conspiracy against him, and they were fined one thousand pounds and costs, the majority of the members incorporated themselves into The London Conveyance Company. This organisation had a short but useful life. It instituted cheap and frequent services, but was later forced into liquidation. Hazardous indeed was the career of small proprietors in these early days, but the 'associations' which they formed were the starting point of all subsequent co-ordination.

II

Competitors who survived the 'nursing' and cutting of fares that was practised against them were usually allowed to join the association on payment of a large fee, which was divided between the other members. The schedule for the route was carefully reorganised and the newcomer was allowed to take over certain 'times'. As a proprietor he had to provide his own buses, horses, and drivers, the association engaged the necessary conductors, time-keepers, cashiers, 'road director', or traffic manager as we should call him today. After the conductor had deducted four shillings for himself and six shillings for the driver—and these sums were often exceeded—the daily takings were paid into a pool, and divided among the several proprietors in proportion to the mileage travelled by their buses. The association held weekly meetings to deal with problems of traffic management, charges of bad timekeeping or inefficient or dishonest conducting, and any questions that called for negotiation with neighbouring associations, such as payments in compensation for the right to run over part of another association's route.

These payments were sometimes made by allotting a certain number of 'times', or running rights, to the other association. In fact the whole financial set-up of the horse-bus association was based on the 'times' owned by the individual proprietors, which were really their shareholdings in the association, and were bought and sold within the industry, often by auction. When an association decided to increase the number of buses on a route, either to extend it or to increase its frequency, the right to run the additional times would be auctioned and the proceeds distributed to the owners of the existing 'times'.

By the eighteen-fifties a number of these associations had been formed: the Paddington, Bayswater, Westminster, Atlas and Waterloo, Camden Town, Hackney Road, King's Cross and Barnsbury, and many smaller groups. Close on 1,000 buses were running in London before the Great Exhibition of 1851, employing at least 10,000 horses (at eleven per bus) and some 3,000 to 4,000 men. With a tax of three-halfpence per mile on each vehicle, the annual revenue for the Government must have amounted to over £150,000.

As the service grew, the buses became more capacious and more business-like. Luxury fittings disappeared. At the time of the Great Exhibition, the mirrors, clocks, and newspapers with which many earlier vehicles had been furnished were gone, and the 'knife-board' bus, with its back-to-back outside seats, allowed an additional fourteen nimble passengers to scramble up on the roof by means of three or four narrow iron steps. An addition, characteristic of the period, was the 'decency' boards which were presently fitted to protect the legs of outside passengers from the public gaze.

Although some of the buses of this period did long runs, from the West End to Brixton, Clapham and Kennington, and travelled to suburbs as distant as Hounslow, Hammersmith, and Brentford, they were still brakeless, and had to use skids and chains on serious gradients. The floor was covered with straw as an aid to warmth, the conductor rode on a step half-way up the back of the bus so that he could observe the comings and goings of his outside passengers, and the driver, complete with a top-hat, and, already, a reputation for lively repartee, leant against a sloping board to which he was secured by a strap.

Punch's Almanack for 1845 makes a conductor observe:

> Buses is erroneously said to hold only 13 insides; if they like they can hold a great many more, besides bundles and wet umbrellas. Man is a squeezable animal, and buses is like carpet bags, there is no knowing what they will hold till you tries 'em. Consequently, though your 'bus seems full, shove 'em in, and drive on, and they are sure to shake down and fit in as close as wood pavement. Bad sixpences is useful on rainy nights, for stingy women as don't pay more than the fare for themselves and a caravan full of parcels. When short of passengers, stop at the corner of every street to make observations, and dance the polka on the foot-board.

Three Worthing Motor Services charabancs equipped with tiered seating — a Sunday School outing in 1910

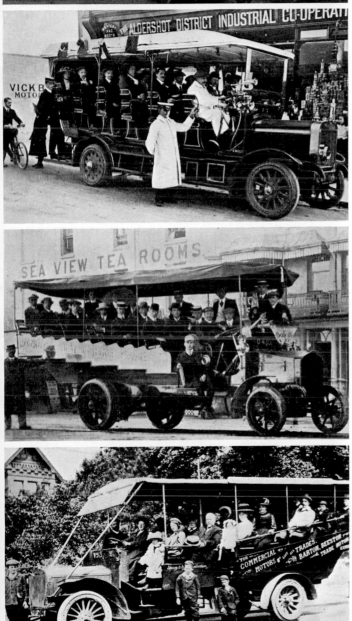

A charabanc named 'Emily' belonging to the Aldershot & District Traction Company —1913

A Halford chain-driven charabanc in service in 1909 for seaside excursions— Maidstone & District Motor Services

A charabanc with a Durham Churchill chassis and an Aston engine. Operated on a regular daily service by Barton Transport in 1908

A 'toast-rack' omnibus powered by a Leyland engine—
Worcester Motor Traction Company—1911

Experimental vehicle, fitted with two petrol engines and of
all-metal construction, operated by 'Midland Red' in 1911

III

The year of the Great Exhibition was a turning point in the omnibus's history. The bus proprietors, operating a remarkable joint service planned by James Willing, took advantage of the enormous crowds, put on many more buses, raised their fares, and made the most of their opportunity. After the Exhibition this boom came to an end, and a slump followed, during which many newcomers, attracted by the boom traffic, invaded the associations' regular routes and the standard 3*d.* fares were cut in many places to 2*d.*, and even for a time to 1*d.* on the Oxford Street routes.

Two astute Frenchmen, Joseph Orsi and Leopold Foucaud, who had seen the financial success of the large omnibus company running in Paris, were, however, convinced of the basic stability and power of recovery of the London bus business and got in touch with several leading proprietors with the idea of forming a public company. Accordingly there was formed in 1855 the Anglo-French Compagnie Gènèrale des Omnibus de Londres, the name being anglicised for public use to 'London General Omnibus Company'.

Not surprisingly, there was at first strong opposition to the idea of such a Company operating in London. Busmen posted up placards protesting at what they took to be interference by foreign capitalists. Many operators declared that the industry was congested already. However, as soon as it became apparent that the new Company intended to buy existing services or 'times' in existing associations at their full value, and to take over the existing staffs, the wind went out of the opposition. A number of existing proprietors agreed to sell their business and in January, 1856, with a French traffic manager Felix Carteret and two leading proprietors, Arthur MacNamara and James Willing, acting as London managers, the Compagnie took over seventy-two buses and in a short time increased their fleet to a hundred and ninety-eight.

The total number of buses in London at this time is still disputed by the various chroniclers. One authority gives it as eight hundred, another puts it as high as fifteen. At all events, the Compagnie acquired some 600 by the end of the year. Amongst the many established proprietors who did not sell to the new company were Thomas Tilling and the Birch family, both of whose businesses have survived to the present day. In 1858 the undertaking was re-registered under the unassailably English form of its name.

G

Yet the original price it had paid, four hundred thousand pounds, of which more than half represented the cost of the 'times', was not written off the balance sheet until 1897.

In their zeal to obtain the best, the Company in 1856 instituted a competition for the ideal bus. The vehicle that won was designed by a Mr. Miller of Hammersmith. This could carry twelve passengers inside and thirteen outside. The vehicle which they produced, however, followed no single design, but incorporated ideas taken from several of the competitors. By June, 1858, some four hundred new buses had been put into operation, and the standard of horses had been raised. There was also introduced a form of through-booking called the Correspondence; under this scheme it became possible to buy tickets for travel between any two points within the Company's system. Also, packets of tickets that could be used on any General route were offered at reduced prices. Neither of these innovations found favour, however, and they were dropped a few years later.

The L.G.O.C.'s articles of association gave it a working area of fifteen miles from Charing Cross. In buying the buses it had been obliged to take over other services, which it proceeded to shed as soon as was convenient, thereby getting a chance to concentrate and improve its own service.

A variety of other amenities were planned, besides cheapness and handiness of booking. The traditional insolence of conductors was to be remedied by the employment of wounded soldiers from the Crimea who, it was thought, would be worthy and suited for such work.

In short, the service, the convenience and the comfort of travellers were to be greatly improved, if not put first. As the *Illustrated London News* observed, when the Company was formed:

> The unprotected female need, therefore, be no longer a strong-minded individual to travel per bus; and even anxious parents will henceforth hazard their fond pledges of mutual affection without disagreeable associations connected with chimney sweeps or dealers in Norfolk sausages.

Early in 1865, *All the Year Round*—the periodical founded by Dickens—makes a comment based on experience:

> I am bound to say that in many respects the omnibuses and their men are greatly improved during my experience. The thirteenth seat,

that awful position with your back to the horses and your face to the door where, in a Mohamet's coffin-like attitude, you rested on nothing and had to contemplate your own legs calmly floating before you, very little below the faces of your right and left hand neighbours, has been abolished; a piece of cocoanut matting is generally substituted for that dank straw which smelt so horribly and clung to your boots with such vicious perseverence; most of the windows are, what in stage language is termed, practicable, and can be moved at pleasure; and a system of ventilation in the roof is now the rule, instead of, as in my early days, the exception. Thirdly, by the salutary rule of the London General Omnibus Company, aided by the sharp notice which the magistrates take of any impropriety, the omnibus servants, the coachmen and conductors, from insolent blackguards have become, for the most part, civil and intelligent men, while the whole 'service'—horses, harness, food etc.—has been placed on a greatly improved footing.

IV

For over half-a-century the General continued to work in close harmony with the old associations in which it had bought 'times', and shared their battles against newcomers. The largest of the associations was the 'Atlas and Waterloo' which had grown from 46 buses in 1868, when it was formed by the fusion of two existing associations, to 357 in 1900, near the end of the horse-bus era. In that year the other associations still existing were the 'Camden Town', 'John Bull', 'King's Cross and Barnsbury', 'King's Cross and Victoria', 'Victoria Station' and 'Westminster'.

One of the most formidable newcomers was the London Road Car Company, which was formed in 1880 by a group of City men who thought there was room for another omnibus company in London. 'Road Car' carried a fluttering Union Jack as a trade sign—contrasting gaily with the scarlet umbrellas sported by the rival buses of M.E.T. 'Road Car' were the first to introduce the garden seat on the top deck. They eventually forced their way into various 'association' and 'General' routes and remained an important operator right through the early days of motor-buses. They started a roll-ticket system which, when the General adopted it in 1891, caused a strike. Both drivers and conductors had inherited from coaching days traditional methods of increasing their wages. At the time the system appeared, they were agitating for a sixteen-hour day to be reduced to twelve, so that they naturally resented the efficiency of any new accounting methods. The problem of conductors and their fares was not overcome, however, until the Bell Punch system was introduced in 1893.

> Punch the ticket,
> Punch with care,
> Punch in the presence of the passenjaire . . .

v

As with the motor car, the development of mechanical power for omnibuses was hampered hopelessly until the man-with-a-flag law was repealed in 1896. Even then oil, petrol and electric-powered motors for traction purposes were in their infancy. The oil-engined vehicle of the Motor Traction Company which appeared in 1899 was purely experimental. So was the Thornycroft steam-car that followed it in 1902. The bodies of both these vehicles were no more than those of horse-buses adapted to the new motive power. Although by no means the most enterprising competitor in this field, the General in 1904 put into service a single-decker steam-bus. A petrol-electric motor-bus, the Fischer, 1903, was tried but did not get into public service. Other companies took up the challenge with various other makes. Soon there were buses on the streets by Milnes-Daimler, Straker-Squire, De Dion-Bouton, Germain, Stirling, Leyland-Crossley, Orion, Wolseley, Clarkson, and Rolls.

At the beginning of 1905 there were one thousand four hundred horse-buses and twenty motor-buses; by the end of it the motor-driven vehicles had increased to two hundred and thirty, and the London Motor Omnibus Company trading under the fleet name of 'Vanguard' had introduced mechanical buses on a commercial scale and which at once forged ahead. It cut fares, introduced route numbers, and put improved double-decker buses on the roads.

Many other operators joined in the competition, first with steam vehicles and then with the petrol-engine. Some were forced into new amalgamations; many into liquidation. This was a grim, hectic period of each man for himself. Every proprietor who meant business had to be ready at any time to scrap his existing vehicles and invest huge sums in an uncertain market. It was a fight to the death: and the public, which should have been the gainer, got little benefit. For one thing, these reshufflings and reorganisations ruined much of the

A 1908 charabanc of the Sussex Motor Road Car Company, precursor of Southdown Motor Services

A Deal and District bus, 1907, constructed with a Brush chassis and a Birch Bros. body

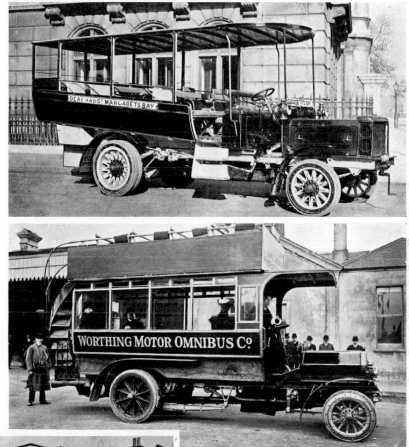

Milnes-Daimler double-decker— Worthing Motor Omnibus Company, 1910

Omnibus run by the Aldershot & Farnborough Company, 1906-10, with the popular Milnes-Daimler chassis

The First Clippies?

Conductresses employed by Barton Transport Company before and during the 1914–18 war. This Company was perhaps the first to employ women for this work. The centre figure is the daughter of the founder of the Company

Left-centre: Petrol shortage compelled this war-time improvisation—a 'gas-bag' omnibus with a Lothian chassis operated by Scottish Motor Traction Company, 1914–18

Below: A war-time improvisation of the Second World War. This producer gas unit was used for a short time by the Southdown Company

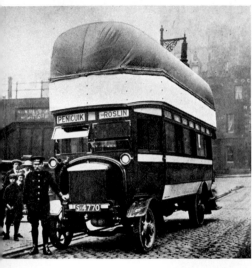

An evacuation scene in the Maidstone & District Company's area early in the Second World War

organisation which the associations had built up. Apart from the fact that whole fleets of vehicles were removed and others put in their place, so that there were always fewer buses than were needed, it was extremely difficult to integrate the timings of horse and motor buses. Proprietors were in such hot competition that many of the more remunerative routes were overworked, to the detriment of others.

The new co-ordination that slowly emerged told, once again, the story of a growing monopoly. It was, at the same time, one of the more remarkable achievements of London's transport. The word monopoly has an ugly sound, and I have yet to find an undertaking that welcomes it as a label. Like any other human institution, it can be used well or badly. If it is well used, a transport monopoly can benefit the public by reducing costs, standardising vehicles, and integrating its schedules so that cross-country journeys lose their terrors and travellers can book for long distances and enjoy carefully arranged connections. If it is used badly, it can make travel costly and inconvenient and prefer its own administrative convenience to the public's comfort. In itself, the word need have no derogatory meaning. At worst, it carries opportunities for abuse. As one experienced commentator has put it, a modern licence is more of a franchise than a monopoly.

London's transport monopoly was, perhaps, inevitable. The operators of motor-buses had many difficulties to overcome. The roads were so bad and tyres so expensive that tyre maintenance alone cost nearly twopence per mile. Drivers and mechanics were inexperienced, and both were costly to train; the motor-buses themselves were expensive and unreliable. As public vehicles more worthy of their task were introduced, the competition between the horse-bus, the motor-bus, the tram, and the underground electric train grew steadily fiercer.

The detailed changes by which these services came to feed one another and give up stealing one another's passengers and cutting one another's throats—see the *Punch* cartoons of the period—lie far beyond the scope of this book; but the main changes were simple. Competition between the buses was greatly reduced in 1908, when the General took over its principal competitors, the Road Car and the Vanguard Companies. The Great Eastern of London followed in 1911.

In 1909 a new bus, the X type, was built and proved unsuccessful. The B type, introduced late in 1910, carried the same number of passengers, thirty-four, but was superior in comfort and performance. Even so, with all the improvements it brought, many of the new services which the General ran were still based on the old

Association routes. The last of the L.G.O.C. horse-buses, which was running between London Bridge and Moorgate, was withdrawn in 1911. In the following year came the second main development: the Underground took over the General.

In this year, therefore, 1912, the railways and much surface transport of the metropolis came under a single control.

CHAPTER XII

London Tramways

'. . . At last I've found out what I am,
A creature that moves
In determinate grooves,
In fact not a bus but a tram.'

MONSIGNOR KNOX.

ALTHOUGH, as we have seen, the bus services had reached a highly competitive state by the middle of the nineteenth century, the progress of tramways was slow and sedate. Trams needed Parliamentary sanction, and for a long time their promoters could not get it. For this reason most of the early schemes in London came to nothing. Trams had been running in New York since 1832, yet in 1858 proposals for a line from Notting Hill Gate to the Bank met with determined opposition.

G. F. Train, the American pioneer who, despite his surname, introduced this form of transport, was also refused permission to lay a tramway in London. Here the provinces took a lead, and the local authority at Birkenhead gave him permission to operate there in 1858. The success of the undertaking impressed the London authorities, so that a further appeal to the Commissioners of Metropolis Roads won him leave for an experimental line, which was to run westwards from the Marble Arch along the Bayswater Road.

The line was opened on March 23rd, 1861. The cars, which were fourteen feet long and drawn by two horses, had one deck only, and carried twenty passengers and twelve standing. Although the rails had an outer flange that was raised half an inch above the level of the road, the cars were frequently derailed, and the track caused so much trouble that its life was short.

A second service, at a fare of twopence, was opened between Victoria Station and Westminster Abbey. For the inauguration ceremony Train issued the following invitation:

An American Breakfast Given by Mr. George Francis Train at the Westminster Palace Hotel on the Opening of the Westminster Street Railway in Victoria Street.

Monday 15th April 1861 at 10 o'clock a.m.

I arrived in England in October, 1859. I opened the Birkenhead Street Railway (with a Banquet) in August 1860; The Marble Arch

103

Street Railway (with a Turtle Lunch) in March, 1861; and today I inaugurate the Third Street Railway this side the New World with a Yankee Breakfast.

I cannot better shew my appreciation for the great kindness I have received in this Country, than by calling my friends about me whenever occasion offers. Several kind friends (I wish I had more enemies and fewer friends) say that I am running the thing into the ground—that the Members of Parliament don't like too much of these things,—that they talk about it in the Clubs—and so forth; such nonsense is unworthy of intelligent minds. I intend to give Dinners, Lunches, Suppers, Breakfasts, just when I please, and if those I invite object, they of course will not honour me with their distinguished company. I maintain that a man has a perfect right to spend his own money, in his own way, providing he breaks no law, and laws are not yet made for Street Railways . . .

Going on to point out that what Mr. Train wanted was Parliamentary sanction for a service that would be a boon to the people, the invitation ended:

Bear in mind there are not many thousands in the Land who can afford their carriage; but there are many millions, if they can have at my expense a pair of greys and an elegant carriage, large enough for their entire family, for two pence each, who will belong to the Hyde Park Party.

I cannot think that anyone would wish to throw any impediment in the way of introducing so great a luxury as the PEOPLES CARRIAGE.

Two months later, Train applied for leave to develop his street railway. Delay and argument followed. Finally, six months later, the Commissioners of Roads not only refused leave, but ordered him to take up the lines he had put down. Subsequently he was fined one shilling 'for injury and breaking up of Uxbridge Road', the Marylebone magistrates holding that the Commissioners of Roads had exceeded their powers in granting him a licence.

Such was the fate of London's first tramways. As one may readily guess, the main opposition, and the most articulate, came from the owners of private carriages, which meant that Authority with a large A was against the innovation. Traders' vehicles suffered the same inconvenience, but their owners could not protest quite so effectively. The general public, having tasted blood, so to speak, was with Train.

Here, obviously, were the seeds of a fine political row. For seven years, however, they lay dormant, the whole subject having been shelved. Later on they were to sprout into an unruly crop.

II

No further progress was possible until, in 1868, Parliament authorised the Liverpool tramway and the line between Brixton and Kennington Gate, and, by the Tramways Act of 1870, established the Board of Trade as the authority which could give assent to all future schemes. Here, however, our native instinct for compromise came out in all its brilliance: for the same Act gave local authorities the power to veto proposals, and to buy up the whole or part of a tramway system after twenty-one years—restrictions which still remain and could not be evaded until the Light Railways Act of 1896 afforded a legal way out. Thus many pioneering companies were severely handicapped in the years that followed.

Nevertheless, after the Act was passed, the Metropolitan Street Tramways Company opened a line between Brixton and Kennington Gate, various other London companies were incorporated, schemes covering more than two hundred miles of tramways were put forward. One Company wanted to put down lines in the centre of the City itself, but could not get the permission of the Corporation. Even the West End was threatened. Many interests were involved here, but it was to a great extent the policy of the omnibus companies that maintained the heart of London for buses rather than for trams. The North Metropolitan Company, for example, made arrangements with the 'General' for the supply of horses, and this fact naturally gave the 'General' a certain degree of influence over the development of tramways.

The cars of the 'seventies were made in New York. Painted in distinctive colours according to their route, and running on improved rails, they carried twenty-two passengers inside, and twenty-four on a knife-board seat on the upper deck. The iron ladder which gave access to this had to be carried from one platform to the other before the tram started its return journey. A foot-brake on the platform worked on a ratchet, and, with its indiarubber block springing, the vehicle swayed uncomfortably on sections of rough track. The rails had to be periodically cleaned of mud by means of a special tool pushed along them by two men. They were without moveable blade points: the only way to switch from one line to another was to jerk the horses sideways. If one car broke down, the rest had to be derailed. This was done by placing iron wedges against the forward wheels, and involved a further struggle on the part of the horses. To put the tram back on the rails was an even more hazardous operation, for it could travel some distance along the road before all four wheels agreed to submit to the line.

However, each tram could cover from fifteen to twenty miles a day, and this schedule allowed at least a double journey on the longer routes. A 'cock' horse waited at the bottom of all serious hills, where the boy in charge of it, with a skill developed by long practice, had to clip his chain to the vehicle without stopping it. Then all three horses cantered as far up the slope as the weight and momentum of the tram would let them.

III

While the North Metropolitan Company tried in vain to introduce trams to the City, and the Metropolitan Street Tramways Company carried its line from Brixton Hill to Westminster Bridge, the Pimlico, Peckham, and Greenwich Company was renamed to form the London Tramways Company. This Company laid a line from Victoria Station to Vauxhall Bridge, which was then privately owned, and there a bus was used to transfer passengers to the tramway on the south side. Not until 1906 were trams allowed to cross the bridge.

In the 'seventies, experimental steam-trams were started on the north side of the river. The first of these had its engine built into a double-decker tram, but later designs, such as those used in north London, had a separate locomotive. The same objections were raised in many provincial cities, for the steam, the noise, and the smoke of these vehicles were a serious nuisance in streets where horses were used, and they were costly to operate; so that some of these experimental services became horse-drawn once again, before they were converted to electricity. Steam-powered cables, however, minimised the nuisance, and were used in the 'eighties to draw trams up Highgate Hill. A similar system was later adopted between Brixton and Streatham.

By 1875, that is, within five years of the Tramways Act, the North Metropolitan Company was operating a hundred and sixty-four cars, the London Tramways Company a hundred and thirty-nine, and the London Street Tramway Company forty-eight. Between them they had fifty miles of track in daily use, and, in a period of six months, they carried twenty million passengers. These were the larger under-takings; and, when we see that in 1889 the tramways of London were still divided between fourteen separate companies, the length and difficulty of the journey towards co-ordination is apparent.

One feature of its slow progress was a continual effort to reduce the fares. In the late 'nineties, some were as little as a farthing a mile. There were frequent early morning services for working men, who found the platforms convenient for stowing their tools and gear. When a man could travel from Bow to his work in Aldgate at the cost of a penny, the rôle of London's tramways was clear. Bus pro-prietors had to accept their competition as permanent.

IV

The electrification of the routes brought immense improvements in speed and comfort, though London, as we shall see, lagged behind many provincial towns and cities. Nevertheless, many tramway companies took advantage of the period in which the bus was slow to develop, and began to exploit the possibilities of electric traction. The London County Council purchased the London Street Tram-ways Company in 1891 and, some eight years later, obtained powers to operate the London Tramway Company's system south of the Thames. With this support it began to think about electrification in 1900.

V

It is all very fine and neat to write statistics of achievement, as if they depended only on legislation and purchase and the improvement of vehicles. The human element remains, obstinate, acquisitive, re-calcitrant. All this activity involved serious and bitter struggles between the operators of the different forms of transport. When, for example, the L.C.C. tried to use buses in order to extend the tram-ways they had laid down south of the Thames to central points on the north bank of the river, many large and small proprietors and the old-established 'associations' formed themselves into the London Omnibus Owners' Federation to oppose it. What is more, they succeeded. At least two attempts by the L.C.C. to carry its tramways across the Thames bridges were defeated.

In 1901, when the London United Tramways had already

electrified sixteen miles of track, a number of undertakings had been welded into a single system, owned and operated by the L.C.C. By 1903 the Council owned a hundred and eighty-nine miles of track in Greater London, which it proceeded to electrify. For aesthetic reasons, the conduit system was used rather than the overhead wires so common in other parts of the country. Incidentally, the amalgamation, and centralisation which it brought about, greatly reduced the capital cost of new vehicles and of generating plant.

First to be electrified was the Westminster to Tooting route in 1903, and lines were laid at last across Westminster Bridge. The Victoria Embankment line followed in 1906, and, two years later, the Kingsway Subway made a link between the southern and northern systems, though for single-deck trams only.

At about this time closed tops began to improve the comfort of the trams and to make them increasingly popular. The buses did not adopt them for another twenty years: with the height of the chassis there were fears for the vehicles' stability, and they would not go under railway bridges. Fares were kept low, despite so much ex-penditure of capital. The L.C.C. made various working agreements with neighbouring organisations, such as the London United Tram-ways Company, enabling services to be extended as far as Wimbledon at a fare of a penny for three and a half miles. Services ran every day of the week into South-West Essex and to Waltham Cross through Middlesex and Hertfordshire and eventually to Purley in Surrey.

So cheap had tramways become that it seemed they would carry all before them. Worried by the workmen's services south of the Thames, for example, the London, Brighton and South Coast Railway decided to electrify the line between Victoria and London Bridge. Even the railways had felt the competition. As the *Daily Mail* claimed in February, 1905:

> London may soon see a triple fight for existence between electric tramways, motor omnibuses and the railways conveying passengers to and from the suburbs. The tramways have robbed the railways of their suburban traffic: motor omnibuses with their greater mobility are threatening the existence of the tramways: and the railways, awakening at the eleventh hour, are hoping to gain lost ground by electrification and the improvement of their services.

Even so, there were many who wrote to the newspapers and maintained that the tramway was doomed.

A familiar sight in London after the First World War— one of the green Daimlers run by the British Automobile Traction Company

Two of the numerous types of buses run by Southdown Motor Services in 1914. The leading vehicle is a 'Scout' followed by a 'Caledon'

An early attempt to solve rush-hour difficulties is seen in this Ribble two door bus of the 1920s

The Potteries Company were proud of their 1d. fare as can be seen from this 1920 single-decker

Piccadilly Circus, 1920. An interesting picture of this busy centre before the present system of traffic control was introduced

CHAPTER XIII

Tramways in the Provinces

'And many people were proud of those cushioned trams. . . .'
ARNOLD BENNETT: *Clayhanger*.

THE point has been made, and more than once, with an emphasis that may invite a momentary wonder about the author's origins, that tramways in the provinces were well ahead of those in London. A successor to Train's experimental line had been laid down in Liverpool in the 'sixties, and although it degenerated into such a state of disrepair that the municipality ordered it to be taken up again in 1874, an amalgamation of concerns eventually brought about the Liverpool United Tramways and Omnibus Company. In due course the system was taken over by the municipal authorities and, for forty years, it operated as the Liverpool Corporation Tramways.

Hull had horse-trams running in its streets in 1873; a combined Omnibus and Tramway Company started a further line a year later. The Leeds system, one of the most progressive, is an excellent example of the many which, after the Tramways Act of 1870, were started by a private company's taking a lease from the municipality. There were difficulties. The inhabitants proved suspicious; they had to be coaxed into the vehicles by the offer of free rides on an experimental track. Although this advertisement had an immediate success, and a route to Headingley was opened in 1871, the company did not prosper. Later the municipality stepped in, and took over the system.

To sum up the position, and escape a mass of local details which would be of no interest to the general reader, we may say that in the last decades of the nineteenth century horse-trams were working in many provincial cities. In some they took the place of the horse-buses that had developed from the short-stage coaches; in others they worked alongside them until, with the coming of electricity, the trams developed fast and the horse-buses became obsolete.

Here and there steam-trams were tried, usually without success. It is said that at Shoreham, in 1884, bus drivers encouraged their horses to smell the engines of the steam-trams so that they would not be frightened. If this is true, the horses must have had the last laugh, since in this case, like many others, the steam-trams had to be withdrawn because they were so unreliable.

Until the introduction of electric traction at the close of the century, both passengers and proprietors preferred horse-drawn trams. The circumstances and the stage of development varied from town to town, so that none can be looked on as typical. Yet, if we are to get deeper into the subject, we shall have to examine a specific case in some detail. An excellent example is provided by the Pottery Towns of North Staffordshire.

II

In the Victorian era, the population of these towns, which had become famous through the work of such potters as Spode and Josiah Wedgwood, had more than trebled itself; and although the towns were distinct and separate, their single industry made for a degree of unity. The inhabitants shared the interest of their work, and the promise of urban development and expansion for each lay within the industry.

During the eighteenth century the pottery had been sent away by pack-horses on miry roads, and the clay had been brought to Liverpool by sea. After 1766 the construction of two canals improved communications. The Grand Trunk Canal gave access to the Mersey via the Bridgewater Canal, and so to Lancashire. Even so, up to the middle of the last century transport services in the area were narrowly limited. Little moved on the roads, and the railway had only just arrived.

In 1861, the year in which he was ordered to remove his tramways from the streets of London, this state of things attracted the attention of George Francis Train. Thwarted in the south, that astute pioneer recognised the opportunity offered by the closely packed little smoky towns. The inhabitants, and the owners of the few horse-buses there were on the local roads, did not at first share his enthusiasm. Train, once more vociferating his theme-song that his cars were the 'people's carriage', attempted to win them over by exhibiting the vehicles and extolling their merits in the market squares.

As in London, Train overcame the initial opposition, and in 1862 the Staffordshire Potteries Street Railway, less than two miles in length, was opened between Hanley and Burslem. The fare was threepence, and the cars ran every half hour in each direction. Although the enterprise ran short of money and changed hands in 1880, Train had started something permanent in the Potteries. He had met an important need, and the inhabitants recog-

nised the fact. Yet when, in 1870, the Loop Line of the North
Staffordshire Railway joined the two towns with the main line
between Stoke and Stafford, there seemed little hope of extending
Train's system.

This district at this period forms the background of Arnold
Bennett's novel, *The Old Wives' Tale*, which has many references to
the horse-tram:

> Incredible as it may appear, there was nothing but a horse-tram
> between Bursley and Hanbridge—and that only twice an hour; and
> between the other towns no stage of any kind! One went to Longshaw
> as one now goes to Pekin. . . . A poor, blind, complacent people! The
> ludicrous horse-car was typical of them. The driver rang a huge bell,
> five minutes before starting, that could be heard from the Wesleyan
> Chapel to the Cock Yard, and then after deliberations and hesitations,
> the vehicle rolled off on its rails into unknown dangers while pas-
> sengers shouted good-bye. At Bleakridge it had to stop for the turn-
> pike, and it was assisted up the mountains of Leveson Place and
> Sutherland Street (towards Hanbridge) by a third horse, on whose
> back was perched a tiny whip-cracking boy; that boy lived like a
> shuttle on the road between Leveson Place and Sutherland Street,
> and even in wet weather he was the envy of all other boys. After half
> an hour's perilous transit the car drew up solemnly in a narrow street
> by the 'Signal' office in Hanbridge, and the ruddy driver, having
> revolved many times the polished iron handle of his sole brake, turned
> his attention to his passengers in calm triumph, dismissing them with
> a sort of unsung doxology. And this was regarded as the last work of
> traction! A whip-cracking boy on a tip-horse.

III

Ten years after the Tramways Act had given encouragement to
this form of transport, the Staffordshire Potteries Street Railway
was taken over by the North Staffordshire Tramways Company.
In 1879 mechanical traction on tramways was authorised. Thus in
the 'eighties, with steam as the new power of propulsion, some five
and three-quarter miles of track were laid down; though the Board
of Trade refused to allow steam to be used in the narrow streets of
Longton. These early vehicles were as noisy and smoky as all the
rest, and quite unsuited for work among horse-drawn vehicles.

The public had things both ways. They took advantage of their
facilities and called them names, until in 1879 an appeal from the
local authorities to the Board of Trade resulted in the licences being
cancelled. But as soon as the people found themselves without their

much-abused tramways, they were more indignant than ever. Further petitions were sent, and the tramways were restored. From this time forward, the lines spread slowly along one side of the narrow streets that linked the principal towns, and some forty steam-cars continued to serve the community.

Arnold Bennett celebrated their importance when he wrote, again in *Clayhanger*:

> . . . people were now talking of the advantages of living 'up at Bleakridge', 'above' the smoke and 'out' of town. The new steam-cars would pull you up there in three minutes or so, every quarter of an hour. It was really the new steam-cars that were the making of Bleakridge as a residential suburb. . . . Land was changing owners at Bleakridge, and rising in price. . . . Cottage property in the centre of the town depreciated.

But the days of the steam-car were short. Some districts found them wholly unsatisfactory and returned to horse-drawn trams. Then, in the 'nineties, electricity brought about a revolution, almost a decade before the carburettor did the same for buses. Leeds, where the inhabitants had taken such a dubious view of the first horse-drawn trams, won back its reputation as a go-ahead city by being one of the first to adopt electric traction. Bristol followed in 1895, and Hull Street Tramways, under the Corporation, started to work an electric line in 1898. Plymouth, Bolton, Glasgow, Coventry, and Liverpool all had electric trams before the century was out and before the electric trams of London were established. (So, though it is outside our scope, had Dublin.) Indeed, it was to the large provincial cities that London looked for guidance and support. In 1898, when the Manager of the London United Tramways was struggling to persuade his local authorities that tramways would not depreciate the value of property and lower the tone of the neighbourhoods through which they ran, he sent a telegram to a number of Town Clerks for their support. The Town Clerk of Dover replied:

'Tramways. No justification from our experience for impression named. Electric cables no source of danger; great economy on all other traction, especially horses. Send critics here. All local opponents converted.'

IV

In considering the problems of the Black Country in particular, we must keep in mind the general conflict which underlay the move to develop tramways as a whole. In 1896 the British Electric Traction Company, the leading exponent of electrification, decided to buy and electrify the tramways of South Staffordshire. Birmingham, Wolverhampton, and Dudley were involved in the project, a year or two later. The B.E.T. Company wanted to adopt a uniform gauge for the tracks and weld the various systems into a comprehensive system which, they argued, could only be achieved and co-ordinated by a single company. This meant that the leases held by the existing companies would have to be renewed, and, since the local authorities showed no desire to take over the system themselves, no particular difficulty seemed to stand in the way.

But, when the necessary Bill was proposed in 1896, the local authorities raised a positive yell of opposition. Their argument was that since the development was to be made by a profit-making company, it would be quicker and more equitable for them to do the work of conversion themselves, town by town, and, by charging low fares, to give the people the benefit of the profit that would otherwise go to the wicked capitalists. The difficulty that some twenty neighbouring districts would have in giving unity to such a system they refused to consider. The argument went on for years—weakening gradually in favour of control by a single company.

Since it was thus impossible for the B.E.T. to get uniform agreement to the scheme, it had to overcome, one by one, the objections of the individual companies who owned the tramways, and then to tackle the local authorities. Even when their permission was secured, it had to promote Bills for the necessary licence to operate in each particular district. Some particular towns stood firm; Walsall and Wolverhampton, for example, insisted not only on owning their tramways but on running trams on them—a situation never envisaged by the Tramways Act. Still, by 1899 the B.E.T. Company was in control of thirty-six tramway projects. These were scattered from Croydon to Greenock, from Devonport to Rothesay, but the greatest concentration of them was in the Black Country. The National Electric Construction Company took over responsibility for many others.

v

When the B.E.T. obtained a controlling interest in the North Staffordshire Tramway Company, it was not indulging in an incidental speculation. On the contrary, the deal was an integral

H

part of the whole scheme. Agreeing with Mr. Train, who had first cast his eyes upon it, the B.E.T. Company realised that the area was particularly suited to tramways. The welfare of the public, the Company maintained, would be furthered by their development.

Once it had obtained the approval of the many local authorities, and, as demanded by statute, the consent of the people whose houses faced the proposed route, the B.E.T., in 1898, formed the Potteries Electric Traction Company—known locally as the 'P.E.T.' Generating plants were installed, a host of technical difficulties overcome, and in just over a year the first electric line was opened.

Unhappily, however, the ceremony was less impressive than that which greeted the opening of the railway at Stockton. When the leading car, which was proudly carrying the Company's directors, reached a slight gradient, it came to an undignified halt. The spectators were delighted, and the officials, tilting their tall hats over their eyes, did their best not to seem disconcerted.

But this was a mere token setback. The electric tramcar worked, effectively, regularly, predictably. By 1903 some twenty-nine miles of line were working in the Potteries, and some eighteen million passengers a year were being carried on them. The Chairman of the B.E.T. felt confident in saying to his shareholders, 'We must consider that the electric traction industry has now established a firm hold on the country, and I think I may justly say this—that our company may be looked upon as the leading representative of the industry.'

Gradually the enterprise grew, each line supplementing the system, until there was scarcely a village in the district that was not served by the Potteries Electric Traction Company. Throughout, of course, the P.E.T. with its parent company had to meet stern opposition both from local authorities and from the Railway Company, which claimed that it had lost eight hundred thousand passengers in a single year. The tramway pioneers retorted that the short-stage journeys were of vital importance to the public, and that the trams had created more traffic than the railways claimed to have lost. This view was supported by the increasing number of people who rushed towards the trams as soon as the factories closed, stood waiting at the roadside for them in the early mornings, and protested loudly if the extension proposed for their particular street could not be put into working order in the space of a few weeks.

Soon the fleet of cars had grown to a hundred and ten—all single-deckers because of low bridges, and drawing their power from over-head trolleys. Fitted with wheel, slipper, and rheostatic brakes, the new cars were reasonably comfortable, safe, and fast. The tracks

were paved with granite setts, and this made the going better for
other road users, particularly the steel-tyred carts which carried
coal, clay, and merchandise between the collieries, the wharves, the
factories, and the goods depots.

The P.E.T. services included an Express delivery for parcels and
newspapers, and special vehicles for carrying coal and merchandise.
All ran regularly throughout a seven day week. Half-price fares were
provided early and late for factory workers. Time-tables were faithfully kept, even in the early years, and often at considerable cost.
In winter the Company had to clear its own tracks with improvised
snow-ploughs.

Although passenger services are our concern, a word should be
said about this parcel service, which was unique at the time. To start
with, bags were hung beside the platforms of the trams; but as the
business developed, the Company introduced baggage cars in the
form of trailers. Charging sixpence for a parcel weighing fifty-six
pounds, this service began by dispatching about three hundred
parcels a week. Within a year the figure had increased to two
thousand five hundred. The local newspaper opined that 'such a
Titanic and all-comprehensive scheme suggests an American origin'.
In fact, the scheme was worked out locally by the Company's representatives, in answer to a genuine need. Later the service was
developed by motor-buses and taken up by other subsidiaries of the
B.E.T. Company. It was the development of Pickfords, ultimately,
which put an end to the parcels service in this area.

VI

As happened in many other districts, the P.E.T. introduced
motor-buses early in the century to act as a feeder service for the
trams. Two Straker-Squire steam-buses were tried out in 1901, but
were a failure. The double-decker chain-driven buses that were later
put on the road in the Trentham area did little better. Like the early
motor-buses in London, they were unreliable and expensive; and
spare parts were hard to come by. Nevertheless, with these experiments the Company was preparing the way for the bus service which
was to be an important part of its provisions before 1914.

In these buses, as subsequent chapters will show, lay some of the
strength that this and similar tramway undertakings needed, in order
to face the widespread bus competition that followed the First
World War. Though tramways in the Five Towns were firmly

established in the first decade of the century, though their cheapness had been proved, and they had done great things for the social and industrial life of the district, the motor revolution had rumbled and snorted its way into London, and, as with every other revolution, its effects were likely to spread. Motor-buses could be used to supplement trams, and many small operators came to realise that they

LIVERPOOL CORPORATION TRAMWAYS.

TOP COVER FOR TRAMCARS

NOTICE TO PASSENGERS

The Curtains are provided for the purpose of affording protection in inclement weather.

In order to secure uniformity of use and avoid disagreement amongst passengers, Conductors alone will be allowed to manipulate them, and the attention of the public is called to Bye-law No. 11:

No person other than the Conductor or Driver shall change or remove the route indicators or destination boards, or interfere with the controllers, brakes, lights, ventilators, trolley cord, or any part of a Car or its equipment, or signal a Car to start.

C. R. BELLAMY,
General Manager.

6, SIR THOMAS STREET,
LIVERPOOL, 1st December, 1902.

W. H. Lloyd, Printer, 61 Dale St. Liverpool. Tel. 2012.

A Notice issued in 1902 by the Liverpool Corporation Tramways. It is evident that there had been cases of hardy travellers who objected to protection against inclement weather. To avoid argument, conductors alone were given authority to decide (a) when the weather was inclement, and (b) when protection should be afforded.

offered a road to rapid success; small outlay, quick return. The Potteries Electric Tramway Company, casting a covetous eye on these possibilities, began to build up its own fleet of buses.

But trams were hard to dislodge. It is curious how, quite apart from their utility, they endeared themselves to their users. The farewell ceremonies which in our own day attended the closing of tramways all over the country had a warmth of affection no bus service has succeeded in generating for itself. Early in the century, they were in their heyday. It was the golden age of the tram, the great galleon on the noisy street, the dependable, sociable, clanking, rocking, preposterous vehicle on rails that became a menace to other traffic and so rallied the tram-riders in a body against all their rivals.

So, in 1914, it was the tram, the tram, the tram, and especially in the north. Thirty-two million passengers a year were being carried in Bolton, a hundred and twenty-five million in Liverpool—most of them for a twopenny fare. What had been achieved in the Potteries was repeated elsewhere by the B.E.T. Company, and the National Electric Construction Company was also triumphing in other parts of the country. And in 1914, whatever was worrying the pioneers of tramways, more serious problems overhung the land.

CHAPTER XIV

Early Transport in Manchester

'Wm. White, hackney coach proprietor, most respectfully
announces to his friends and the public that he has added to his
establishment of coaches a new eight-inside omnibus, which he
intends to commence running on Monday, March 30th, 1835, from
the "Robin Hood", Church Street, Manchester, to the "Golden
Lion", Harpurhey and which he hopes will give entire satisfaction.'

From an advertisement.

WE chose the Potteries to show how tramways developed in a
region to which they were particularly suited. Now for a single
city: Manchester, 'noble town' of the old ballad.

From the days when stage-coaches pulled out for London, York,
Aberdeen, or Bristol, Manchester provides an excellent example of
the growth of passenger transport in a provincial city. The development can be considered in three stages, which are clearly defined.
For some fifty years after long-distance coaches had been killed by
the coming of the railways, horse-buses, depending on the initiative
of individual proprietors, provided most of the nearby districts with
a modest service. By the 'seventies most of these small operators had
merged into a single company.

In the second stage, which lasted until round about 1927, the
omnibus, in spite of its competitive vitality and the protests of those
who supported it, was gradually eclipsed by the tramcar; first by the
horse-drawn kind, and then by the electric.

The third stage, which, obedient to our plate-spinning technique,
we shall look at in a later chapter, is one in which the tramcar was
superseded by the motor-bus. The pattern of development in
Manchester, therefore, is simple and straightforward. Different types
of service replace one another. If this seems too obvious to be worth
saying, since it must be in some measure true of all cities and towns,
our justification is that in Manchester the development was classic,
clear, and on the grand scale. To see the process of traffic evolution
in all its variety, we should look at Manchester.

II

The man who first realised the possibilities of a local service
which would link the rural villages and the new Victorian suburbs to

the town was an ex-toll-gate collector called John Greenwood. Having watched the coaching traffic through the Eccles Old Road and the Bolton Road gates shrink to a trickle, Greenwood recognised his chance.

His first service ran between Pendleton and Manchester in the 'twenties, several years before Shillibeer's first omnibus. Two or three vehicles, each holding eight or nine passengers, were soon on the road, and one man combined the duties of driver and guard. The fares were paid at an office in the yard of the Horse Shoe Inn, where Greenwood had his stables; and the proprietor is said to have suggested that his drivers should allow him 'one wheel in four, considering that he had to find all the expenses'. And although factory workers were then poorly paid—Peterloo was only a few years behind—the sixpenny fare was much cheaper than that of Manchester's hackneys. Among all but the worst paid, at any rate, Greenwood's buses became popular.

Other operators were quick to follow his example. They had the whole area to divide between them, so that there was little need for their routes to overlap. Nevertheless, in their own particular and local way, these buses, just like those in London, cut their fares to win the public's favour and to put one another out of business. After the Stage Coach Act of 1832, which officially recognised the short-stage vehicle plying for hire as it went, regular accommodation coaches began to serve the suburbs at a fare of twopence a mile.

When the Liverpool and Manchester Railway was opened in 1830, four specially painted buses, owned by a stage-coach proprietor of the Royal Hotel, served the railway station, making it possible to take a 'through' ticket to Liverpool from various parts of the town. This is an early example of co-ordination between the two forms of transport; co-ordination often easier to achieve in a town than in deep country, where, in many cases, the railway was obliged to provide its own buses.

In a growing industrial area such as Manchester, where the population increased by fifty per cent in ten years, this developing passenger service had two important effects. People in outlying districts could be brought to work at regular times. Those who lived in the notoriously dark and miserable back-streets—many buildings in which were later converted into warehouses and offices—were enabled to move further out, where they could at least be within sight of the country. In fact, the horse-buses of a hundred years ago first encouraged the 'commuting' which is a fundamental part in the lives of so many in modern industrial towns.

From this time, the development of transport services and the development of the town went side by side, each supporting the other. The result, whether we like it or not, is the modern housing estate, lying much further from the centre than the Victorian suburbs that were being built at the time we are discussing. The centre of the city was affected too, for the congestion caused by traffic in the 'fifties and 'sixties compelled the authorities to widen and replan the streets.

As though to celebrate these rapid beginnings, Manchester was provided in 1852 with a remarkable double-decker bus. Drawn by three horses, it was able to carry forty-two passengers, and its owner astonished his competitors by reducing what had become the normal fare of sixpence to threepence. The cheapest and best transport, in the interests of both the public and the proprietor, now became the object of any operator who wanted to survive. The services that were wanted were most of them short-stage street-to-street routes, for, although some bus proprietors were running services to places that the railway could not reach, the development of the railway was steadily cutting out the need for the long-distance bus.

In other respects, Manchester's development at this stage followed the pattern set in London, not, one need hardly say, by imitation, but because of a similar evolution. There were various attempts to control the way in which conductors collected fares, followed by strikes when the conductors resented such interference. Owing to their resistance —to take but one example—the numbered ticket system, invented in the 'thirties, was not in fact adopted until 1901.

At one time a reward of ten pounds was offered to anyone who could bring about the conviction of a conductor for taking a passenger's fare in his hand, when the rule was that the passenger should put it into a glass-topped box. In other words, relationships between owners and staff, and staff and public, were for years uneasy, despite a general tendency towards goodwill.

More important, however, is the fact that in 1865, when the competition between these independent operators was at its height, the majority of them formed the Manchester Carriage Company. This included Greenwood's business and that of the City Omnibus Company. The lesson implicit in the London 'associations' had been learnt in Manchester, as it was learnt wherever competition reached its logical conclusion. From that point the services as a whole were on the way towards co-ordination, and Manchester transport reached the end of its first phase.

III

The second phase concerns the coming of the tramways, and the violent objections which preceded their arrival. A writer in the *Manchester Guardian*, commending the city's buses and condemning Train's experiments at Birkenhead, had doubted whether the trams could be successful. Members of the Corporation, though equally perturbed, had commended themselves for having open minds.

An attempt to introduce trams was made in 1872, and failed. The following notice, posted while tramways were beginning to make progress in other parts of the country, is typical of the attitude people were asked to take:

The Great Tramway Nuisance

Fellow Sufferers,

we have long been subject to this dangerous and crying evil. Some good men and true have at last taken the matter up, and if we support them as we ought,

THE ODIOUS TRAMWAY MUST COME UP.

Attend the Meeting on Wednesday evening next, at half-past seven and show that you are determined that our principal Highway shall no longer be encroached upon; that life and limb shall not be endangered; that the public traffic shall not be taken away for the purpose of filling the pockets of a clique of greedy and monopolising speculators.

A Poor Cabby.

That the first tramway, from Bury New Road to Pendleton, was not laid down until 1877, and that it was then operated by a Yorkshire company, is some indication of the tenacity with which many Manchester citizens held on to their opinions. Once it was introduced, however, the service was soon taken over by the Manchester Carriage Company; and, with the help of the Corporation, which laid new lines within the city while the Company was laying them outside, the system was rapidly extended. To proclaim the advance, the Company changed its title to The Manchester Carriage and Tramways Company Ltd.

But the battle of the tramways was not over. As though to launch a further attack, an independent operator encouraged various of his fellows to introduce wagonettes, drawn by two horses, which were called 'penny jiggers'. With young women to collect the fares, these wagonettes undercut the tramways.

The Company's riposte was to bring out three-horse buses, and charge the same fare. Later they reduced the tram fares also to a penny. When another individualist brought out a conveyance with wheels designed to run along the Company's rails, the Company 'nursed' every one of his vehicles with two of their own, and ran him off the road.

In the 'eighties, reversible cars, so built that they could be swung round on the chassis without unhitching the horse, were put on to augment the fleet of trams. Horse-buses were now used on a few minor routes only. In 1895, after considerable negotiation with Oldham, Ashton, Hale, Stockport, and Salford, the Corporation decided to take over the tracks that had only been leased to the Company, and to run them as an electric system. The conversion was completed in 1903, when a hundred and thirty-eight miles of track came under the Corporation's control.

IV

From 1906 motor-buses were working on the Northenden and Cheadle routes. Their preliminary trials and vicissitudes need not be described, for they followed a similar pattern to those met elsewhere: but by 1910, as in the Potteries, their value was established as auxiliaries to the tramway system. In Manchester, it must be noted, the whole organisation came under the control of the Corporation. By 1914 the horse-buses had been driven into retirement; although, when war started and the motor vehicles were needed for service abroad, they came out again for what was, positively, their last appearance.

CHAPTER XV

Early Transport in Birmingham

'To rule a country of a thousand chariots, there must be a reverent attention to business, and sincerity; economy in expenditure, and love for men: and the employment of people at the proper season.'

The Analects of Confucius, quoted—very happily—by the Chairman of the Birmingham and Midland Motor Omnibus Company at the annual general meeting in 1954.

F EW things are more dangerous than to suggest comparisons between one city and another. Citizens of both are apt to rise in anger, protest the unique virtues of their own city, and, if they admit any faults at all, to claim that these are inimitable too. In any case, they aver that no outsider can possibly understand.

So, with a due sense of the risk, let me remark that although Birmingham has certain points of similarity to Manchester, its transport tells a very different story. The two accounts illuminate each other, when we look at them side by side; but their chief lesson is the astonishing variation in stages of development that can occur even within dense urban areas.

Passenger transport in Birmingham means the Birmingham and Midland Omnibus Company Limited, known as the Midland Red—an undertaking second only to London Transport, the largest in the country. With its one thousand nine hundred vehicles, served by nearly nine thousand employees, it now carries each year four hundred and eighty million passengers over some seventy-nine million miles. Midland Red is important not only because from it sprang many other undertakings, but because in its agreements with local authorities, the technical development of its vehicles, and its general policy, it has had an influence on the whole industry.

Its growth was difficult and devious. Not only had it humble beginnings: it arose out of chaos.

The development of tramways in Birmingham had been particularly slow, largely through lack of co-operation between their promoters and the Corporation. Two men had acquired a controlling interest in the City of Birmingham Tramways Company with the intention of electrifying the system, but in 1898 the Corporation decided not to let them do it. This left the problem on the Corporation's hands; and the members found themselves with a dense

population urgently needing better transport facilities, and with
short lengths of horse tramway which it was difficult to electrify
cheaply.

After negotiation, the British Electric Traction Company acquired
the interests of the two frustrated planners, and pressed for the city's
tramways to be linked up with the comprehensive system for the
Black Country, much of which the Company itself controlled.

All this took a considerable time, and occasioned much argument.
Meeting followed meeting in which steam-trams were deplored and
the progress in other cities envied. The Chairman of the Tramways
Company and the Mayor, agreeing only that the unprofitable routes
were a disgrace, filled the newspapers with their arguments about the
best way forward. Many people wanted to adopt the overhead
trolley system and have the benefit of cheap tramway fares, but no
one seemed ready to oblige them. Newspapers protested that the City
Council were wasting time. Public and private enterprise were at
loggerheads; and the controversy was no milder in Birmingham than
elsewhere.

II

By 1903, it became clear that some measure of co-ordination
was necessary in order to knit the diverse tram and horse-bus
services into an undertaking of reasonable efficiency. From this
sprang the Birmingham and Midland Tramways Joint Committee,
which was formed from the Boards of five of the local companies
associated with The British Electric Traction Company.

About the same time, the Birmingham Motor Express Company
were operating some rather uncertain motor-bus services on the
Hagley Road and Harborne routes and in June, 1904, it was
arranged for this business to be amalgamated with the horse-bus
departments of the Joint Committee's undertakings. For this
purpose, a new Company, the Birmingham & Midland Motor
Omnibus Company, was formed, and it was from this embryo,
struggling to maintain a fair service with its wayward experimental
motor-buses, that the mighty Midland Red was to grow.

Nine of these double-decker buses, some Milnes-Daimler and
some Brush, with their open tops and solid tyres, were run in
Birmingham during the next three years; but they were a complete
failure, and the Company decided to transfer them to more suitable
country in East Kent. Here they were useful, and presently helped

to give rise to an undertaking later incorporated in the East Kent Road Car Company.

The point to notice in this incident, however, is that the parent operator, the British Electric Traction Company, was in a position to transfer these buses, instead of having to go out of business, as a small local proprietor would probably have done after such a

CAUTION.

At the Birmingham Police Court, on Tuesday, October 30th, 1900, a Passenger, R.P., was charged with Assaulting an Omnibus Inspector, and **FINED TEN SHILLINGS** and COSTS. In default of payment the Defendant was ordered to undergo **FOURTEEN DAYS' IMPRISONMENT, WITH HARD LABOUR.**   *RICHARD R. FAIRBAIRN,*

Birmingham General Omnibus Offices, 118, Dale End, 1/11, 1900.   *Manager.*

A Notice issued in Birmingham in 1900. Whilst no doubt the penalty was intended to fit the crime, the alternative of fourteen days' imprisonment with hard labour, gives some idea of the value placed on a half-sovereign in those days

disaster. Furthermore, as Birmingham gave up its experiment with motors and returned once more to horse-buses, the Company's receipts immediately doubled. The citizens of Birmingham had no love for the internal combustion engine at that stage. All the same, the word 'Motor' was retained in the Company's title, to be a token of things to come.

In view of the citizens' distaste for them, motor-buses did not return to Birmingham for five years; years in which over a thousand buses were running in London. Meanwhile the Board of the Midland Red wondered what they were losing, and brooded over their immense forage, veterinary, and shoeing bills, and the pittance they got for the carcase of every horse past use.

The working conditions of the men were little better than they had been in stage-coach days. Each driver had twelve horses attached to him, to allow three or more changes during the day; his hours were long, his wages poor. Far from being supplied with a uniform, he had even to provide his own waterproof. Although the Company was obviously waiting for motor-buses to become a good deal more predictable in action than they had been in 1907, they decided, when the last of the horse-buses were leaving the streets of London, that it was time for Birmingham to take part in the revolution.

III

Though the technical development of motor vehicles lies beyond the scope of this book, it is important at least to mention the organisations that were responsible for aspects of this work. In 1905, for example, the British Electric Traction Company, realising that in some areas tramways would not develop as fast and as effectively as the founders had expected, formed the British Automobile Development Company in order to carry out research into motor-bus design on behalf of the group. In one design, made in association with the Brush Electrical Engineering Company, the driver sat above the engine, and an all-metal body was developed. The firm of Thomas Tilling, whose story looms ahead, did a great deal to perfect the vehicle with which the Midland Red Company supplied itself in 1912.

Naturally the evolution of the motor-bus was more complicated and protracted than can be suggested by giving the names of one or two organisations and describing a vehicle or two. But the organisations must be mentioned; they have important parts to play in the later stages of the story. Both Tilling and the British Automobile Development Company made contributions towards the bus with which we are now concerned.

Although the Tilling-Stevens petrol-electric vehicle rode as roughly as most of its predecessors, it was mechanically an advance on them. It was easy to drive, if not to control when moving at speed, so that members of the old horse-bus and horse-tram staff could be trained to work it without any great difficulty. A petrol engine drove a dynamo which generated power for the motor that propelled the bus. Less noisy than some earlier types, the model had drawbacks, especially when on a gradient. When it climbed, the dynamo, moving too slowly, did not generate enough power. When it ran downhill, the engine could not be used as a brake, so that it was easy for an inexperienced driver to lose control. Nevertheless, in their second attempt with motor vehicles the Midland Red was more persistent. It used motor-cycle combinations as first-aid units, so that breakdowns could be dealt with wherever they occurred; and the public lost its chance to jeer at the ignominious sight of a bus being towed back to base.

Still, the drivers soon learnt more about their vehicles, and defects were overcome, so that the number of these buses in Birmingham increased rapidly. Just before the outbreak of war the Company entered into an agreement which at first looked like another serious set-back, but turned out to be the start of its eventual expansion. As had happened in Manchester, it was agreed that the existing services and vehicles should be taken over by the Corporation. The result of this was that the Company had to find new headquarters, study the needs of the people in outlying districts, and pioneer new routes in the countryside round about the city.

These routes were opened up more quickly than might have been expected, for during the 1914-18 war the gearbox-drive buses belonging to the British Electric Traction Company, which were working in Worcester and Kidderminster, were thought by the War Department more suitable for foreign service than the petrol-electric buses. The Midland Red was therefore able to take over the services in these towns.

For the same reasons the services in Leamington and Warwick were included a little later. Wartime conditions made it necessary to run some of the vehicles on coal-gas, with results more picturesque than workmanlike; a driver and conductor chasing a gas-filled balloon across the fields was not an uncommon sight. Even so, the undertaking made more progress than many others during the First World War. After an uncertain start, it had begun the expansion which was eventually to carry it throughout the length and breadth of the Midlands.

IV

What happened to the nine buses B.M.M.O. abandoned in 1907 is a pendant to this part of the story. They were transferred, as we have seen, to territory in East Kent, which was judged more suitable. There they were taken over by Mr. Sidney Garcke, the son of the

British Electric Traction Company's first Managing Director, Emile Garcke. Living in a Kentish village and watching the people walk, cycle, and ride in horse-brakes the three and a half miles between it and Deal, he had seen the possibilities of motor-buses in unspoilt country. The question that worried him was whether these particular vehicles would be any more useful than they had been in Birmingham. To put it crudely—would they go?

They were of an earlier vintage than the Tilling-Stevens model, and the only thing that was proved about them was their ability to give trouble. Technically, they belonged to the bonneted type, powered with Peter Brotherhood four cylinder petrol engines which developed thirty-five horse-power, and they ran on heavy wooden wheels. They had a three-speed gear-box, and a gate-change. The bevel type of axle gave endless trouble, not only because the shafts broke, but because, if the brake was applied suddenly, the bevel pinion key had a habit of shearing off. This meant that the foot-brake, working on a transmission drum, was put out of action. Thus on several occasions the agonised driver found himself careering down a steep hill with inadequate steering and a hand-brake of purely decorative value. Small wonder such vehicles had been found wanting in Birmingham.

When Mr. Garcke led his convoy into Deal, one fine spring evening in 1908, each vehicle striking its double-toned gong, those of the Town Council members who were present regarded them sombrely, wondering how they had been persuaded that such spluttering monsters were safe, reliable, and fireproof. The journey from London, diversified by its complement of breakdowns, had taken all day. The spectacular entry ended in anticlimax, as the garage was too small to house the buses, and the police, suddenly alert to their duties, reported them for driving after dark without lights.

Nevertheless, on the very next day three of them started a time-table service to Kingsdown, Walmer, and St. Margaret's Bay. Mr. Garcke very wisely held back the rest as reinforcements. But, in their new climate, the old buses prospered. Further services were added in 1910, and the small enterprise was taken over by the British Automobile Development Company.

v

Once again, the pioneer was not left to enjoy the fruits of his foresight unchallenged. Having given such a lead in an area where motor-buses had never been seen, the Company met with competition. The same kind of thing was happening in many country districts at this time. The Folkestone and District Road Car Company, begun in 1914, was being operated by Thomas Tilling, already a force to be reckoned with. A firm of coal merchants was running a bus from Herne Bay to Canterbury and Whitstable, and there was a further company known as the Margate, Canterbury and District Motor Services Limited. To complete the picture, a farmer was running a primitive service between Ramsgate and Margate.

The 1914-18 war brought about shortages of manpower, fuel, and spare parts. These difficulties, plus the motives we have observed elsewhere, brought the competitors together in the East Kent Road Car Company in August, 1916. By then they had a fleet of seventy-two vastly improved vehicles including Tilling-Stevens, Daimlers, Commers, Leylands, Straker-Squires, and Albions. In eleven years services were built up in East Kent which carried four-and-a-half million passengers a year over routes measuring one hundred and eighty-five miles. In addition, as far as the industry was concerned, the East Kent Road Car Company had brought together the interests in that area of the British Automobile Development Company (which in 1912 had changed its name to the British Automobile Traction Company) and of Thomas Tilling. Such a merger could be expected to have important influences on other services elsewhere.

Soon after the First World War, the Company was taking advantage of the holiday trade, running express services between London and the coastal resorts, and so starting the extensive excursion business which, with a fleet of over five hundred buses and coaches, it continues to this day.

So a disaster in Birmingham brought about a triumph in Kent. The moral, if there was one, lay in the difference between the needs of a dense industrial area and those of a countryside which—at that date—was still unspoiled.

CHAPTER XVI

Thomas Tilling

'What is it that roareth thus?
Can it be a Motor Bus?
Yes, the smell and hideous hum
Indicat Motorem Bum!'

A. D. GODLEY.

ALTHOUGH the story of this remarkable man is connected both with London and the provinces, his influence was so far-reaching that we must depart from our plan and give it a chapter to itself. His work, continued by his family, has built up one of the most important organisations in the industry; one which played a sterling part in the later stages of its development.

Soon after Shillibeer's omnibus had astonished the Londoners, Thomas Tilling, a young man in his twenties, was managing a dairy in Walworth. If Shillibeer's venture interested him at all, it would be on account of its horses and the work which buses would provide for them. Tilling's love of horses sprang from his Gloucestershire fore-bears and grew during his early years in the countryside at Hendon. Horses were in his blood; and the great business of Tillings' can be said to have started on the day he bought his first horse and harnessed it to a cart to ease the work of the women who used to deliver his milk with a yoke and buckets.

The hiring out of that cart and its successors soon eclipsed the dairy business, and offered opportunities young Tilling had not dreamed of. By the 'seventies, after a great deal of this kind of work, he had moved to Peckham; and there, for seventy years, one of the greatest transport organisations was to have its centre.

First and foremost, Tilling was a man of courage and moral strength. Not only did he mean to succeed, but he meant to be scrupulously honest in a trade where honesty often counted for little. In the end, his fair dealings, both with his employees and his rivals, were an important factor in his success.

At first, when he started a horse-bus service, he had to struggle against the usual pilferings of conductors and the unscrupulous practices of his competitors. Yet before long he was able to buy, from a small firm in financial difficulties, a service that became almost as famous as the man who owned it. This was the *Times*, which ran between Peckham and Oxford Circus four times a day and charged eighteen pence for the journey. To begin with, Tilling himself sat on the box; but he soon made two important innovations.

The first was to run at a fixed time, whether his passengers were ready or not. The other was to keep to a specified route, no longer turning aside from it to pick up 'regulars' or because some passenger was ready to pay for a particular diversion. Although Tilling was not the only operator to do this, he had to be prepared, like many of the early owners, to lose business in order to institute a basic principle. As a result, his buses were punctual. The word went round, and this, together with the discipline he instilled into his employees, greatly increased his reputation.

In addition to his *Times* service, which he bought in 1851, Tilling opened new routes serving Rotherhithe, Bermondsey, Lewisham, Clapham and Wandsworth, and was one of the principal proprietors to refuse to sell out to the London General Omnibus Company.

II

Buses, however, were only one part of his business. Soon he was supplying horses for almost every occasion. He had large contracts for supplying sturdy, grey horses, together with their harness and fodder, to the London Fire Brigades. Many famous people came to him for coaches, landaus, and every other form of Victorian carriage. In a single year in the 'seventies he was supplying two hundred horses and a hundred vans to the Army, a hundred and thirteen horses for the Board of Works, and a number of carriages for the Lord Mayor's Show. Soon he was augmenting and reorganising the Royal Stables. This, and other duties, later earned the firm of Tillings' a Royal Warrant.

By the 'eighties, Thomas Tilling was not only known as one of the biggest and most reliable horse-masters; he was recognised as a leading authority in matters of transport throughout the country. In 1893, when he died, aged sixty-seven, he had some thirty depots in and around London.

When the motor vehicle was about to start its revolutionary career, Richard Tilling, Thomas's eldest son, took over the business and developed it into a national enterprise. In 1897, fifty years after the business was started, a Limited Liability Company was incorporated with a capital of a hundred and thirty-seven thousand pounds; and, although the Articles of Association made plain the firm's intention to develop the business on a basis of horsedrawn traffic, the Directors reserved the right 'to introduce any present or future automatic inventions when (if ever) they may become of practicable utility'.

Practically useful or not, the 'automatic inventions' soon came. In 1904 the Company introduced its first motor-bus to London—a Milnes-Daimler which carried sixteen passengers inside, and eighteen on 'garden seats' on the upper deck. This vehicle ran on the famous *Times* route from Peckham to Oxford Circus. Though it turned out to be one of the less temperamental makes, when other buses augmented the fleet the Company developed the use of 'leading drivers', versatile men who were ready at any time to exchange their vehicle for one that had broken down and, if they were lucky, coax the defaulting vehicle home under its own power.

Equally important, as buses became more reliable, was the introduction of motor transport for the Royal Mail. Tilling helped to persuade the Post Office to adopt this innovation, with the result that, by 1910, vans were running regular services to Birmingham and other large cities, and letters were being sorted *en route*. In view of road conditions and the nature of the vehicles, the delay caused by breakdowns was surprisingly small. On some of these long-distance services, logging some forty thousand miles a year, the percentage of miles lost was as little as 0.19.

Thus in 1906, at a time when the motor revolution was driving many undertakings out of business, when Birmingham was giving up its motor-buses, and those in the Potteries were little more than an uneasy experiment, Tilling had a garage containing thirty-six buses where, by day and by night, every form of mechanical repair was carried out in order to keep them on the road.

Still, talented and enterprising though they were, Tillings' were not magicians; and it was soon clear to the directors that if motor-buses were to be developed efficiently and to be worked by drivers who were not skilled engineers, both the mechanical design and the maintenance would have to be simplified. Thus they helped to start the petrol-electric vehicle. This, as we have already explained, had an internal combustion engine to drive the dynamo which operated the propulsion motor. Some of the earliest models were built in the Tilling garages in Bull Yard, Peckham, the electrical equipment being provided by W. A. Stevens. From this collaboration came the Tilling-Stevens vehicles which have already been mentioned. Whatever their shortcomings, these reduced the labour required for maintenance by half.

A 55-seater double-deck bus belonging to Liverpool Corporation, 1919. Note influence of tram design

Single-deck omnibus of South Wales Commercial Motors outside Cardiff City Hall, 1920

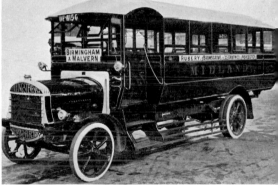

Tilling-Stevens petrol-electric single-deck omnibus, 1920. Body designed by 'Midland Red'

Tram and bus, Potteries Electric Tramways, 1925. The omnibus is of the S.O.S. type, designed and manufactured by 'Midland Red'

Model T Ford open charabanc operated by Messrs. Mills & Seddon of Bolton, 1920

HOW THE COACH DEVELOPED FROM THE CHARABANC

Albion coach of Lewis & James Ltd., 1928, with 'all-weather' head

Leyland 6-wheeled coach built and operated by Birch Bros., 1936—permanent head with opening roof

III

Though Tillings' were continually extending their services with motor-buses to such places as Sidcup and Farnborough in Kent, and reinforcing them with various 'cross-country' routes as well, the business still relied to a large extent on horses. Richard Tilling and his brother Edward were as good judges of horses as their father had been. A different pair was sent to take them to and from their home each day so that, in the course of a week, they came to have personal knowledge of four dozen horses. When two thousand animals were requisitioned in 1914, Tillings' still had five thousand in the stables to carry on with.

Although the business entered into an agreement in 1913 with the London General Omnibus Company over the number of buses to be run in London, for the most part it had been able to stand alone. In the country districts its scope had been enormous. Services were developed in the Brighton district, where Tilling, after starting a small fleet based on Hove, without Brighton licences, in 1915, bought a year later an undertaking that dated from 1884. We have already noted how the East Kent Road Car Company brought together Tilling's Folkestone and District services with those of the British Automobile Development Company.

However, just as the new motor services were coming into their own, war-time restrictions began to hamper them, and extensive ambulance and military services had to be organised both at home and abroad. Shell cases were made in Bull Yard, special 'munitions' services were run into the heart of Woolwich Arsenal, and, to the astonishment of all who saw them, women conductors with heavy serge uniforms and peak-caps took the place of men on the platforms of the buses. The last Tilling horse-bus left the streets in 1915, after more than sixty years of service.

As soon as the First World War was over, the Company was ready for the further expansion and development, which we must look at presently.

CHAPTER XVII

The Country Pioneer

'Enthusiasm, hard work and the never-say-die spirit are prime
ingredients in almost any success story. The pioneers in Passenger
Road Transport needed these qualities in full measure.'
The Coaching Journal and Bus Review, March 1954.

THE city dweller usually finds it impossible to realise the conditions that confront the countryman. This psychological
truism is behind most of the evils of government from Whitehall. To
take a very small example, I was responsible during the war for the
fire precautions in a rural area. The instructions sent to me bore no
relevance whatever to the conditions I had to face. Had I obeyed the
rule on which most stress was laid, most of my faithful helpers would
have kept watch up to their necks in brambles.

Thus the growth of passenger transport in country districts was
different in almost every particular from that in the cities, or even
in an area like East Kent at the turn of the century. There can be
little in common between such services and those that look after,
say, the mining valleys of Wales, the moors of Northumberland, the
fishing villages, and the agricultural areas that have no need of main
roads. In such districts the rise of passenger transport was *sui generis*.
It followed no law, save that of adaptation to what it had to do.
Nor had it much to do, initially, with the major companies; they
naturally concentrated their efforts in places where the population
was dense and where working conditions made transport essential.
Elsewhere, through the length and breadth of the country, it was
left to individual men of enterprise and initiative to provide the
local service that was needed.

Many of them began with a single bus or car, little knowing the
extent to which their business would grow or the difficulties and
competition they would have to meet. These men, preserving the
traditions of the carrier and the short-stage country coach, built up
simple services that depended entirely upon a local need. A few have
survived. The stories of all of them reflect a spirit which, cocking
snooks at the centralisation and control that have since developed,
gives the industry much of its life.

The careers of these pioneers did not follow straight lines, or
even develop in one place. The running of early motor-buses was a

precarious job, and a man could be led far from his starting point by luck, good or bad. Some failed because a regular service did not fill their bus, and, when they accepted individual bookings, for picnics, choir outings and the like, their few regular patrons were driven in disgust to look elsewhere. Others went under for want of capital. Vehicles had to be sold when times were hard or the local authority refused to grant a licence. A sudden chance to develop a service would present itself elsewhere, and the kind of man we are concerned with would get another vehicle how and where he could, and rush off in a cloud of dust to forestall every possible competitor.

The career of each of these early pioneers is unique, and although a close study of many of them makes interesting reading, an outline of one must satisfy our present purpose. This is the story of one T. H. Barton, who, together with other members of his family, developed a business centred at Chilwell, near Nottingham, into one of the leading independent undertakings of today.

II

T. H. Barton, having trained as an engineer at University College, Nottingham, became manager of the oil-engine department at Richard Hornsby and Sons of Grantham. On the death of his father, he left this job to take over the family quarry business between Little Eaton and Duffield. Illness soon caused him to abandon this and to move to Mablethorpe, where he rented a smallholding. Here, in 1899, he conceived an idea similar to Thomas Tilling's, and decided that a pony and trap would help to augment the family's income. He therefore gave a guinea to his eleven-year-old son, now Mr. T. A. Barton, the present Managing Director of the business, and told him to fetch the animal and its vehicle from Little Eaton, some eighty miles away.

As if resolved to show that he had the spirit and enterprise for the work that lay ahead of him, the boy completed the double journey in four days. Pony and trap were then employed as a hackney for people going to and from the station; they also collected scrap iron, for which the Bartons found a market in Sheffield. Alas, the supply of scrap iron at Mablethorpe soon ran out, and the inhabitants who used the railway station seemed to prefer walking. In any event, the pony and trap was not a success, and, as an expression of their views about pioneering passenger transport, the Bartons turned their attention to poultry.

A chance revived the spark. Nor very long after this, Mr. Barton noticed an advertisement offering for sale in London a nine horse-power Benz Campion six-seater wagonette. He could not drive such a vehicle, but that was a trifle; he decided to go and buy it. The initial difficulty was overcome by having the vehicle driven out through the horse-buses as far as Barnet. After that, Mr. Barton was left to his own resources; and the journey home was a matter of trial and error. When tyres burst, they were stuffed with grass. When one of the belts broke, it was taken to the nearest village saddler, who put stitches in it. The journey to Mablethorpe took four days, and there, whenever it could be persuaded to go, the Bartons' first motor vehicle carried passengers up and down the main road at twopence a time.

A little later, ill health again caused Mr. Barton to move. This time he went to Weston-super-Mare. On the journey the Benz gave so much trouble that the engine was sold for what it would fetch. The Bartons travelled the rest of the way to Weston by train, and the wagonette, fitted with shafts, ignominiously ground out the rest of its life behind a horse.

III

But Barton's spirit was only whetted. Doubtless with a prophetic notion of what the motor industry was to become, he soon found in Weston a six horse-power twelve-seater Daimler wagonette which had been built in 1898 and long since dismantled.

The indefatigable father and son paid seventy-five pounds for it, put it together, and found it to be more reliable than they had dreamed. After a brief test, they started a service between the Old Pier and the New, and ran excursions to Cheddar, Wells, Glastonbury, and Clevedon. This happy enterprise soon died, however; the owners of local horse-brakes and wagonettes petitioned the Council to withdraw the Bartons' licence. This was the Bartons' first experience of licensing difficulties as they were in the early years of the century, and it put an end to their transport activities in Weston.

Their blood was up now. They returned to the Midlands, where the eventual sale of the quarry business produced the necessary two hundred pounds to pay for a twenty-seater char-à-banc, which they proceeded to run from Derby, especially at the weekend, for football matches and private parties. This venture was just getting on its feet, so to speak, when the Bartons were offered a price for the vehicle which they were in no position to ignore. They used the money to buy a 28-seater 1908 Durham Churchill char-à-banc, with a four-cylinder Aston engine. With this they inaugurated their stage-carriage route between Long Eaton and Nottingham for the 'Goose Fair' traffic. Permission was obtained from the local councils, time-tables were printed and circulated, and the service, starting quickly to catch the sudden demand, was a great success.

The success outlasted its occasion. The vehicle was adapted for wet weather and, sometimes by working all night on it, father and son did their utmost to keep it on the road for seven days a week. They had made a start as recognised bus operators. At last the tide was running in their favour.

Soon they were able to buy an additional bus, an eighteen-seater Scott Sterling. They had to fit wooden tyres to it, because rubber at that time cost about a hundred and thirty pounds a set. The disadvantage of this lay in the fact that, when the soft wood became worn, the lumps of hard wood that remained gave passengers a rough ride. However, the Bartons were soon able to develop and improve their transport. When a London omnibus company went into liquidation —and there were many to whom this happened during this first decade of the century they managed to buy a number of double deckers for fifty pounds each. A company failed in Burton-on-Trent; Mr. Barton bought some of their fleet, sold at a profit, and so began to build up a reserve.

On the chassis of one of these vehicles father and son themselves built a body and carried out various experiments in seating. Meanwhile they had introduced services between Draycott, Long Eaton, Sandiacre, and Nottingham, with Mrs. Barton and her three daughters pressed into service as conductors. The *Daily Mirror* made a 'sensation' of this fact.

IV

Barton passenger services were now firmly established, but many disappointments lay ahead. A road-train with a tractor and a number of trailers, designed to run on the Beeston and Nottingham route, was a complete failure. The engine used too much petrol and was far too slow. During the First World War the firm, like many others, fitted gas-filled bags to their vehicles and, by continuing to run both passenger and goods services, maintained their position.

After the war the Bartons sold their vehicles and re-equipped themselves with ex-Army Daimlers that had been used as workshop lorries. With the sixty-four seater, double-decker bodies which were then fitted to them, these Daimlers gave admirable service, meeting with success the competition of numerous owner-drivers which was characteristic of the 'twenties. To deal with this competition, the Bartons bought twenty Lancias from Turin, and converted them into the first six-wheeler passenger vehicles to be used in the industry. Two years later, they were running seventy-five. They showed no less enterprise with the heavy-oil engines which were developed and introduced in the 'thirties.

From that time onwards the business made steady progress. It developed its local services and extended to the Continent the long-distance tours which had begun in such a haphazard way in Weston. Today Barton Transport operates three hundred vehicles, and is one of the most important independent undertakings in England. Its interest for us is the way in which the business sprang from small beginnings and, through its owners' enterprise and determination, became what it is now.

v

Many similar instances could be given. Even today, in deep country, rural services are bringing the countryman increasingly closer to the town. As an instrument of social change, the country bus has had no equal. The lads of the village who forty, even thirty years ago sat on the bridge dressed in broadcloth, can now run into town and are as well dressed as the townsman. The girls have like-wise every chance to dress as their fashion paper tells them. Whether this, and the cinema, are good or bad is beside the point, which is that country dwellers now can choose. Sheer isolation no longer condemns them to yokeldom.

But at the time with which we are here concerned, the first three decades of the century, the factors which brought success or failure to these transport pioneers varied little from place to place; although, since the basic problem was the human one of building up a business, each operator had his own peculiar difficulties. Where opportunities were good, the local operators had to face competi-tion from one another and, as time went on, from bigger under-takings based upon the cities. They had to face licensing authorities, which, to put it mildly, were not always fair. They had to work for a public which opposed Sunday traffic, obstructed many other attempts to improve local services, and often regarded the operator's buses as a joke instead of as an enterprise in which he had staked every penny. These country operators were often garage proprietors, who had to find out about their vehicles the hard way and to work night and day in order to keep them on the road. Witness, for example, Mr. Tom White's early services in Barry, which later became a part of the Western Welsh Omnibus Company.

In those days country folk had ambitious ideas about the kind of parcel which it was reasonable to take with them on the journey. These, on market-days at least, could range from piglets and calves swathed in sacking to sides of bacon and bags of cat's meat. The last was the attractive kind of burden that the driver was expected to swing upon the seat beside him.

The cheers which greeted these drivers on their journeys often included the abuse of competitors. This, in a few ill-chosen words, was likely to include a brief description of the offending vehicle, a reference to its owner and, no doubt, injurious speculation as to the ancestry of its driver. And the abused one gave as good as he got.

In addition to the jolting he received from solid tyres, the driver had little protection from wind or rain, and, after nightfall, had only the aid of two guttering oil lamps. Conductors, too, made use of oil-lamps attached to a strap, acquiring from them a somewhat bearded aspect after they had spent a few hours fumbling for fares in the semi-darkness. On country routes, it is recorded that a few more enterprising conductors carried guns, and considered the route a bad one if it did not provide a rabbit for the pot.

VI

Before the First World War was over, many of these pioneers were in competition with services from neighbouring towns, which they themselves were not allowed to enter. They were opposed by local authorities whose plans were often vague and ill-considered. Long distance char-à-bancs cut across their areas and, on popular routes, a bewildering number of driver-operators drove their small vehicles at what was then a break-neck speed in order to kill each other's chances. The confusion of the early horse-bus days had returned in another form.

The way in which this confusion ended, and both areas and licences came to be more equitably controlled, leads logically to the next stage of the story.

CHAPTER XVIII

The Development of the Industry
in the 'Twenties

'. . . in spite of an out-of-date and inconsistent licensing system, the road passenger transport industry was developing rapidly and on sound traffic principles, and there were many sensible working arrangements between operators for the provision of better service to the public. . . .'

RAYMOND BIRCH: From a paper read to members of the Public Transport Association in May 1946.

THE competition between free-lance operators after the First World War makes an exciting story, but we must resist the temptation to elaborate it and so draw attention from the co-ordination which, paradoxically enough, was developing within the industry as a whole. One might say that a confused shower of sparks was flying from the rim of the wheel, but the hub and the spokes were beginning to feel their strength and the first sense of their unity.

Before we can understand the co-ordination which had been achieved long before the passing of the Road Traffic Act in 1930—the first thorough overhaul which the industry had to undergo—we must take a look at the expansion and regrouping of the major undertakings. And although, to the unskilled eye, this at first offers a bewildering spectacle of hard bargaining and political controversy, the attentive observer will soon see that a much greater and more important process was taking place. What looks like a series of success stories in some sort of individualistic free-for-all turns out to be a major movement in our economic evolution. Power was passing from the many to the few and, through the enterprise of the men who now held the power, the whole industry was becoming more streamlined and efficient. There was an insistent public demand for more and more buses, and the response of the operators was correspondingly robust. They saw the need, and exerted all their energies to meet it.

The need arose from a variety of causes. The war had left a bad shortage of vehicles. Food was scarce in country areas, so that the shoppers flocked to the nearest town. Country folk yearned for the bright lights and other amenities of city life. Housing shortage in the towns drove people further and further out to live.

Typical Leyland double-decker of 1930

Double-deck omnibus operated in London by one of the many independent companies before the creation of the London Passenger Transport Board in 1933

Six-wheeled front entrance double-decker Western Welsh—1933. This omnibus had 60 seats

Above: Modern double-deck Leyland omnibus operated by R. Chisnell & Sons ('King Alfred' Services), Winchester

Above: East York-shire double-decker emerging from Beverley Bar. All double-deck omnibuses passing through this arch must be shaped as shown in the illustration

Right: A Leyland P.D.2/3 'White Lady' double-deck coach—Ribble Motor Services, 1951

Guy double-deck omnibus with Metropolitan - Cammell - Weymann body — Northern General Transport, 1955

Experts within the industry may find what follows an over-simplification of the facts, but if it is clear to the reader no apology is necessary. He will have a sketch of the background to the industry's development, without which the details would mean little, or be misleading.

II

Voluntary organisation between operators is once more the theme-song, as it was in the days of the horse-buses. Long before anyone took seriously the idea of a national authority or of regional boards to control public transport, voluntary organisation between the owners of trams and motor-buses carried the industry a long way forward. This organisation, as we have seen from past chapters, was always directed towards smoother and more economic working. Companies who did not have to spend money in wasteful competition could spend it on improving their services.

Mechanical transport, bringing with it an increased range, made it necessary for the major undertakings to divide the country into areas and to come to some agreement as to their provisional boundaries. With the rapid development in the 'twenties of the major omnibus groups, such as British Electric Traction, Tilling, and Scottish Motor Traction, these areas were more clearly defined. Furthermore, their existence helped to define the boundaries that were later required by the Road Traffic Act of 1930. Another boundary, also agreed initially by the undertakings concerned, was that fixed by Parliament for the London Passenger Transport Board when it was formed in 1933.

During the Second World War these areas were planned as self-governing regions. In the event of an invasion, they would have been capable of dealing with their own transport problems. Thus the War speeded up a process which had begun in the early years of the century, and which was to have far-reaching consequences afterwards. To a great extent the initial movement sprang from the group in which the British Electric Traction Company had financial interests.

In 1907, for administrative purposes, the Company had divided its transport interests in the British Isles into eleven territories, which were placed under District Superintendents. Ireland and Scotland formed a territory each, and the remainder were arranged roughly into London and the South East: Birmingham: Manchester (two districts): Newcastle: the Midlands (York, Derby, Nottingham, Leicester): East Anglia: the South West: South Wales.

III

.Readers closely interested in these matters may remember that the British Electric Traction Company, anxious to develop motor-bus operation, had formed the British Automobile Development Company in 1905, renamed in 1912 the British Automobile Traction Company; and that this undertaking, gaining control of the Deal and District services, had helped to bring about the East Kent Road Car Company. While the railways were developing bus services in the years preceding the war, the British Automobile Traction Company acquired further interests in bus operations involving the Aldershot and Maidstone districts, Macclesfield, Reading, and Preston. The chief reason for this was because the British Electric Traction Company had decided to take over more and more bus undertakings, and, as in the Potteries and Birmingham, to foster motor-bus feeding services for its tramways (see Chapter XIII). The usual procedure was to form a new local company in order to develop bus services that would take account of the interests of the tramways. Thus the Scottish General Transport Company was formed in 1913 to foster such interests in the Greenock, Airdrie, and Rothesay tramway regions: the Northern General Transport Company, incorporated in 1913, had similar work to perform for the Gateshead, Jarrow, and Tynemouth tramways; and the South Wales Transport Company, incorporated in 1914, had to develop motor services to support the tramways of Swansea.

Although this was the work of British Electric Traction only, it placed on the loom the first strands of the elaborately woven network of interlocking bus services which exist today. These feeder services in the Gateshead and Jarrow districts—to take but one example—had to meet on common ground, and, through co-operation and mutual agreement, to work out adequate services for the towns concerned. Their aim was to serve the public. That was how they made their living. Since they came under one control, competition was no longer a reason for their failure to do so. The Northern General Transport Company wanted the maximum takings, and British Electric Traction wanted the efficiency that can result only from an economic service.

In 1913, the larger provincial operators formed the Provincial

Omnibus Owners' Association in order to promote and protect their part of the industry. After its incorporation in 1913, with a council of fifteen to twenty members, the association concerned itself with litigation that promoted or opposed the general interests of its members. It is important in this context, because it helped to develop inter-company legal agreements.

Its original members were companies associated with the British Electric Traction Company, the Bristol Tramways and Carriage Company, and Tillings'. Another important member was United Automobile Services. Their first offices and garage were rented from the Great Eastern Railway when the railway's bus service between Lowestoft and Beccles was taken over by U.A.S. in the years before the First World War. Later, the company struck out into Yorkshire and Northumberland, to cover territory which was then also served by the L.N.E.R.

Much later, in 1929, Tilling and British Automobile Traction Limited acquired an equal controlling interest in this Company with the railway, and the railway made working agreements to co-ordinate the bus services it had acquired along the North-East coast. This is worth recording, to show the way in which companies affiliated with the Omnibus Owners' Association made clear their intention of meeting the challenge of the railways not by wasteful competition but by co-ordination on the basis of equal partnership.

IV

Another important undertaking to run buses in co-operation with the railways was the National Omnibus and Transport Company. Formed in 1911 as the National Steam Car Company Limited to develop steam-driven buses, at the end of the war it expanded rapidly with services in Bedfordshire, Essex, Somerset, Dorset, Devon, and Cornwall. By 1928 it owned fifty-five garages, and had taken over so many enterprises that it was obliged to split its working interests into the Eastern, Southern, and Western divisions. The parent company remained separate from the main groups until 1931, when Tillings' obtained a controlling interest in it.

Thomas Tilling Ltd., as we have already learned, had expanded rapidly even before the First World War. Its Folkestone and District Road Car Company merged with the British Automobile Traction Company's interests in that area to form the East Kent Road Car Company, and this brought the association between

Tillings' and British Electric Traction one stage closer. The same process of amalgamation had produced the Southdown Motor Services in 1915, with the purpose of developing bus transport along the southern coast. The merger included the British Automobile Traction associated, the London and South Coast Haulage Company, and the Worthing Motor Services; it took in also two services of the Brighton, Hove and Preston United Omnibus Company, which contributed its char-à-banc business.

In 1916, Tillings' took over the town services of Brighton and Hove from the last-named company. A year later, after surrendering their char-à-banc business to the Southdown Motor Services, Tillings' obtained an interest in that undertaking. Once again the interests of Tillings' and the British Electric Traction Company were brought together. Since 1935 Tillings' have continued to operate the Brighton and Hove services, and have a co-ordination agreement with Brighton Corporation, the Corporation operating its own municipal buses and trolley-buses.

v

Before the 'twenties were out, and before legislation had made any really effective contribution towards the problems within the industry, the balance of power between the two largest groups was about even. The interests of Thomas Tilling and the British Electric Traction Company were so closely interlocked that Tilling had substantial holdings in eleven out of eighteen of the British Electric Traction Company's undertakings. Both companies therefore considered that it would be well to redistribute their interests. In 1928, they decided that the British Automobile Traction Company, with increased capital, should become Tilling and British Automobile Traction Limited, Tillings' acquiring their share of the new venture in exchange for their interests in various provincial services. Mr. Sidney Garcke, who had pioneered much of the work of the British Automobile Traction Company, became chairman of the new company, and Tillings' and British Electric Traction had equal representation on the Board. The broad plan was that future acquisitions of bus companies by Tillings' and British Electric Traction would be channelled through the newly formed joint undertaking—Tilling and British Automobile Traction Limited.

In the same year, however, there was a further development. The Railways (Road Transport) Act of 1928 gave the railways wide

Northern General
37-seater S.O.S.-type
single-deck bus, 1928

One-man operated 'pay-as-you-enter' single-deck
omnibus — Sunderland
Corporation, 1955

The first single-decker to
seat 44 passengers has
now found a place in the
British Transport Commission's Museum. Strikingly modern in design,
it was produced as early
as 1934 by the Northern
General Transport Company.

A new use for an old railway station—Southport Omnibus Station
—Ribble Motor Services, 1954

A country bus station—Aldershot—Aldershot & District Traction Company, 1953

powers to acquire and run road transport. Many, as we have seen, had been running local services to their stations before the First World War, and for some years had been appealing unsuccessfully for these powers to be increased. At last they were in a position to compete with the major bus undertakings. Thus the hundred and thirteen vehicles owned by the G.W.R. in 1913 increased to three hundred and seventy, and the L.M.S., by purchasing the Crosville undertaking, obtained bus services as far off as Aberystwyth and Lampeter. Perhaps the best example of the type of service which railways were now able to develop was the Cheltenham to Oxford coach, which was scheduled primarily to connect with London trains.

Obviously this sort of thing might have led to a great deal of wasted energy on both sides; and it is clear that at this point the railways must have decided to seek partnership with the bus operators instead of competing with them. Competition would have been wasteful, and not in the railways' best interests. Accordingly many undertakings came to be held jointly between them, the railway companies acquiring a share interest equal to that of British Electric Traction or of Tilling and British Automobile Traction. Working agreements were entered into between the railways and the operating bus companies for the close co-ordination of their respective services. At last the conflict between the two industries, which was by now nearly a century old, began to be resolved.

These agreements are not only a milestone on the long road of co-ordination between road and rail transport. They are remarkable in that both parties, while naturally looking after their own interests, agreed to abide by certain principles which directly profited neither of them, but were expressly designed to safeguard the interests of the travelling public.

In the long run, of course, all transport depends on the public it serves: but the administrators who run it do not invariably keep this fact before their eyes, much less acknowledge it in their commercial relationships one with another.

In 1931 the British Electric Traction Company bought the greater part of the issued share capital of the National Electric Construction Company, its rival in tramway development since the 'nineties. And since this undertaking had many associates that had working agreements with the railways—a good example is the Western Welsh Omnibus Company, in which the G.W.R. had been interested since 1929—this further strengthened and simplified the position as far as the main operators were concerned.

K

VI

So much, then, for the expansion and regrouping of the chief undertakings which had taken place by the early 'thirties. What did it all boil down to, in terms of the day-to-day working of the buses? The answer is largely self-evident. The agreements brought about by these mergers limited unnecessary competition and arranged a satisfactory sharing and co-ordinating of traffic on the boundary lines between the different areas. The powers granted to the railways in 1928, and the agreements that followed, speeded up this process. That is as much a fact as the chaotic competition which arose after the war.

This earlier competition was inevitable. It belonged to the general situation of the day: and until the Road Traffic Act of 1930 appointed Traffic Commissioners and gave them the powers of licensing Justices, it could not be overcome. Previously the licensing authorities—the Watch Committee of each Borough—were likely to take a parochial view; and although a few of them issued licences to one main operator only, many seemed to enjoy the confusion and issued them to everyone who asked. Thus, at one extreme, the Slough to Windsor road became notorious for its 'jitneys', and at the other—to take but one example—the Southdown Motor Services' vehicles did not run on routes served by Tilling in Brighton, except by some special arrangement which meant that the trespassing operator had to charge a higher fare.

The boundary line, in some of these early agreements, was intended to run through points where the respective companies considered it convenient to have an exchange of traffic. Where 'through running' became necessary from one area to another, a contingency which does not appear to have been fully considered when many of the agreements were made, the companies were usually expected to provide a joint service and to pool their receipts. Maidstone and District and Southdown, for instance, operated a joint service between Hastings and Eastbourne on a fifty-fifty basis. Many other examples could be given of the same kind of friendly and practical agreement.

Trouble arose in cases where services were interrupted, since independent operators were given a chance to fill the gap. Many of them did it usefully: but there were too many. Rushing in they often created the sort of competition which the licensing authorities could not then control. The problem looks easy enough today, but we have to remember that, although before the passing of the Road Traffic Act operators applying for licences indicated the route they intended to follow, it was quite another thing for the authority to make them do it, and ensure that they did not take other routes where they were sure to get more passengers. So, in areas where neither party to an agreement had yet developed a service, many independent companies sprang up.

VII

Further problems were introduced by long-distance coaches. These, the modern counterpart of the stage-coach, developed in the late 'twenties. To start with, most inland towns were connected with one or two seaside resorts only. As far as London was concerned, the London General Omnibus Company's limits being strictly defined, it was left to provincial operators to provide the services to the south coast. Thus, just as Midland Red had run coaches to Weston-super-Mare since 1921, Southdown developed services between London and the coast towns from Eastbourne to Portsmouth. All these services were designed for passengers going the full distance, but it was soon obvious that long-distance runs, closely interlocked with other services using or crossing their route, would provide useful intermediate facilities for the public. The Northern General Transport Company started a syndicate which successfully worked a scheme of this kind between Liverpool and Newcastle, and although the Margate to Portsmouth Coastal Service (competing with the Royal Blue) was for a long time the only comparable syndicate in the south, the possibilities of these inter-service co-operative plans had been established, and formed yet another part of the industry which called for co-ordination.

By the time of the Road Traffic Act of 1930, therefore, the measures of co-operation introduced by the larger bus organisations, and the steps taken to connect them more closely with the railways, had made a real advance towards co-ordinating the services. Although there were many problems still to be solved if the industry was to reach the maximum efficiency, numbers of the small operators, who knew and understood their public and what that public expected of them, were linked with the larger companies. This linking had overcome the worst aspects of cut-throat competition and had simplified the difficulties of 'through-working' between one company's area and the next. Thus the danger of setting up uneconomically large units, which would destroy the intimate service and efficiency that can be given by a local operator who knows his job, was seen and avoided.

But that is ahead of our story. Although there were to be further regroupings between Tilling and British Electric Traction in the 'forties, by 1930 the first stage of co-ordination within the motor-bus industry was complete. Its basis was sound, as is proved by the fact that the territories then held by the main provincial operators have remained more or less unchanged.

Despite the growth of the large operating units, a great many bus and coach operators have continued as small or medium-sized 'independents' in the strict meaning of the word.

Particularly in rural areas bus services are often still run by a family who own only a very small number of vehicles, and cover routes which in many instances could not be covered satisfactorily by the big local bus company.

'Coach' operators, that is, those who keep vehicles specially for private party work or for operating long-distance express services, still abound, and while a limited number own twenty or more vehicles, most of them are in the five to ten vehicle category.

Many of these small 'independents' have a fascinating background of struggle, particularly in their battles with their big competitors, but it is encouraging to know that they have survived and continue today to offer 'coaching' services of a nature not so very far removed in fact from the pioneers who started off the coaching era in the seventeenth century.

VIII

One more factor remains to be noted—the growth of municipal undertakings. The Road Traffic Act of 1930 expressly recognised the importance of these undertakings, by giving special power to Local Authorities whereby they might enter into agreements with other bus operators so as to co-ordinate their services.

Details of these agreements, which have proved of great value to the industry, will be discussed in a later chapter.

CHAPTER XIX

London in the Roaring 'Twenties

'. . . the greatest urban transport system in the world, the only one
to combine the ownership of omnibuses, motor coaches, tramways,
trolleybuses, underground and surface railways.'

VERNON SOMMERFIELD: *London Transport.*

IN 1912, when the London General Omnibus Company passed
into the control of the Underground, a number of buses, especially in the suburbs, began to connect with the Underground
stations. Through-bookings were started, and communication
between Central London and the suburbs was greatly improved.
On Sundays, when the townsman takes to the country, and on
weekdays too, services ran as far as Epping Forest. Buses to Windsor,
St. Albans, Watford, Farnborough, and Sidcup ran every day.
Villages in the chalk hills of Surrey were connected with their nearest
town, and many which had been neglected since the days of horse-
buses, or had never known a public service at all, could be reached
from Hyde Park Corner in the course of a morning. People whose
daily work was in London could live, not only at some distance from
a station, but off the railway line altogether.

The bus companies which had built up businesses in the home
counties and whose services ran into the fringes of the London
area, were naturally concerned at the prospect of new competition
from the expanding 'General', and, to placate them, the 'Thirty
Mile Agreement' was eventually negotiated. Under its provisions,
the provincial companies agreed not to operate within that distance
of Charing Cross. The main area of Greater London was thus,
in theory, left as the preserve of the London General Omnibus
Company, but in practice it was shared with a number of other
undertakings; while the National, the East Surrey, the Thames
Valley, and the Amersham and District undertakings by agreement
worked some of the outlying sections. In fact, however, except for
the years between 1916 and 1922, when the London General Omnibus Company and its associates had almost complete control, independent operators were competing—as they had every right to do
in most parts of the Metropolis. London was not to be exempt from
the law of competition which prevailed in the provinces.

In 1914 the London General Omnibus Company had a fleet of over three thousand 'B' vehicles, soon, like the fleets of many other operators throughout the country, to be seriously depleted by War Office requirements. Some one thousand three hundred vehicles were taken to Flanders, and over three hundred reserved for defence purposes. Many women had served as conductors in order to keep the buses running, as with the services of Tilling, Barton Transport, and, indeed, most others, for ten thousand members of the London General Omnibus Company staff were serving with the Forces. If garages were empty, buses were commandeered in the streets, and the Chief Commissioner of Police had to allow the vehicles that remained to carry extra passengers.

All this started on rather a small scale. In September 1914, in response to a sudden call from the First Sea Lord, who was then Mr. Winston Churchill, seventy-five buses and their crews were lined up on the Embankment and prepared for Antwerp. Those were days in which the famous 'B' type 'Generals', their sides bedecked with optimistic legends—'London to the Kaiser's Palace and return—6d.'—ambled genially down a London street for the last time.

II

Once the war was over, the London General Omnibus Company at first ran a number of open 'lorry buses' to supplement their depleted bus fleet; but technical development was surprisingly rapid. 1919 saw the introduction of the 'K' bus, an improved design in which the driver was placed above the engine rather than behind it. This model had transverse seats inside, and was able to carry forty-six passengers.

The 'S' type, in 1920, was even bigger, and was followed in 1923 by a design (the 'N.S.') which, having a lower centre of gravity, allowed a covered upper deck. This innovation, which took the road in 1925, was at first unpopular, although it had long been used on trams. Loud English complaints about the need for fresh air were soon silenced by English weather; the majority of customers quickly realized the usefulness of a shield from wind and rain, and the covers were soon accepted and taken for granted. Once this had happened, and it did not take long—and many operators were using covered tops and pneumatic tyres from 1925 onwards—upholstered seats could be put on the upper deck; and the comfort of the bus was greatly improved.

It was at this time, in the upsurge of private enterprise after the First World War, that the London bus business once more attracted the attention of newcomers. The powers of the Metropolitan Police to license buses never included any right to restrict their numbers, but only to control their design and their standard of maintenance, in the interests of public safety. Accordingly in August, 1922, a Mr. Partridge surprised Londoners with his chocolate-coloured 'Express' plying for hire amongst the red 'Generals'. His example was quickly followed and by the end of 1923 the new generation of independent owners had put nearly 200 buses on the London streets in liveries of all colours and these within a few months had grown to 500.

Names such as 'Admiral', 'Ambassador', 'Express', 'Prince', 'Fleur-des-Lis' and 'Peraeque' became familiar sights; some recalled the names of the horse-bus era: 'Royal Blue', 'Favorite', 'Atlas' and 'City'. Naturally the London General reacted in the traditional manner and themselves put on many more buses to deal with the competition. All this increase of service undoubtedly attracted a great many more passengers to bus travel, many of them at the expense of the tramways and the underground railways.

In 1924 the Minister of Transport took wide powers in the London Traffic Act to control the number of London buses and their routes, and the position was very largely stabilised. Unfortunately, much ill-feeling followed when the Minister ordered actual reductions (in some cases as much as by two-thirds) in the numbers of buses on long lists of 'restricted streets', which included many tram routes. The independents defied the order, objecting that this was using retrospective legislation to ruin established services which had been legitimately 'scheduled' under the new Act, and that the public's preference for buses instead of trams was being ignored. They organised a monster petition to the 'Honourable Commons' which collected two million signatures, and was delivered to Parliament in two double-deck buses. In the end, under pressure from indignant M.P.s, the Minister dropped the prosecution of the recalcitrants and eventually the 'reduction' Orders were revoked.

For the twelve months up to the end of February, 1925, the Commissioner of Metropolitan Police licensed 4,269 motor-buses to the 'General' and its associated companies, and 1,209 to other operators. In the following two years the 'General' acquired a few of the smaller concerns, but in July, 1927, the proprietor of the 'Admiral' buses, Alfred Bennett, together with the Marquis of

Winchester, formed the London Public Omnibus Company with the avowed object of combining the remaining independent buses in one undertaking; he succeeded in acquiring a fleet of 271. A few months later the 'General' had obtained a controlling interest in Bennett's company and within three years the blue buses with their fleet name of 'Public' disappeared, to be replaced by 'red 'uns'. The idea of 'fight's a good dog but settle's a better' persisted, and in the early nineteen-thirties there were the beginnings of co-ordination and through-booking between some of the independents and the Underground group itself. But these commendable arrangements were soon to be overshadowed by further action on the parliamentary plane.

In 1927 the London and Home Counties Traffic Advisory Committee (set up under the London Traffic Act) had recommended that all passenger transport undertakings in the London Traffic Area—buses, trams and railways—be put under common management and public control, and as a first step, in 1928 the Underground Group, the four main line railways, the Metropolitan Railway, and some smaller undertakings agreed to pool their revenues in the area. The following year the Underground Group and the London County Council (London's largest tramway operators) promoted private Bills in Parliament to unify the managements of their undertakings and pool finances, but a sudden change of Government prevented them passing into law.

A new and much more ambitious measure, the London Passenger Transport Bill, was introduced by the new Labour Government in 1931, and, with very little alteration, was passed by the National Government two years later as the London Passenger Transport Act 1933.

That Act swept into one net of compulsory acquisition all the undertakings, large and small, providing regular local passenger transport services in the London Area—the Underground and Metropolitan railways, tramways run by London County Council and by companies and other municipalities, trolley-buses run by the London United Company, buses run by the London General Omnibus Company, Thomas Tilling, British Automobile Traction and a host of independent owners. Opposition to the Bill had been long and severe, not only on principles but on the area to be covered and the scale of compensation to be awarded. Six months after the Act several 'listed' undertakings were still running on their own, the last to 'hand over' being Birch Bros. and the City Motor Omnibus Company in 1934, both of which, however, had also developed provincial services which were not affected. One hundred and ninety-seven independent operators had been in business in 1925. Only fifty-five survived to the last round. From 1933 onwards, stage carriage operation in all London streets was reserved for vehicles of the London Passenger Transport Board.

When the Bill proposing the formation of the London Passenger Transport Board was put before Parliament, many of the undertakings working in the Home Counties opposed it, largely because the area proposed for the monopoly was bigger than that agreed between these companies and the London General Omnibus Company. As a result, the Bill was amended so that the area corresponded almost exactly with that defined by the boundaries on which both sides had voluntarily reached agreement. Outlying areas operated by the London General Omnibus Company associates were sold to the appropriate provincial company—Southdown and Maidstone and District both benefited in this way—and, with some minor adjustments, the new Board began to work the area that the London General Omnibus Company and its associates had been working for years.

The years of intense competition in London were also years of intensive improvement in bus chassis and body design, in which all parties shared the credit. As one busman has put it recently:

'We started with open-top, solid-tyred, normal-control, 48-seater, petrol-engined double-deck buses looking very much like their 1906 counterparts, and finished only nine years later with covered-top, pneumatic-tyred, forward-control, 56-seater, diesel-engined double-deck buses, looking very much like their counterparts today. In no other decade, before or since, has bus design improved so fast as during the "Roaring Twenties".'

CHAPTER XX

Transport in Scotland—I

'I'm now arrived—thanks to the Gods!—
  Through pathways rough and muddy:
A certain sign that makin' roads
  Is no this people's study.

Yet, though I'm no wi' scripture crammed,
  I'm sure the Bible says
That heedless sinners shall be damn'd
  Unless they mend their ways.'

ROBERT BURNS.

IT is unlikely, despite their reverence for Burns, that his country-men so laid his words to heart as to become the roadmakers they turned out to be; but they certainly 'mended their ways'. Today, their road passenger services are the equal of any in Britain.

Though the greater part of this achievement took place in the twentieth century, and Scottish motor transport was never behind the times, it must not be forgotten that the roads, especially in the northern parts of Scotland, gave the pioneers a formidable task. For want of roads and bridges, and because of the rainfall, General Wade in the first decades of the eighteenth century had found the Highlands 'impracticable'.

The name of Jeremy Wade does not always resound happily in Scotland, yet generations who warmly dislike his motives have had reason to bless his achievement. Sent to the Highlands in 1724, after a successful military career under Marlborough, he established a powerful system of metalled roads, building no fewer than forty stone bridges to carry them over rivers and ravines. His motives were strictly military and anti-Jacobite, but his roads survived their primary purpose and found peaceful uses at the hands of the people they were meant to keep quiet. It is to Wade's credit that he handled the clans with tact and with humanity, in addition to serving the impersonal and sacred ends of transport.

In 1763 there was still only one stage-coach a month from Edinburgh to London, and it took anything from twelve to fourteen days to make the journey. Away from the industrial south, tracks that had served for centuries and which, with their twists and turns and treacherous surfaces, were difficult enough even to the drovers, remained almost unchanged till the coming of the motor car.

On the other hand, Scotland has a few trunk roads which were made later than those in England, and were therefore better surveyed and graded. Most modern vehicles can cover the road from Carlisle to Edinburgh in top gear, though the most up-to-date gearbox may seem inadequate on a cross-country journey in some parts of the country.

The problem which faces the industry today, however, is the fact that many of these trunk roads, cut through rock as they often

A L L that are desirous to pass from EDINBURGH to LONDON, or any other place on their road, let them repair to the 'WHITE HORSE CELLAR', in EDINBURGH, at which place they may be received in a STAGE COACH every Monday and Friday, which performs the whole journey in eight days (if God permits), and sets forth at five in the Morning.

Allowing each passenger 14 pounds weight, and all above, 6 pence per pound.

February, 1754.

An advertisement appearing in Edinburgh in February 1754. It shows a concern for detail as regards weight and charges which will be familiar to those accustomed to air travel, but unlike modern advertising it introduces a note of uncertainty by frankly admitting that safe arrival at the destination was dependant on Higher Authority

are, would cost an impracticable sum to widen, or cannot be widened at all. Bottle-necks occur, even in the Glasgow area, for example, and unpredictable traffic jams are a terror to a Traffic Manager who is trying to run his buses to a strict schedule. Thus the roads of Scotland, good as some of them are, have often been a serious problem to the organiser of road transport. South and north, many of them bother him still.

Before 1928 there was no co-ordinated organisation in the Scottish branch of the industry. Up till then, the principal undertakings, which were concentrated in Edinburgh, Glasgow, and the industrial areas of Lanarkshire, had overlapped and competed like their colleagues to the south. And although our concern is with all that these services have given to the social and industrial life of Scotland, an outline of the whole story must precede it if we are to understand the importance of the Scottish Bus industry.

The first step will be to consider the co-ordination given to the industry by the development of the Scottish Bus Group. The development which has taken place since 1932, and the more recent purchase of these companies by the British Transport Commission, will come later.

II

In the days of horse-tramways, almost all the Scottish undertakings were local and self-contained. Until 1898, when the British Electric Traction Company began to develop tramways in a number of Lowland Burghs, none of the English pioneers had touched Scotland. The moment they did so, they met with characteristic opposition. It is not surprising that the Scots should have had decided views about their own transport and the way in which it should be run. We need not trouble ourselves long over their horse-bus and horse-tram services, as their development followed a pattern described already.

Before the trams reached the Hamilton, Motherwell, and Wishaw districts of Lanarkshire, the only form of transport, apart from the railways, was horse-drawn. For many years to come, horses provided the only form of transport on the roads to the Western Isles. Even in the Border country in the 'nineties, many of the roads were so soft-bottomed that there were often two distinct tracks—one for vehicles moving in each direction.

In winter these Lowland roads were like those described by Defoe a hundred and fifty years earlier. When cable-trams ran in Edinburgh, steam-cars began to rattle between Hamilton and Blantyre in 1902; but it was the road which made the experiment a failure. At this time, the townsman who did not walk made use of such horse transport as his burgh provided.

With a view to electrifying the horse-tramways, especially in the area of the Clyde, the British Electric Traction Company placed Scotland as a district under one of its superintendents (*see* Chapter XVIII). But Scotland in the 'nineties was a stronghold of municipal trading. Thus although, between 1898 and 1902, the British Electric Traction Company developed successful schemes in

Greenock and Port Glasgow and in the Airdrie and Coatbridge areas, establishing services which later helped to form the basis of the Western S.M.T. Company Limited and Central S.M.T. Company Limited, it met with even more stubborn resistance in Paisley and Stirling than in the south. The local authorities would not grant the necessary leases.

Scotland, the Scots proclaimed, was capable of running her own trams, and, in many cases, of operating them on municipal lines. An Act of 1900 authorised trams between Blantyre and Wishaw in Lanarkshire, and the eight miles of track was covered by some twenty-five cars. In the years that followed, services were extended to Larkhall, Cambuslang, Uddingston, Bothwell, New Stevenston, and Holytown. Cameronians and Highland Light Infantrymen, returning from the Boer War, were recruited to operate this system, and their smartness and discipline won distinction and popularity for a service which, in 1900, became the Lanarkshire Traction Company.

III

There was only one 'group' in Scotland at this time, comprising the companies in which George Balfour was interested. These undertakings started similar tramways in Falkirk, Dunfermline, Wemyss, Dundee, and Dumbarton. In 1919, they formed what was to become an important concern, the Scottish General Omnibus Company. The other tramway pioneer of note is the British Electric Traction Company's earlier competitor, the National Electric Construction Company. This, through the Musselburgh and District Electric Light and Traction Company, extended Edinburgh's tramways as far as Port Seton.

Nothing in all this makes Scotland's story very different from that of England. Tramways suited these small towns, and with the few exceptions named, they were developed by their local authorities. It was the introduction of the motor-bus, first in conjunction with the tramways and later with the railway companies, that brought about the grouping of Scottish companies as they are today. And, as it did in England, the motor-bus caused a revolution in the travel habits of the Scottish people.

Edinburgh had the distinction of possessing a more firmly controlled traffic system than any other part of the country. Indeed, some of the main provisions of the 1930 Road Traffic Act, which has been called the bus operator's Bible, had been adopted in Edinburgh before the century began. The Edinburgh Municipal and Police (Amendment) Act of 1891 made the licences granted to omnibus operators control the stands that the vehicles should use, the routes they should follow, and the times at which they should run. Not only was it illegal for a licensed vehicle to ply for hire at any other time or place, but the vehicle itself had to conform to rigid specifications and to be passed by a Hackney Carriage Inspector. Edinburgh was forty years ahead of the times.

IV

The Great North of Scotland Railway Company was first in the field with motor-buses, running Milnes-Daimler vehicles between Ballater and Braemar in 1904. However, when the Scottish Motor Traction Company began to develop services in and around Edinburgh during the years that followed, these were considerably more than a haphazard enterprise.

In the first place, they were under the direction of William Johnston Thomson, a man of unusual foresight and business acumen. From the outset he aimed at making the Scottish Motor Traction Company the hub of Scottish transport. Within a year, it had developed services to Dalkeith, Gilmerton, Broxburn, and other surrounding towns. The first circular tour of thirty-two miles was introduced as early as 1907, and it was not long before a vehicle called the 'Lothian', designed by William Thomson and assembled by the Scottish Motor Traction Company, was so far ahead of the time that it influenced all designers for some twenty years.

The introduction of the 'Lothian', a notable event in Scottish bus history, calls for further comment. Necessity mothered its main features. The rigid regulations governing such things made twenty-three feet the maximum length for any passenger vehicle. Thus, if the company was to carry the number of passengers it wanted, William Thomson realised that the driver must be set further forward, at the side of his engine. The 'Lothian' was therefore the first 'forward drive' vehicle, giving the driver a position and a view of the road which at that time was unique. Moreover, it had a four-speed constant-mesh gear-box with dog clutches. Small wonder, therefore, that the 'Lothian' in 1912 should have given the Scottish Motor Traction Company a lead.

As in the Potteries and other English towns, tramways were considered the most suitable form of road transport, and bus services were developed to supplement them. The greater part of this work was concentrated in the industrial area of Lanarkshire, a fact which, for one who is not a Scot, may require explanation.

The area which embraces Glasgow and extends into Dumbartonshire and Lanarkshire is the chief production centre in Great Britain for heavy industries. There are the coal-fields and steel works of Lanarkshire, the engineering firms and ship-building yards of the Clydeside and Dumbarton. There are also the massive industrial and commercial businesses of Glasgow, with their world-wide mercantile associations. Though the light engineering businesses of the area have been developed in more recent years, these great industries, together with the thickly populated towns to which they have given rise, were a formidable problem for the pioneers of transport, even in the early years of the century. How the motor-bus operators tackled the problem must now be considered.

By 1911 the British Electric Traction Company had developed feeder services for its tramways in Airdrie and Coatbridge. When Greenock and Port Glasgow offered competition, the company formed the Scottish General Transport Company Limited as a holding company to develop motor-bus services in that region. The buses of this undertaking were soon in competition, on the Coatbridge Fountain to Hamilton route, with the petrol-electric buses of the Lanarkshire Tramways. This rivalry, with all its time-honoured ruses, lasted for some time; and the agreement which these companies eventually reached over the route was the first of its kind in Scotland.

These undertakings, together with the Scottish General Omnibus Company, had been primarily concerned with tramways. All three were rapidly developing bus services by the end of the 1914–18 war.

V

They were not alone. In Scotland, as everywhere else, this was a time of intense competition, especially from small independent operators. Their efforts were encouraged by the coming of the pneumatic tyre, and by the ex-Army Italian and American buses which were cheap, could be obtained on hire-purchase terms, and so offered a quick return. The licensing authorities controlled them

little better in Scotland than they did in England, and, although
the safety and trustworthiness of their vehicles were the last things
to be considered, the public welcomed this sudden spate of comparatively fast motor vehicles and the cheap fares with which they
tried to cut each other's throats. Among most operators it was a
fight to the death.

But the major undertakings were developing too. The Scottish
Motor Traction Company acquired services in Dundee in 1920, and
got a controlling interest in the Peebles Motor Company in 1925.
By this time it had added to its 'Lothian' vehicles a number of
fourteen-seater ex-Army Fiats, which were light and well suited to
the competitive work of the day. Through the purchase of various
businesses in the south, including the firm of Brook and Amos in
Galashiels, the Company's control of the important south-eastern
part of the Border Country increased rapidly. By 1926 it had gained
an entry into Glasgow. This was a crucial move. Everyone was
trying to get buses into Glasgow.

Until 1924 Glasgow Corporation's cheap and efficient tramways
had satisfied the transport needs of the City: buses had only been
used as feeders. However, as soon as the public realised that these
ex-Army vehicles were faster, they became very popular. The number of driver-operators competing with the tramways was fabulous.
By 1926 there were six hundred buses in the City, including those
of the Scottish Motor Traction Company; but only a small proportion of them belonged to Glasgow.

One important competitor in the district was the Midland Bus
Company, established in 1924. For two years it had run buses from
Paisley and was developing services to Saltcoats and Ardrossan.
Within the City area itself, a new undertaking, under the direction
of Sir Thomas D. Pile, a former director of the London General
Omnibus Company, was struggling to establish itself. This was the
Glasgow General Omnibus and Motor Services Limited. The Com-
pany started in 1926 with thirty A.E.C. vehicles. Two years later,
running as far as Hamilton, Motherwell, Wishaw, Stonehouse,
Strathaven, and along the north bank of the Clyde, it had over two
hundred.

The overlapping of interests was grotesque, and, of course,
grossly uneconomic. The picture can be completed by reference to
the important business of W. Alexander and Sons. This enterprise,
with a chain-driven Belhaven char-à-banc, had started in 1914 to run
Saturday and Sunday services between Falkirk and Bonnybridge.

Alexanders', soon to become an important part of the Scottish

Single-deck tram—
Blackpool Corporation,
1956

Double-deck 6-wheeled
trolley-bus — Wolver-
hampton Corporation

Single-deck centre-
entrance trolley-bus—
Mexborough & Swinton
Traction Company, 1955

London Coastal Coaches Ltd., Victoria. Office and *below* starting point, 1927

London Coastal Coaches Ltd., Victoria. Office and *below* starting point, 1927

Left: The London Coastal Coach Station, 1930

Victoria Coach Station, 1956

industry, at first knew all the hard struggles of a pioneer. In a dark garage on Sunday nights, the char-à-banc body had had to be un-bolted and a platform body put in its place, so that throughout the week, unless the vehicle should be wanted suddenly for a private party, it could run as a goods lorry. In wartime it added to its many uses by collecting ammunition from the factories of Falkirk.

During the mêlée that started in 1919, however, Alexanders' services were developed with Leyland vehicles; and their solid-tyred char-à-banc which bumped its way to John o' Groats was said to be the first to make such an excursion tour. By 1920, time-tables had been printed and published, and special six-day tours were running from Falkirk to Inverness and Aberdeen. Thus, by the mid 'twenties, Alexanders' services had fought their way to an important position in the centre of Scotland. With a fleet of over twenty vehicles, the firm was running buses not only from Kilsyth to Glasgow and Stirling but also to Dundee and Aberdeen.

In the south, English competitors had stolen a march. The Caledonian Omnibus Company, which started operations in Gallo-way, was promoted by our old friends the British Automobile Traction Company. Though this outpost of Sassenach enterprise operated joint services between Dumfries and Edinburgh with the Scottish Motor Traction Company, it would be disingenuous to suggest that these agreements lacked a tinge of rivalry. And when, following the Road Traffic Act of 1930, the Caledonian Company's application for licences in Edinburgh was upheld by the Traffic Commissioners, every Scottish Motor Traction busman felt the irony.

VI

This situation had, however, been modified sharply in 1928, when the railways were given powers to run road transport services. As in England, every operator knew the strength of the new com-petitors who had entered the field. Fortunately the railways, instead of adding to the confusion as they might have done, took the wiser course and obtained financial interests in a number of well-estab-lished bus undertakings.

So, in 1929, long before legislation had any major influence on its affairs, Scottish road transport, through the wisdom and enter-prise of its directors, had reached a most creditable degree of co-ordination. The Scottish Motor Traction Company, under the direction of Sir William Thomson (as he became when Lord Provost

L

of Edinburgh), joined forces with the L.M.S. and L.N.E. Railways
to acquire a financial interest in Alexander and Sons. This move
united these two major undertakings, and the regrouping had
far-reaching effects. Alexander's services extended into Fife and
to Pitlochry in Perthshire. The acquisition of the Scottish General
Omnibus Company, which belonged to the 'Balfour Group' and
was in keen competition, brought in further services in Perth, Fife,
Aberdeen, Moray, and Inverness.

In this way the Scottish Motor Traction Company consolidated
their position to the north and east of Glasgow. Alexanders', with
its additional services—this was one of the merits of the regrouping
—continued to function as before; in 1930 it took over the buses,
garages, and certain road services of the railways. Thus the group
co-ordinated the services for central Scotland, from Glasgow and
Edinburgh in the south to Aberdeen and Inverness in the north.
During the following years, the purchase of a host of subsidiary
undertakings completed many of the local meshes in a widely cast
net.

VII

Another development of 1929 was the granting of powers for the
Lanarkshire tramways to be superseded by buses: and the Lanarkshire Company began to suffer from the resulting competition. The
confused position in the Glasgow area was not resolved until the
Road Traffic Act obliged many of the minor operators to sell out or
retire. This they had to do because neither their vehicles nor their
maintenance systems were adequate and, under the new provisions,
they could not qualify for licences. Thus by 1932 most of them were
out of business; and the major undertakings, now in closer liaison
with the railway's requirements, decided to regroup. The Glasgow
General Omnibus Company, together with two other important
undertakings, was reformed into the Central S.M.T. Company; and
the L.M.S. and L.N.E. Railways each took roughly a quarter share
in the new undertaking. The range of operations included Peebles,
Douglas, and Muirkirk, and later reached Helensburgh in Dumbartonshire. New services were developed for schools, for collieries,
and for Public Works. During the rush-hour of a working day in
Hamilton, two buses a minute were passing through the town. This
regrouping not only meant that fares could be at a minimum: it
kept them from increasing until 1950.

By 1932 most villages in the south and west of Scotland had a bus service. The British Electric Traction Company's subsidiary, the Scottish General Transport Company, had extended its range, and the Southern Bus Company had been taken over by the Midland. The first phase of co-ordination was thus complete when, in 1932, the Scottish General and the Midland were merged to form the Western S.M.T. Company, and the new undertaking took over the services of some fourteen smaller operators.

Thus, within two years of the passing of the Road Traffic Act, and as a result of their efforts to develop co-ordinated services throughout the country, such undertakings as survived the chaos of the years before had been incorporated into the Scottish Bus Group. A sensible policy of de-centralisation allowed each branch of the group to give to its public the intimate service which, over the years, it had learnt to give. At the same time, the administrative control was in the hands of the three associated companies of the Scottish Motor Traction Company. The main areas of operation can be roughly defined as follows:

(a) The Scottish Motor Traction Company operated south and east of a line Bo'ness, Glasgow, Biggar and Carlisle.

(b) Alexander and Sons, on behalf of the parent company, operated north of a line Bo'ness, Glasgow, Helensburgh.

(c) The Western S.M.T. Company operated south of the Clyde and west of the line joining Glasgow to Muirkirk, Dumfries and Carlisle.

(d) The Central S.M.T. Company, concentrating on Glasgow and Lanarkshire, was bounded roughly by the circle—Glasgow, Biggar, Muirkirk, Glasgow. Services were later extended along the north bank of the Clyde to Dumbarton and Helensburgh.

VIII

This record, with its names and details, is likely to be of no interest whatever to the general reader. Still, the interests of the student or the man who is looking for local information require it: and, to the best of our knowledge, it has not been set down before in any form which is at all easily got at.

A reader interested in the details may remember the tramways of Musselburgh, which had been developed by the National Electric Construction Company. In 1931 these were bought by the British

Electric Traction Company and later sold to Edinburgh Corporation. The corresponding bus line was later taken over by the Scottish Motor Traction Company.

By 1930 coaches were running daily from Edinburgh and Glasgow to London. Collaboration with the Ribble Company enabled services to Blackpool, Liverpool, and Manchester: and, in conjunction with United Automobile Services, coaches were running from Edinburgh and Glasgow to Newcastle. A hundred diesel-engined buses had been put on the road, and the Scottish Motor Traction Company had increased its annual mileage of sixteen thousand two hundred in 1906 to over ten million. Every aspect of its services was improved. A high degree of co-ordination had made possible much closer attention to the detailed needs of the public.

What all this development has meant to Scotland in the last two decades will be considered in Chapter XXV.

CHAPTER XXI

The Days of Uncertainty

'Here and there, men of some vision training and business
acumen considered . . . deeply the immense possibilities lying behind
the fevered competition of these early post-war days.'
WALTER DOWDING: *A History of the Red and White
Group of Omnibus Companies.*

WRITERS hate abstractions. The poet, the novelist, the play-
wright shun them, less because they lack precision than
because they convey so little meaning of any kind. The parable
says far more to us than the revelation it humanises. The myth
transcends the truth that inheres in it. 'Give me a practical example.
Then, maybe, I'll understand.'

Teacher and journalist depend on their skill in answering this
age-old request. We care less for the principle than for the instance:
less for the rule than for the demonstration of how it works: and our
writers must know this, if they are to reach us.

Historians also fall to the lure, in a different way. Their temptation is the vivid phrase, which identifies a period or a movement
for us at the cost of misrepresenting it. Our attention is drawn to
one aspect only. We are encouraged to over-simplify. This is one of
the paradoxes of any kind of history: to make his subject vivid and
memorable, the writer needs to stress something about it which is
less important than the broad general movement of events, the
working of cause and effect, which it is his business as a historian
to make clear.

So, when we come, legitimately and without intentional bathos,
to our special context in the history of the bus industry, it would be
tempting to label the 'twenties as the time in which the Scottish
Bus Group found its strength. More particularly, we could celebrate
them because, within their span, after uncounted Board Meetings,
the interests of Tillings' and the British Electric Traction Company
were aligned. Or—sounding the journalistic, human-interest note—
we could portray the 'twenties as the era in which hundreds of ex-
Servicemen bought buses on hire-purchase terms and put them on
the road, either in hopes of making an easy living, or because buses
fascinated them, whether they made a living or not.

Each of these things happened, and was in its way remarkable,

165

but they are only a part of the story. The solid, prosaic core, the real truth lies in hard work on the part of the forty or fifty leading companies, plus a host of small but reasonably equipped firms, to maintain a decent service and expand it. Much vital groundwork was put into the industry during these years, and in all parts of Britain. Garages, works, depots, and bus stations were built; new vehicles were designed and put into production; and a great deal was done to improve the working conditions of bus crews and administrative staff. Undramatic, general, not to be summed up in a phrase: the bread-and-butter of history: the sober, factual truth of what in fact was happening to the industry as a force in human progress.

Every day brought fresh problems about fares, routes, licences, or the movements of competitors. Not the least of the worries, on a frosty morning, was to get many of the buses to start. These difficulties give point to Mr. W. J. Crosland-Taylor's account of the Crosville Company, *The Sowing and the Harvest*.

> The Lacres started fairly easily . . . but wouldn't keep going. The Daimlers were more stubborn to start, but seldom gave trouble once they were nice and hot. We used to heat petrol in a tin (God help us!) and pour it into the induction taps whilst somebody was swinging the engine. This ensured a start, but washed the oil off the sleeves, so it was immediately followed by a dose of engine oil and thus all was well. Bill Smith was the mechanic, and Mrs. Hughes, who had worked through the war, was in the office. She taught me all there was to know about waybills, which was not much as they were simple affairs—just a card with about eight values down one side and spaces to book in ticket numbers at the end of each trip. No parcels, returns, exchanges, vouchers or any of the modern complications that harass a conductor nowadays. At the end of the day a man was over or short and his punch was right or it wasn't.

In these days, Mr. Crosland-Taylor points out, the inauguration of a new route gave little difficulty. The journey was first of all made in a car, in order to decide the most favourable places for stages and to measure the intervals between them. The time-table and fare-table for the vehicle were then worked out, with an allowance of the necessary time for meals. Handbills were printed, and, in pursuance of the Crosville Company's practice, distributed at every house within half a mile of the route.

> It was just as easy as that. The bus crew kept the same vehicle as far as possible. They cleaned it, too, and because it was theirs and

they were always with it, the public got to know the whole outfit.
How different times are now.

II

During the 'twenties, the railways were developing too; and if
we are to see the period in its true perspective, we must say a little
about them. The Railways Act of 1921 had amalgamated the principal undertakings into the four groups whose names are still remembered; the Southern, the Great Western, the London Midland
and Scottish, and the London and North Eastern. A Rates Tribunal
had been formed to authorise rates and fares, in the hope that any
excess revenue could be returned to the public in the form of reduced fares. Just as railway equipment and services were beginning
to improve, however, the General Strike of 1926 paralysed the
country and began a trade depression which lasted for several years.
Coal became so expensive and in such short supply that during the
coal strike the railways could run skeleton services only.

All this offered an unexpected opportunity to the operators of
road transport. Imported fuel for motor vehicles was far more plentiful than coal, and the industry went rapidly ahead. When the railways at last disentangled themselves from the disaster, they had
little hope of recapturing the traffic they had lost. Non-stop expresses
were improved, and many lines in the south were electrified, but
the work that had been taken over by the country bus, by the long-
distance coach, and by road haulage dealt a heavy blow to the
railways. So heavy was it, that agitation was raised for powers to
operate road transport, and these, as already stated, were granted
by Parliament in 1928.

III

Since motor-coaches could be run at this time for about a shilling
a mile, they became a popular investment for operators. The public
seemed to enjoy this way of travelling in and out of cities. No longer
was a passenger obliged to go to a main-line terminal in order to
start his journey. Like his forbears in the days of stage-coaches, he
could be picked up by one of the latest pneumatic-tyred vehicles at
the stopping point that suited him best.

Much of this bus business was newly created traffic, and a good
deal of it due to the spread of population in suburban housing

estates. Even so, it has been estimated that this stopping facility alone, especially near London, cost the railways twenty per cent to forty per cent of their comparable traffics. Nearly all bus undertakings were fast developing their coach fleets. Three examples of the speed at which they were doing this will explain what the railways had to worry them. The East Kent Road Car Company had acquired three hundred vehicles in ten years; the Thames Valley Traction Company was carrying nine million passengers a year, while the United Automobile Services, now one of the Tilling Group of Companies, was in 1929 covering two thousand route-miles and had services from Lowestoft to Bishop Auckland.

We can readily understand why the Great Western, once the necessary authority was granted, wasted no time in joining forces with the National Omnibus and Transport Company in order to develop its road services. Other railway companies followed their lead; and for the most part, as we saw in an earlier chapter, the railways were wise enough to invest their money in existing passenger transport companies, rather than add to the confusion by forming their own. By 1932 they had invested nine million pounds in road services.

IV

The popularity of buses had a drastic effect on other forms of transport beside the railways. Many towns were forced to replace their trams with buses or, following the example of the British Electric Traction Company in the Potteries, to extend them with 'feeder' services. A representative case of this sort of development is that of Torquay.

Torquay's surface-contact tramway system, introduced during 1907 and 1908, caused a good deal of alarm. The studs in the centre of the track sometimes remained 'live' after the skate on the tramcar had passed over them, with the result that one day a cab-horse was electrocuted. Conductors were often obliged to dismount and place insulating material over the studs, and the company is reputed to have employed a man whose job was to kick them and see whether he received a shock. Not surprisingly, this somewhat hazardous system was in 1911 replaced by overhead wires.

Soon after the First World War, Torquay's tramways were affected by the bus services of the Devon General, which had been started by a Mr. John Mill in 1919. The Tramways Company therefore obtained a controlling interest in this venture, and, as the Devon General expanded rapidly into one of the largest organisations in the south, the work of the trams was gradually taken over by buses.

Torquay was not alone in realising the disadvantage of tramways. Leeds and Bradford had introduced trackless trams, to work up subsidiary routes until they justified the laying of tram track, in 1911. Ipswich and other towns were beginning to use them in the 'twenties: the first wholesale conversion was at Wolverhampton. In Manchester, traffic on the tramways increased steadily until 1928, when it began to decline; and since at the same time the revenue on the buses was trebled, the Corporation decided to try the necessary conversion on one route. It was a success, and they went ahead with others. The result was to increase by two and a half million the number of passengers carried by bus. These are not isolated instances. Between 1921 and 1930, the number of municipalities operating buses increased from forty-eight to one hundred.

Even so, the 'twenties must not be looked on as the era that sounded the death-knell of the trams. The tramways' day was drawing to a close, but they were by no means finished. Trams and light railways in 1926 carried the astonishing number of four thousand four hundred and sixty million passengers. The last new tramway, Dearne District Light Railway, in the West Riding, belongs to this period, and lasted only eight years. Even at the end of the decade, the London trams were still returning record figures. Nevertheless, though the tram continued to provide cheap transport in a large number of cities, the motor-bus was beginning to overtake it, and, as already shown, to offer serious competition to the railways.

The investments and mergers that followed the various Acts giving road transport powers to the railway companies were the main answers to this situation, though the railways were moved to improve their express services in an attempt to strike back at the long-distance motor-coach. Contrariwise, local motor-bus services made it necessary for them to slow down other 'express' services with stops at intermediate stations. For the first time road transport was drawing level with its rival.

v

Though they were expanding rapidly, the bus undertakings met with all manner of difficulties, especially in the matter of licences. Local authorities often took an unfavourable view of men who wanted to open new bus routes or extend old ones. Political issues, passionately voiced by individual councillors, could often make the local authority an unfortunate arbiter in these matters. Intransigent competitors were a continual menace to the larger undertakings, who called them pirates.

Partisanship could be violent, too: there were instances when a newcomer to an area, even though duly authorised by the local authority, had stones thrown at his bus by the supporters of his rival.

It is on record that at one time Brighton refused to grant licences to a Worthing company's buses to ply for hire in Brighton. Worthing retaliated in the same way. As a result, each of the companies concerned could only 'pick up' in the other's territory the passengers they had brought. Obviously such a situation could not continue for long. Thus each company, arguing that there would be no illegal 'plying for hire' if they allowed would-be passengers to book in advance, set up a booking office in the other's area. Indeed, the Worthing company went so far as to sell books of tickets, and maintained that there was no law against a driver stopping anywhere to pick up a passenger who held a ticket. This ruse was so effective that the Worthing drivers decided to go a stage further. Before leaving the town, they drove their vehicles round the Aquarium, in a manner that attracted the maximum of attention. Then, in order to avoid the accusation of 'plying for hire', they obliged everyone who wanted to board the bus to walk as far as the booking office and buy a ticket there.

When a local authority ran its own transport, it was naturally chary of issuing a licence to an independent operator who wanted to run a service through the area. There was no agreed standard of roadworthiness. Some local police gave vehicles the most perfunctory examination; others were stringent beyond reason. It was not uncommon for a bus to be passed by one examiner, and be failed in a town on some other part of the route it wanted to run. This often happened to reserve vehicles, which could take over certain duties but not, as luck would have it, the task of the bus that had broken down.

The point is underlined by a case in Yorkshire. One authority insisted that vehicles should have a sliding window behind the driver, for use in an emergency. The neighbouring town held that it should not be possible to disturb a driver in any circumstances, and refused to allow the device. So, when buses serving both places had to be prepared for inspection, the unfortunate company did not know what to be at.

But the bus companies had their own ruses. In towns where there was a police examination involving the weighing of buses, it was not unknown for the petrol tank to be removed from under the driver's seat and the engine fed from a two-gallon petrol tin. If the bus was still too heavy, doors were sometimes removed and replaced with pieces of painted plywood before it reached the weighbridge. If the police examined vehicles in their garages, there was some significance about the way in which vehicles were arranged in rows, nose to tail, making the row in the middle extremely hard to reach. The police soon got on to this one—and made a point of calling for the less accessible vehicles.

Inconsistencies and prejudices about licensing were not the only hindrances. By the mid-'twenties, motor vehicles could reach a speed that made ridiculous the old limit of twelve miles an hour for solid tyres, and twenty for pneumatic, imposed in 1903. Still more archaic was the ten-mile limit which they were supposed to observe in towns. In any case, buses and long-distance coaches had multiplied the traffic on the roads to such an extent that the legislation on transport was ludicrously out of date. The Ministry of Transport knew this, and, in the public interest, a Royal Commission was appointed to investigate the whole position. The ultimate result of its work was the Road Traffic Act of 1930. This act, one of the most important features in the story, must be discussed in detail.

CHAPTER XXII

The Road Traffic Act

'Transport is the Circulatory System of the Body Politic and is
just as essential to it as the Circulatory System is to the body of
every human being.'

W. H. BOULTON: *The Pageant of Transport through the Ages.*

AFTER a survey of the conditions described in the last chapter,
the Royal Commission reported, among other things, that the
existing system of licensing was out of date and useless. This is
hardly surprising, as it was based on Acts made law before the motor-
car existed. The Commission pointed to the careless and inconsistent way in which some eleven hundred licensing authorities in
England and Wales exercised their powers, and drew attention to
the increasing number of public transport vehicles which the licensing authorities, owing to the deficiencies of the Town Police Clauses
Act, found difficult to control. The Commission's report on these
matters was well received, and most of the recommendations were
drafted into the Road Traffic Act, which became law in 1930.

The new Act abolished the speed limit for private motor-cars and
motor-cycles. It raised the minimum age for drivers to seventeen in
the case of cars, limited to five and a half hours the length of time
the driver of a heavy vehicle should be continuously on duty, and
fixed his maximum period of driving to eleven hours a day. It
introduced compulsory third-party insurance, dealt with conditions
of employment for men in the industry, and gave local authorities
powers to abolish such toll charges as still remained in force on
certain roads and bridges.

By far the most important provisions, in our present context,
were the regulations that related to licensing of buses and coaches.
These fell into three classifications: Stage Carriage, Express Carriage,
and Contract Carriage. The Act divided the whole of Great Britain
into thirteen areas, which the operational boundaries had helped to
define. These areas were presently reduced to twelve—ten in
England and Wales, and two in Scotland.

Over each Traffic Area there was set up a body of three Commissioners, a whole-time Chairman appointed by the Minister,
and two other Members appointed by the Minister from panels
nominated by Local Authorities, not less than two Members to be
present at the hearing of any application. These Traffic Commis-

sioners became the sole arbiters for the licensing of services, vehicles, drivers and conductors, but within the Metropolitan Traffic Area the licensing of drivers and conductors is still done by the Commissioner of Police.

Though the Act removed at a stroke so many of the industry's ailments, two which followed its passing into law gave anxiety to every undertaking. No matter how long it had been established, as from 1931 each undertaking had to apply to the Commissioners for a Road Service Licence to cover every route it meant to run. The Commissioners were not bound by agreements made prior to the Act, nor had anyone the right to run a vehicle until a licence had been obtained. Applications had to be made on the appropriate forms and supported by the necessary time-tables and schedules. The details were published—they still are—in a publication called *Notices and Proceedings*, so as to give other operators, railway companies, and local authorities the chance to lodge an objection within fourteen days, and the right to voice it when the application came up for hearing. Hearings were to be held in public, with procedure like that of a normal court, except that evidence was not required on oath. Every detail concerning the proposed route had to be disclosed, every arrangement affecting the parties had to be made plain; and the right of appeal to the Minister of Transport, which existed under the old system, was reaffirmed. It still obtains today.

II

Naturally the initial phase, in which hundreds of applications had to be heard and their results co-ordinated, confronted both Commissioners and operators with a tremendous task. For many months the courts sat until late at night. Compared with proceedings once the basic arrangements had been hammered out, the work was terribly arduous, for the right to operate almost every route was at issue. Local authorities who ran tramways did all in their power to get their services protected, and sometimes to put buses off them altogether.

Every public service vehicle must still have a Certificate of Fitness before it can be used, and the Certifying Officer for the area must ensure that the numerous regulations are obeyed. For instance, a four-wheel vehicle must not be more than thirty feet long and no more than eight feet wide. The seats must allow adequate leg room and be at least sixteen inches wide, though even this does not meet the problem of the corpulent and heavily coated passenger, who overlaps the inside seat and leaves room for half the posterior of his unhappy neighbour.

The Certificate of Fitness is normally valid for five years and, on payment of the fee, a Public Service Vehicle licence automatically follows provided the holder is 'a fit and proper person'. As a guard against careless owners, the licence has to be renewed at the end of each year and the vehicle re-examined to ensure that it is road-worthy. A paper disc of the same dimensions as the Road Fund licence is now carried behind the windscreen and alongside the Road Fund licence indicating that the licence has been granted.

After five years the vehicle is again examined in detail, and a fresh Certificate of Fitness issued for whatever period the examiner thinks fit. Today the passenger's safety depends on something more tangible than the reputation of the operator.

III

The work of Public Service Vehicles falls under three categories: that of the Stage Carriage, the Express Carriage, and the Contract Carriage.

Stage Carriage work includes the normal street-to-street services provided by urban buses. The Stage Carriage is defined as a vehicle which carries passengers at separate fares, stage by stage, and stops to pick up or set down all along the line of the route. This is, of course, the most common of Public Service Vehicles. Even a few long-distance coach services, running through deep country, come under this heading, because they cater for passengers travelling short distances.

The Express Carriage—the modern equivalent of the Stage Coach—is distinguished by the fact that it carries passengers at a fare of not less than one shilling to destinations specified in advance, and, as a general rule, does not take up or set down passengers other than those who have paid for the journey in question. In practice this category covers the long-distance services of fifty miles or more, on which coaches can keep up an average speed of twenty-two to twenty-five miles an hour. In both cases licences for the routes must be applied for. Nowadays an interval of about two months must elapse before a proposed route can be published in *Notices and Proceedings* and the case heard and decided by the Commissioners.

As soon as the owner of a Public Service Vehicle has paid the excise duty on the vehicle, as every motorist must, he is in a position to carry 'private parties' from one place to another. This is termed

Contract Work, and as long as various regulations are observed and the vehicle does not ply for hire on its journey, no further licence is needed. One of the most important provisions in the Act was the distinction drawn between the purposes for which Public Service Vehicle licences would be issued. To the layman Contract Work sounds straightforward enough, but there has been a good deal of legal controversy about it, and particularly about the meaning of the words 'private party'. In practice this refers to the type of journey made by a football team or by a village outing, when the route, cost, passengers and timings are planned in advance and without public advertisement.

The advertisement prohibition is strict. A vicar may not even announce on his church notice-board the hour at which the coach leaves on the choir's jaunt to London, nor the secretary of the Women's Institute proclaim in spidery handwriting on a notice the time at which members are to be at the appointed bus stop.

IV

The majority of undertakings, of course, have vehicles which do all three types of work. In addition to their normal stage-carriage or bus services, they run Express services to, say, a number of sea-side towns, and a summer programme of Excursions and Tours which entail careful booking and planning for months in advance. Private hire or contract work, which naturally fluctuates from season to season, has its special difficulties. The problems which the planning and co-ordination of these three types of service present to a Traffic Manager are discussed in Chapter XXVI.

The most important result of the Road Traffic Act of 1930 was that it brought the whole question of licensing into open court. All in all, it was of great benefit to the industry. Although it put out of action many small operators whose vehicles could not comply with the regulations, and obliged others to sell out to larger undertakings, it gave everyone a fair chance. Many a small business found its feet in the early 'thirties and, with its competitors under similar control, was able to go ahead.

There is no doubt that the Act gave the industry the thorough overhaul it needed, and offered some degree of stability and security to all concerned. But no Act can do everything. The voluntary co-ordination of interests which has been described in Chapters XVIII, XIX, and XX was equally important. Today, the Road Traffic Act is the busman's Bible.

CHAPTER XXIII

The Days of Promise

'It is the Road which determines the sites of many cities and the growth and development of all. It is the Road that gives its framework to all economic development. It is the Road which is the channel of all trade and, what is more important, of all ideas.'

HILAIRE BELLOC.

VICTORY is sweet—but its results make duller reading than battle. In nine life-stories out of ten, the account of the early years of struggle is far more interesting than the chapters which deal with achievement. Once the man's position is established, once the actor or singer has won fame, a routine of triumphant appearances sets in; the characteristics which were brought out in the fight to succeed are blotted by success.

With suitable qualifications, this is true of the constructive and useful period which began as soon as the Road Traffic Act had overhauled the industry and laid down limits and rules which every busowner must observe. The time and the idea at last were matched; the industry found its strength and, within a year or two, was providing buses and coaches in numbers which the public came to take for granted.

In London, in provincial cities, and in the deep country, such companies as were to go forward did so rapidly. In the nine years before the outbreak of war in 1939, British Electric Traction and Tilling Groups, which had come together in 1928 in the Tilling and British Automobile Traction Company, the holding company in a large number of undertakings, came to control some thirty-six leading subsidiaries in every part of the country. Of these the United Automobile Services, to mention one only, had itself absorbed over a hundred neighbouring concerns at a cost of more than a million pounds. Though some important independent operators survived, it is true to say that at the beginning of the war the Tilling and British Electric Traction Groups held most of the provincial omnibus interests outside Scotland.

An important break in this partnership, which was to shape the grouping of the industry for some years, occurred in 1942 when Tilling Motor Services and B.E.T. Omnibus Services were formed to 'take over the respective interests of the partners in the Tilling and British Automobile Traction Company'.

Tours charabanc, Scottish Motor Traction Co., 1914—
photographed outside the Mound, Edinburgh

38-seater Bristol touring coach—Scottish
Motor Traction Company, 1955—on tour
in Perthshire

Part of the fleet of 30-seater A.E.C. coaches
—Scottish Motor Traction Company—
leaving Edinburgh for London

LATEST
DEVELOPMENTS
IN
DOUBLE-DECK
OMNIBUSES

Top left: An Atkinson central-entrance vehicle—Stalybridge, Hyde, Mossley and Dukinfield Joint Board

Top right: The first 'Routemaster' to be placed in service by London Transport

Bottom left: The standard omnibus designed and manufactured by 'Midland Red'

Bottom right: A Bristol 'Lodekka' operated by the Western National Company

This period of swift expansion came about because the possibilities of the latest types of coach and bus could at last be realised. Pneumatic-tyred vehicles, fast and comfortable, were easier to provide. Cheap, long-distance travel by road was changing from a novelty into an everyday need. People living in the country had come to want the amenities of the towns. Townsfolk demanded to reach the country whenever they wished. Given a public that would use them, there was therefore no limit to the number of interlocking services which bus-owners could build up, in, through, and around almost every town in the country. Ribbon-development and housing estates were taking people further and further into the country, and the buses had to follow. Moreover, within the towns themselves, the abandonment of the tramways began to throw an unexpected volume of traffic on the buses. These, and a host of smaller factors, helped to bring the bus and the coach into their own.

Yet all this general prosperity did not mean that everything within an individual undertaking at last ran smoothly. The traffic staff, with the Commissioners and the new licensing law before it, had almost to start all over again. Agreements with Local Authorities—greatly encouraged by the Road Traffic Act—had to be worked out by Standing Joint Committees, and agreements between one company and its neighbour for the operation of joint services. Problems of peak-period traffic, split services, regular vehicle maintenance, and the distribution of crews whose normal working day was now limited more precisely than by the existing Trade Union agreements—all these and a hundred other worries thrown up by the Road Traffic Act had to be faced and overcome.

The only possible answer was hard work, and hard work by men who found themselves increasingly busy when everyone else was on holiday.

A comprehensive account of the growth of the industry during this period would be flat and tedious. Fortunately the most important points are shown in the stories of the undertakings the early growth of which has already been described. It is enough therefore to refer briefly to the way things went in Birmingham, in the Potteries, and in Manchester.

II

After its uncertain beginning, the progress of Midland Red in the 'thirties was both quick and sure. Figures tell the story: the fleet

M

of three hundred and twenty-six vehicles, which had carried thirty-four million passengers a year in 1924, had by 1939 become a fleet of one thousand three hundred and nine vehicles which was carrying two hundred and ten million passengers annually throughout the Midlands. During the same period two thousand nine hundred and sixty motor-buses were built by the Company to its own designs. This number included enlarged single-deckers, six-cylinder double-deckers, and, after 1933, compression-ignition vehicles using heavy oil, which were ultimately to make the petrol engine a thing of the past.

When the Worcester Corporation decided to abandon the tramways which were owned by the British Electric Traction Company, it was eventually agreed that Midland Red should operate buses in their place. The Company was already operating in the area, so that this arrangement avoided the competition that might otherwise have broken out. In any case, the arrangement was both convenient and economical.

The Worcester Agreement was important, not only as the first step in the replacement of tramways by Midland Red buses throughout the whole of the Black Country, but also because it gave a lead to other undertakings and encouraged them to start similar work in conjunction with local authorities. By 1939 all the tramways owned by British Electric Traction in the area had been replaced by the motor-buses of its most modern and progressive subsidiary, and many new garages and depots had been built. The tramway between Kidderminster and Stourport was superseded, and the Company took over the services of the concern which had operated trams between Leamington and Warwick. Agreements on the same lines as that at Worcester were made with a number of local authorities, including those at Dudley, Oldbury, Rowley Regis, and Tipton.

At the outbreak of war, the Company's fleet was working from some thirty garages in places as far apart as Stafford in the North, Leicester in the East, Shrewsbury in the West, and Banbury and Hereford in the South. Associated Motorways, which Midland Red had helped to form, was contributing to a network of long-distance coach services that extended all over the country. In short, the small company which in 1907 had failed with its nine buses and been driven from its native city, was now serving, with the most up-to-date equipment, an area of about twelve thousand square miles.

Midland Red also offer a good example of the many undertakings which were putting into effect Partnership Agreements with the Railway Companies. These, as has already been shown, became common when, for their own financial benefit and in the interests of travel by rail, the railway companies decided to give up the management of buses and increase their investments in suitable bus companies. Today, when British Railways form part of the British Transport Commission, these Agreements with individual bus undertakings represent the middle course between private enterprise and outright public ownership. The important thing about them for the man in the street is that their objects and principles, agreed by privately owned companies long before the present position was dreamed of, show that obligations to the travelling public were fully recognised.

The aim of these Agreements was to co-ordinate and arrange the necessary road services between the parties and to avoid the wasteful competition that would otherwise have been inevitable. The Railway Companies agreed to purchase fifty per cent of the holding of the main shareholders, and their representatives joined the Board of the bus undertaking. Thus both became equal partners. To deal with the details of co-ordination between road and rail, a Standing Joint Committee was set up. The Committee agreed that the factors which should bind the Committee's decisions (and those of any Arbitrator it might refer to) were (a) the needs and convenience of the public; (b) the public's demand for a particular form of transport; and (c) the usefulness of any transport already in existence.

Thus the parties, in legal contract, agreed of their own free will not to overrun and damage existing services in the furtherance of their own interests, but to strive after what would benefit the area as a whole. In practice these Agreements led to schemes for mutual assistance in the event of break downs, to arrangements whereby road and rail tickets should be 'inter-available'—a horrible word, but the one known to the public—and to the development of combined road and rail trips.

Apart from the large number of services which the Midland Red ran in partnership with the Railways, sixteen other subsidiaries of the British Electric Traction Group and many of Tilling had similar agreements. Today, Halifax, Huddersfield, Sheffield, and Todmorden Corporations have Joint Committees with the Railways; and in Plymouth, Southend, Luton, and Brighton, where the Corporations and Companies concerned both provide local transport, a Joint Committee supervises the pooling of receipts.

We have had more than one occasion to note that in many places tramways were gradually losing ground. Since 1925 the Potteries Electric Traction Company had been appealing against freelance motor-bus competition in its district, without achieving much result. The day of tramways in the Five Towns was coming to an end.

That trams should fail in a district where, twenty years before, they had achieved so much, was due to many causes. Narrow streets had made double tracks impossible, so that the services were very slow. Low bridges had meant the use of single-deck vehicles, which as traffic grew became inadequate. Cheap fares, which had done so much for factory workers in the early years of the century, yielded too small a profit. Reserves were low; and the whole system now wanted a great deal spent on it.

It was therefore decided that the Company's buses should gradually replace the trams. Since the fleet had been started before the 1914–18 war, this meant that operations were not disrupted by a wholly new undertaking, and that the work of a company which knew its area could go on. In July 1928, the last tram rattled its way into the depot. Generating stations were dismantled, overhead wiring and cables were removed, and the local authorities were compensated for the work that was needed to make good the roads.

In 1933, a year after its capital had been considerably reduced, the Company resumed the paying of dividends and, in view of its new work, changed its name to the Potteries Motor Traction Company. Large garages and offices were built in Stoke-on-Trent, and use was made of the space formerly occupied by the old tramway smithy and welding shops. The building of garages and depots in other towns, the provision of rest-rooms and canteens necessary for bus crews who had no regular meal-times, was only part of the work that had to be done as quickly as possible. A Joint Committee of all Omnibus Operators in the Potteries and in Newcastle-under-Lyme greatly helped the co-ordination of services for the district; and, when a service involved more than one operator, it helped to arrange for the interchange of tickets.

Many of these other operators have gone out of business since the costs of working began to mount so heavily, because of the increase in the tax on fuel oil, and the repeated rises in the wage rates of omnibus employees. As a result, the Potteries Company has had to increase its own services. It now runs five hundred vehicles.

IV

In Manchester, where the Corporation had taken control of all public transport in the 'nineties (*see* Chapter XIV), a motor-bus was a rare sight in the City centre as late as 1927. Nevertheless, the Corporation soon realised the limitations of its tramways. Their passing loops made the cars a menace in fog, the services were continually obstructed by other traffic, and by the 'thirties the whole system called for the spending of a deal of money, if it was to cope with the ever-increasing number of passengers.

Express bus services ran to the suburbs, intended for those who were prepared to pay a little more for comfort and speed; and, a year or two before the passing of the Road Traffic Act, agreements with neighbouring municipal and company operators made it possible for districts outside the City to be linked up by bus services which reinforced the trams.

Once again, the operators concerned voluntarily agreed upon a basis for sharing and operating services, many of which ran through the City from one side to the other. After the Act, these agreements were developed and increased, for it was an express purpose of the Road Traffic Act to harmonise the interests of local authorities and other operators. Manchester is a good example of the many cities and towns in which this worked well.

It is not surprising that the fundamental and costly step of abandoning the tramways, first proposed in 1929, should have had its critics. The result was a steadily mounting revenue for the buses. Route by route, some thirty-eight miles of tramway track were abandoned, and the buses soon showed an increase of nearly seventy thousand pounds in their takings. Moreover, by this step the Corporation saved the City expenditure of the four hundred thousand odd which would have been necessary to overhaul and develop the system; and since many routes, unsuitable for tramways, were quickly taken over by buses, the change brought great improvements.

The rest of the work carried out in Manchester during the 'thirties differed little from that in many other cities. Before the outbreak of war, a bus station capable of dealing with a thousand buses a day had been built, and a fleet of some eight hundred vehicles was carrying about two hundred million passengers a year. The peak periods of traffic in the morning and evening soon made Manchester's transport problems comparable to those of London—and every other large city—problems which, from a Traffic Manager's viewpoint, have yet to be discussed. The immediate point, however, is that by 1948 all the trams had been replaced by buses or a limited number of trolley-buses.

Some twenty-four local authorities in England were operating trolley-buses by 1935. A discussion of the technical points for and against these vehicles would lie beyond the scope of this book, but their entry into the story needs some comment. Like their petrol and diesel-engined counterparts, these vehicles were improved so rapidly that many operators took more of them into permanent service than anyone expected at the start. They continue to do important work, though some authorities are replacing them with ordinary buses.

It is not hard to see why the trolley-bus comes into the picture. In the first place, the existence of overhead wiring and of generating plant suggested the use of an electric vehicle more mobile than a tram. After all, there was nothing very new about trackless trams. Leeds and Bradford had had a primitive type as early as 1911. Moreover, though depots needed modification in order to accommodate trolley-buses, maintenance staffs were already trained and accustomed to the repair of electric motors; and in districts where mining is the principal industry, it is not surprising that local authorities should have favoured a vehicle whose power is obtained from coal.

A further advantage lay in the fact that, once authority had been granted for the operation of trolley-buses, detailed supervision of their route by the Traffic Commissioners was not required by the Road Traffic Act. Instead, they came under the control of the Ministry of Transport as light railways.

But there are objections to the trolley-bus. Though quiet and smooth running, it is very much less flexible than a vehicle with a form of propulsion which is self-contained. This means far more than the inconvenience that a trolley-bus cannot be taken away from its power supply. It means that trolley-buses are difficult to link with the motor-bus services of a neighbouring authority, or to divert in order to meet a sudden emergency. The football match or political meeting for which special services are required may be off the trolley-bus route. Even if it is not, to collect and park a large number of trolley-buses in readiness for a home-going crowd is no simple matter.

This lack of flexibility, rather than the relative cost per vehicle-mile, can mean that trolley-buses are more expensive to work. Their cost does not depend simply upon the number of units of power they consume, but upon the particular traffic problem and the degree to which they fail to solve it.

In any event, whatever we may have since learnt about these vehicles, in the 'thirties many authorities took the bold step of adopting them. Others took the even bolder step of abandoning the whole of their electric system, and of purchasing motor-buses to re-place the trams. Quite a number, finding their answer in the British principle of compromise, took some of each.

V

Thus the 'thirties was a period of rapid expansion and hard work. If success is the theme song, this certainly does not mean that every undertaking found itself prosperous, with every vehicle fully employed. In these years the economics of running large fleets had to be learnt through bitter experience. When fares, time-tables, and schedules had been worked out, and vehicles purchased to meet an apparent need, a company might discover that for every fifty hours the men were paid, the wheels of their buses were turning only for thirty.

This problem was serious. It is still with the industry, and remedies are not always easy. There is a great deal more in the best deployment of vehicles and crews than the layman would imagine. It may sound easy enough to buy buses and to put them on the road; but how to employ them so that the public is satisfied and, at the same time, costs are kept to a minimum, is only one of the problems which, in the 'thirties, most bus undertakings had to learn in the hard way.

CHAPTER XXIV

The Second World War

'Whether in peace or war time, transport is the life blood of civilized society.'

CAPTAIN EUAN WALLACE.

THE task which faced the entire bus industry between 1939 and 1945 was so enormous that it is hard to know where a short account of it should begin. Heroic efforts by bus crews and garage staffs in bomb-shattered streets; improvised arrangements to meet such emergencies as the evacuation of a whole district; regular services that had to be maintained to docks, to shadow factories, to airfields, by dwindling fleets of vehicles; all this, against a background of black-out, rubble-blocked roads, and griping shortage of men and buses, was the common experience.

Different parts of the country varied in the severity of the attacks they had to bear, but, at one time or another, all transport undertakings met with comparable hardships. Bouquets for the triumphant way in which they were tackled have been distributed elsewhere. Our purpose is simply to point out the problems that imposed so cruel a strain on vehicles and staff, and thus to give some impression of what the industry achieved.

While Mr. Chamberlain was hoping to secure peace at Munich the staffs of many aeroplane factories were being doubled and trebled, and the bus companies concerned had to work feverishly to provide the needed emergency services. Factory managers had to stagger working hours, so that the buses might cope with the work that was suddenly thrust upon them. In many parts of the country, increasing numbers of workers had to be taken to factories by fleets of vehicles which were soon to be weakened to meet army requirements, and by staffs soon to be cut by mobilisation. All this made a worthy prelude to the difficulties that lay ahead. Meanwhile, Regional Commissioners and Civil Defence authorities in each area wasted no time in laying plans to meet the more grievous emergencies when they came.

II

In 1939 Red and White Services had a hundred and fifty of its three hundred and fifty vehicles engaged exclusively on factory services, and it was not long before most companies had many of their single-decker vehicles converted into ambulances. The whole of the Green Line fleet in London was set aside for this purpose. Yet the contractors' men had to be taken to scattered sites for the building and enlarging of war factories, to which thousands of additional employees were soon to be carried.

When the staff of the Railway Works at Crewe was suddenly doubled, the Crosville Company found itself not only with intense morning and evening 'peak periods', but also facing the fact that, in this particular district, thousands of men had the habit and intention of travelling home to their midday meal. The problem called for adroit staff work, but the transport was supplied.

During the anxious summer of 1939, anti-aircraft gun-sites had to be effectively manned, and the urgent movement of troops made sudden demands on all forms of public transport. One midnight, in Ryde, members of the local company's office staff had to be rushed into drivers' seats so that the unexpected soldiers might be taken to their defensive positions in the island.

All over the country, men whose job was no longer driving but who happened to hold P.S.V. licences soon found themselves called on when the number of regular drivers was inadequate. And on this occasion, at Ryde, while the local manager supervised and volunteers used the tram to carry baggage the length of the pier, vehicles were provided and the soldiers duly dispatched. The incident was typical of the way in which the bus companies behaved when they realised their country was on the brink of war.

By September the Evacuation Scheme was in progress, and buses had immense tasks to perform in distributing thousands of children from the railheads. For this and similar emergencies that presently arose, undertakings within the main Groups pooled their vehicles, so that a sudden demand on one company could be assisted by the vehicles of a less harassed associate. So it came about that over a thousand buses were ready to move children from Bristol into the surrounding villages. The same thing happened in many parts of the country, and a great many normal services had to be curtailed, so that the children could be carried to safety with the speed that was then thought necessary.

Meanwhile fuel rationing came into force, long-distance services had to be cut, and companies had to accept the fact that they would be unable to make or buy new vehicles until the war was over. Maintenance routine could no longer be kept up, vehicles were being requisitioned and borrowed at short notice, more and more of the regular staff went off to join the Forces. Faced with these problems, those who were left to run the companies began to feel the determined spirit of the pioneers. It inspired them to astonishing feats. Again and again, in circumstances that would have justified a total breakdown in services, buses appeared at the bus stops and ran more or less on time.

III

Then France fell. As the little ships came back from Dunkirk, the bus companies had to collect thousands of weary soldiers and take them to their camps. Hundreds of vehicles had to be rushed to assembly points in a single night; and, since almost every army unit had lost its own transport in France, it was some time before most of them could return. Meanwhile other fleets stood by to carry troops to the danger-points on the eastern coast, to meet the invasion which all thought to be imminent. The planning of commanders could have achieved little without the transport to make it possible.

For many undertakings, shortage of vehicles was an overwhelming problem; but numbers of civilians were clearing out of some of the danger areas, so that some services were relieved—those at Southend, for instance—and a few buses were set free for the companies that had most need of them.

IV

When the blitz brought its nightmare to London, Plymouth, Portsmouth, Bristol, Glasgow, and the dozens of other cities and towns that had their sirens moaning night and day, then, if life was to be maintained, the transport industry had, by heaven knows what means, to keep its wheels a-turning. Petrol tankers ran the gauntlet through blazing streets; bus drivers, urged on often by their passengers, kept one eye on the flak, the other on an almost invisible kerb, and pushed on through falling shrapnel. Such journeys were routine; their hazards were what everyone expected.

In the morning after a raid, there were hurried inspections to see what vehicles had been put out of action, what streets were impassable—and for how long—and what new routes had then and there to be improvised. Severe raids naturally imposed the greatest strain upon the staff of every transport undertaking, who had to recover from them, like everyone else, and at once set about restoring services.

No one knew what would happen next. The men who had to bear it report that this was the part of the strain that memory will not hold. No one in the crowd in Bristol's Old Market Square, that summer's day in 1942, knew that the bomb from the lone raider overhead would set fire to three out of five double-deckers, kill forty-four passengers, and seriously injure as many. Yet someone had to deal with the disaster, and see that the services went on. If the regular buses had been buried under rubble and twisted girders, staff would find vehicles of some kind, somewhere, somehow, and see that a service was provided. A theatre curtain must rise, no matter what the back-stage difficulties may be. The buses—what was left of them—went on.

v

A driver's account of his journey from Bournemouth to London, in November, 1940, shows the spirit in which thousands of his kind faced their task. The details of the incident may not have been common, but the attitude is characteristic. This man had heard the sirens in the suburbs, and had seen enough in the sky to know that London was 'having it'. Still, as all was reasonably quiet in Kingston-on-Thames, he decided to carry on.

I had hardly got clear before things began to happen in real earnest. Anti-aircraft guns began firing from unseen positions near the road and mingled with their firing were the explosions of falling bombs. I thought the only thing to do was to keep going and to trust in luck. I was actually on Putney Heath when it happened—one terrific explosion and the coach seemed to shoot away from underneath me. I felt as though I was flying through the air with the coach. I clung on to the steering wheel, although this did not stop me from being severely bumped around inside the cab. I remember wondering what had happened and then I saw I was rushing towards some trees. The coach swerved and hit a wall and fence. My first thought was what had happened to my passengers? They were shaken, but uninjured. I went back to find the cause of the trouble—there was a crater nearly covering the road where I had passed a second before.

Though he says little about himself after this point, the driver was taken to hospital suffering from shock. Many of his mates suffered the same kind of thing. There were the bombed and machine-gunned buses of Dover, the 'Busman's Malta', where the local bus depot was destroyed by shelling, and the local traffic and cashier's office consisted of a double-deck bus which stood in a square by day and retired out of gun-range for the night. There was the driver who was delivering fuel-oil to the London Passenger Transport Board garage in Leyton when a high-explosive bomb set it on fire. The man, having picked himself out of the debris, ran through the flames, disconnected the hoses, and drove the tanker away. And there were the everyday, humdrum, unheroic deeds which showed the same devotion to the job. When the centre of Southampton had been flattened, and most of the people evacuated, some four thousand in the surrounding countryside had still to be taken every day to work. To make this possible, every night a number of crews took their families aboard their buses, and had taken a thousand men to the docks before seven-thirty in the morning.

Yet, cruelly though they battered transport, the blitz and all that came with it were not the only trouble. Labour shortage was a continual problem. It could be overcome only by employing thousands of women as 'clippies' and, in a few cases, as drivers too. As the years dragged on, women did duty increasingly as cleaners, as supervisors, and as traffic controllers.

But even the women, gallant and resourceful as they were, could do nothing about the crippling shortage of spare parts. Broken crankshafts had to be bolted together and put back into engines: engines were modified to fit chassis they had never been designed for: obsolete vehicles of every kind were routed out, patched up, and brought back into service. Fuel was short too, making it increasingly difficult for the industry to keep pace with the demands of the time. Services, especially over long distances, were worse and worse restricted: some villages lost their buses altogether.

And all this while, the number of passengers who wanted to travel kept steadily growing. In some areas the increase was over a hundred per cent. 'Perimeter seating' which made it possible for a thirty-four-seat single-decker to carry sixty-four passengers, was sometimes used as a makeshift. For a time the Ministry of Transport had to wink an eye at the breach of regulations by standing passengers.

VI

But seating arrangements, however drastic and accommodating, could be only a partial remedy. One attempt to solve the problem was to develop Producer Gas Units. Various undertakings experimented with different designs of trailer and equipment. Although companies in the Tilling Group developed a single-decker with its own built-in gas plant, the gas-producers were a great advance on the gas-filled balloons which often came adrift from their vehicles during the 1914–18 war, but many of the experts who had to use them look back on them with scorn.

Such, then, were a few of the trials and difficulties which the industry had to suffer in the years of war. To do justice to all that was done would need a book of an encyclopædic size. A chapter catches nothing of the atmosphere, the debilitating, prosaic, heart-breaking fatigue in which depleted staffs, month after month, struggled to keep their worn-out buses on the road. It says nothing of the Traffic Managers and their teams who, drawing a deep breath at last after adapting themselves to the emergency on hand, were suddenly called on to revise their schedules once again because a yard-full of vehicles were needed for some unexpected reason. It says nothing of Home Guard and Civil Defence duties doggedly and often humorously carried out in garages after hours of driving in the black-out, or of the endless waiting and the boredom enlivened only by moments of sharp fear.

All this and a great deal more sounds in the words of Lord Leathers, appointed in May 1943 to be head of the Ministry of War Transport, when he paid tribute to the whole of the Transport industry.

'At every stage of the struggle,' his message said, 'the maintenance of transport services has been an indispensable condition of the defence of our homes and of victory in the field, and, realising this, the enemy has sought to smash the lines of communication and destroy the means of conveyance.

'It will not be forgotten that through the worst air attacks you kept the wheels of transport turning and thus enabled the country to gather its strength for the offensive. You maintained the flow of essential supplies to our industries and people while carrying the greatest military load in our history.

'To all men and women who have worked on the railways and roads, in the docks, and on the inland waterways—I offer my sincere thanks, knowing that I voice the feelings of the whole country.'

CHAPTER XXV

Transport in Scotland—II

'We have a definite and clear responsibility to the people of this country. We intend to carry out our obligations to maintain and, wherever possible, improve the standards which we have set ourselves. . . .'

JAMES AMOS: From a paper read to the Institute of Transport (Scottish Section), January 1953.

WHEN the Road Traffic Act of 1930 had consolidated the progress described in previons chapters, the Scottish Bus Group settled down to a period of steady development which continued until the beginning of the Second World War. The general picture was not unlike that in England. Many small and inadequately equipped operators had been bought out and their businesses acquired; countless local licensing authorities had been abolished; the licensing of routes and staff, and the supervision of fares and time-tables, passed to Area Traffic Commissioners.

As we have emphasised already, the Road Traffic Act did not bring unity to the industry by a single stroke; it extended and enforced the co-ordination and the standards of service which the leading operators and undertakings had been struggling to bring about by their own exertions.

Many more undertakings were incorporated into the Scottish Bus Group during the 'thirties, and arrangements made with the Burghs of Perth, Kirkcaldy, Ayr, and Kilmarnock for modern bus services, each run by the appropriate company, to take the place of tramways. In cities where the Corporation ran its own services, the Group entered into agreements which co-ordinated its joint efforts and gave Corporations some measure of protection.

This protection varies according to the circumstances. One example of it is the complete monopoly enjoyed by Glasgow Transport authorities within what has become known as the 'monopoly area': Glasgow having secured an Act to that effect. Another is in the additional 1½d. fare which must be charged when the Scottish Omnibus Company's vehicles run on the tramway routes in Edinburgh.

Through the length and breadth of Scotland the Bus Group

steadily developed. In 1935 the capital of the S.M.T. Company was increased. With the other companies, they spent substantial sums on diesel-engined vehicles, and on garages and bus stations which in the cities were beginning to deal with fifty vehicles per hour.

No less important than the comfort and efficiency of the vehicles, however, were the improvements made in the working conditions of drivers, conductors, and administrative staff; and it must be put on record that throughout the Scottish industry's efforts to improve the lot of its staff—many of whom, incidentally, held shares in the undertaking—the friendliest relations were enjoyed with the Trade Unions concerned.

During the early 'thirties, also, the Touring business, which had begun with a thirty-two-mile tour in 1907, began to develop enormously. Places of beauty and historic interest, which had only been names to many of the people, were now within the reach of all who could afford a seat in a small char-à-banc. Visitors, especially Americans, were more than enthusiastic; six- to sixteen-day tours of the Highlands were run with the co-operation of various hotels and the Travel Association of the time. These light, swift vehicles raised dust-clouds in the glens, dragged their sightseers up precipitous mountain tracks, and brought a new industry to Scotland. Today the touring business brings thousands of visitors to the country, acquaints the Scottish townsman with the life of the crofter, and brings money and work to places that had been remote, depopulated, and unknown.

II

During the anxious autumn of 1939 all this touring had to stop, and the development of normal services was impeded. Hundreds of vehicles were requisitioned, as they were from undertakings in all parts of Britain; drivers and conductors were recruited from the Services, and fuel was short. Over and above the wartime production accomplished in their workshops, the companies had to provide the vital day-to-day traffic upon which so many industries depended; and, although their services were not so frequently interrupted by bombs and shelling as those near the English Channel, the Scottish buses had their share of trouble. Over sixty double-deckers were hurried to London to help with the evacuation which followed the blitz; others did similar work in Greenock and Glasgow. Incidentally, the fares charged for normal day-to-day services at this

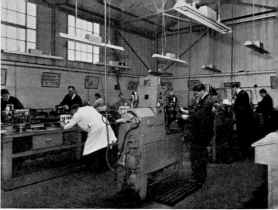

Potteries Motor Traction Company upholsterers at work

Re-calibrating fuel injection units—'Midland Red'

Dock shop and pits—'Midland Red'

Body overhaul shop at the new Aldenham Works of London Transport

General engine reconditioning shop — Potteries Motor Traction Company

A.E.C. chassis with Metropolitan-Cammell-Weymann "Fanfare" body—North Western Road Car Company

Bristol chassis with body by Eastern Coach Works—operated by the Eastern Counties Company

EXAMPLES OF LATEST TYPE COACHES

Leyland Royal Tiger chassis with Burlingham body—Hebble Motor Services

A.E.C. chassis with Bellhouse-Hartwell body—Sheffield United Tours

Leyland chassis with Harrington body—one of the 'Grey-Green' fleet of George Ewer & Sons

time were no higher (and in some cases less) than they had been in 1912.

During the winter of 1940, some six hundred vehicles were prepared for the support of our slender coastal defences, and the Scottish Bus Group decided that it could contribute something more positive. In spite of long hours of working and driving in black-out conditions, about two thousand men volunteered to form a Scottish Home Guard Transport Column. Under the command of Lieutenant-Colonel Amos (the present Chairman of the Group), this column was capable at short notice of providing transport for two Army Divisions.

That the strength of this voluntary organisation was never called upon for more than long and arduous rehearsals is a mercy that in no way lessens its achievement. In those days, when so much depended on the enterprise of individuals, the Scottish bus crews made a characteristic contribution to the defence of their country.

III

As soon as these difficult years were over, the pre-war complement of 'workers' ' and normal stage-carriage services was restored and slowly extended. The touring and long-distance services, cut off by fuel rationing, were resumed and developed. The volume of traffic steadily increased until, by 1947, the companies' reserve of overworked vehicles reached its lowest level.

The situation was difficult. To restore the Group's vehicles to pre-war standards would have cost a staggering sum. The effect of the crisis upon the Scottish Bus Group was clear and simple. When the part of the Scottish Motor Traction Company concerned with bus operations had been formed into a separate company, now known as Scottish Omnibuses Ltd., its shares were voluntarily sold to the British Transport Commission.

Continuity in policy and working methods was, however, made possible by the fact that, in principle, the same Board of Directors, with additional representatives from the Commission, still guided and co-ordinated the work of the same companies, decentralised in the areas in which they grew up. The Chairmanship of the Group and of each individual company passed at this time from Sir William Thomson to Mr. James Amos, whose original company in the Border area had become part of the Scottish Motor Traction Company's organisation in 1926. Under a closely knit form of direction,

N

therefore, each unit within the Scottish Group continues to maintain its day-to-day contact with the particular sections of the public which it alone understands.

This principle has about it nothing abstract or academic. The needs and interests of the public are constantly studied by Traffic Managers. Inspectors are continually investigating complaints and suggestions. Conductors on the platforms of their vehicles are incessantly dealing with people in all their moods and difficulties. The public is not slow to complain if things are not to its liking, and no organisation can flout it as long as there are other ways of travelling.

At times, even if he has the patience of Job, it would seem difficult for a conductor to do right. Attention to the public, to his tickets and his waybills are not the end of his job. He has almost to have eyes in the back of his head.

> Sir,
>
> I beg to report that on the 7.20 p.m. journey from Glasgow today I was booked by a police officer—the offence being 'picking up passengers at an unauthorised stopping-place, i.e. —— Street.' (I subsequently learned that the police officer who booked me had previously directed the passengers to that picking-up point. This entirely sets at nought the popular theory that policemen, like cats, live only in the moment, as it indicates considerable forethought.)
>
> The part in parenthesis is quite irrelevant to the report and is quoted merely as an interesting sidelight on Corporation officials and their methods.
>
> > Your obedient servant,
> > John McDonald.

Though few conductors may be quite so philosophical as Mr. McDonald, their attempts to help and look after their passengers can lead to countless incidents of this sort.

In recent years further important developments have taken place. Liaison with the railways has made it possible for a passenger travelling by coach from Edinburgh or Glasgow to London—the cheapest service of its kind in the country—to return by train if he so desires. Other express services have been extended. Today, thanks perhaps to their window-roofed coaches, specially designed for giving the best views of a mountainous countryside, the Scottish Omnibus Group claim to have the largest touring business in Britain. Having developed arrangements with hotels and worked in close co-operation with the Scottish Tourist Board, the Bus Group runs vehicles bringing thousands of visitors from all parts of the world into the heart of Scotland. By this means alone the Group has done a great deal to develop trade in towns and villages and to bring the country's scenery and places of historic interest within the reach of all. Naturally the buses have a great deal to offer those who come year by year to the Edinburgh Festival, and use this opportunity to visit different parts of the Highlands.

IV

Yet touring is by no means the principal activity of the Group. First and foremost, this tightly co-ordinated part of the industry, with its combined fleet of just over four thousand five hundred vehicles, provides people in all parts of the country with the daily services they need. In the industrial cities it brings workers to the factories; it stands by with extra vehicles to meet peak traffic periods; it enables artisans to bring up their families on the new housing estates, away from smoke and grime. In remote districts it links villages with the town, providing numerous services which run and must continue to run at a loss.

Many other tasks in the operation of buses today, problems which we have still to discuss, contribute to this total achievement; but enough has been said to show why the Scottish Omnibus Group faces the future with confidence. Over the years, its growth has been shaped by many brave pioneers, by the needs of the Scottish public, which that public was never hesitant to voice, and by the form of control, gradually evolved, which is most appropriate for Scotland. Today in a number of areas buses are gradually replacing branch-line trains. And when the bus industry, already powerfully organised, begins to take the place of such railway services as are running at a loss, who can foretell what the future may have in store for it?

CHAPTER XXVI

Traffic Problems

'. . . and so the Traffic Manager was born. The third and perhaps
most important Department of the Bus Company. . . .'

W. J. CROSLAND-TAYLOR.

THE story of the Scottish Bus Group has shown that a steadily
expanding fleet is essential if steadily increasing demands both
for new and established services are to be met. This is a platitude;
but practical experience was needed in order to drive it home.
Every undertaking in the industry has now realised the truth, and
we can leave it with them.

To survey in any detail the expansion of the industry since the
Second World War would be a waste of time. There have been important changes both in policy and ownership, and these must be
discussed; but the main improvements that have taken place in the
majority of undertakings have all run on similar lines.

Trams have been replaced, stage-carriage services have been
restored and have surpassed their pre-war standards, and the luxury
and efficiency of long-distance coaches have offered an increasingly
serious challenge to the railways. In the number of passengers
carried on all types of service there is a widespread and dramatic
improvement on pre-war records, and the various undertakings have
been able to buy or to have manufactured for them the latest types
of vehicle with which to make it. Single-deckers with under-floor
engines and improved seating have been introduced for long-
distance runs and for stage-carriage work; lighter and more spacious
double-deckers are an answer to the problem of rising costs. In order
to extend the life of vehicles, garages and maintenance systems have
been radically improved. Ticket-issuing machines and paying-in
systems are under constant review, since no undertaking can afford
to carry surplus staff. A driver's daily basic rate of pay is more than
twice what it was in 1939, and the fuel tax has risen steadily. The
industry is therefore as heavily burdened as any other with the
problem of cost.

Statistics make dull reading, and a numerical review of the speed
at which the industry has grown since the war would give little idea
of the work it has to tackle day by day. In any case, the man in the
street wants facts, not figures. It will be much more interesting to

glance at the way a representative undertaking is organised, and at some of the operational problems it has to face. Such a glance not only gives some picture of the industry as a whole, but suggests the work that has to be done before each bus can pull out of its depot and start its morning run. On the whole, the public show an understanding of the busman's work, at any rate on the human relations side: but to judge from complaints, a few members of the public would seem to think that all that must happen is for the driver to start the engine and the conductor to hop on the platform.

II

Details in organisation naturally vary from one undertaking to another. They depend not only upon whether the undertaking is owned by the ratepayers or by shareholders, but on the way in which it has evolved. Every undertaking has developed a system to suit its own part of the world, and principles that work in one area may be useless in another. Some undertakings serving compact areas are able to carry on with a large central depot and, perhaps, a few small subsidiary depots. Others serving a scattered public are decentralised into areas, each of which has a complete traffic and engineering staff responsible to those at headquarters.

The difference is not important to the traveller, for the work and problems in each section of an undertaking follow a similar pattern. At its head is a General Manager, whose job is to put into effect the policy he is given by his board of directors (if it is a company) or his transport committee, if it is a municipal undertaking. As in every business, he has the main responsibility for his undertaking's performance. To assist him he has an organisation which falls into three broad sections—Traffic, Engineering, Finance.

The Traffic Section is responsible for routes, fares, time-tables, the frequency and supervision of services, and the staffing of vehicles. The Engineering Section has the duty of providing safe, clean, and properly maintained vehicles wherever and whenever they are required. The Finance Section has charge of the issue and checking of tickets, the recording and the security of takings, wages, accounts, and statistics.

Let us first of all outline the work of the Traffic Manager, and the work supervised by the Chief Engineer. We must bear in mind, however, that, according to the convenience of the undertaking in question, a great deal of this work may be delegated to Area

representatives and thence to Depot Superintendents. Apart from
one or two specific calculations, the Finance Section offers less for
our interest; its work is like that of any similar department in any
kind of business.

III

Whether or not he has Area supervisors to assist him, the Traffic
Manager is primarily responsible for the provision and supervision
of services to meet the requirements of his particular district. In
most cases these will include the three types of service—Stage-
carriage operations, Express or long-distance, Contract or private
hire work. Of these, the stage-carriage work presents the largest
problem.

Though the majority of the stage-carriage routes will have been
built up, licence by licence, over the years, the Traffic Manager has
to study the fluctuations in the number of passengers carried and
consider, week by week, any adjustments that may be necessary.
He has in mind the obvious fact that the most remunerative routes
are those which have a consistent number of passengers throughout
the day; and as these are comparatively rare, he is constantly on
the watch to see whether the frequency of service of every route is
both economic from the undertaking's viewpoint, and in the interests
of the public. He is constantly on the watch to see that the extra
number of buses put on each week for, say, market-day services, or,
day by day, to meet peak-period demands, is both adequate and
necessary. He has continually to reconcile the best interests of his
undertaking with those of the public. In this connection we should
remember that almost every undertaking runs a large number of
workmen's, market-day, peak-period, and similar services at a loss.

The bus industry as a whole is inclined to pride itself on this
piece of public service. The public, on the other hand, regards it as
a bare duty, and expects the loss to be offset by the profit on the
many money-making routes. Still, to its great credit the industry on
the whole has very faithfully accepted and discharged this part of
its responsibility.

Help in watching the fluctuations of the number of passengers
in every part of his area comes to the Traffic Manager from his
Inspectors. Needless to say, the Inspector has many other duties.
Whereas originally he merely checked tickets and supervised time-
keeping, he is now trained to be the company's representative in
dealing with the public. It is part of his duty to assess the growth of

any new type of traffic—for example, children going to a different school—and to look after bus-stands or stations. It may fall to the Inspector's duty to prepare a roster. As a rule, Inspectors tend to fall into two groups, those employed on time-keeping and at bus stations, and those employed on the road. Among this latter class come the mobile squads used by some undertakings to travel about the area and check what is happening at any given traffic point.

Inspectors' reports to their Traffic Manager will indicate stage by stage the number of passengers picked up, the number set down, the number remaining on the bus, and the number for whom there has been no room.

Having studied these reports, the Traffic Manager can decide whether there is a case for reducing or increasing the frequency of the service. The report may stress the need for a completely new route, or suggest that an old route is redundant. If an increase in a service is suggested, he must then study the duty schedules and charts which record the working hours of every vehicle, driver, and conductor. If a vehicle is available, or if he decides to license a spare vehicle which is not at that moment on the road, the Traffic Manager must estimate the probable cost of the service. He must consider whether, in view of the services of other operators, it will genuinely help the public; whether, in short, he has a case for a licence which the Traffic Commissioners are likely to grant.

IV

The factors that affect the probable cost of a new service are many. The length of the route, its gradients, the density of its traffic, and the number of stops that will be necessary, will all influence the speed of the service, and the speed has a direct bearing upon the cost. If a certain number of passengers can be carried over five miles at an average speed of sixteen miles an hour, the trip can pay better than one carrying many more passengers at an average speed of eight miles an hour through dense traffic when the stops lie close together. In some cases the slow urban service can cost twice as much as the other type: since, though receipts may be higher, fuel consumption and wages for both working and waiting time can cost a good deal more. This is a problem with which Municipal Transport authorities are particularly concerned, and it explains why they sometimes wish to develop faster services on the perimeter of a town.

If the Traffic Manager, having made his calculations about a

proposed route, decides to apply for a licence on behalf of his company, he has to follow the procedure established by the Road Traffic
Act of 1930, already outlined in Chapter XXII. Should his application be successful and the licence be granted, it may be two
months or more before the service can get going, because, as we have
already seen, every possible competitor has a legal right to lodge his
objections and to have them considered by the Commissioner.

All this work, when described in such terms, may appear simple
enough. But in addition to his other duties a Traffic Manager may
have to keep a check on a hundred or more routes, week in, week
out, and be alert to every possible improvement in the deployment
of his fleet. And since the changes that he might like to make are
dependent upon the question of 'overtime', upon the possible re-
cruiting of additional drivers who may be wanted only for an hour
or two each day, and upon the number of vehicles that the
engineer's department has to take off the road for maintenance
work, it is clear that his calculations are anything but simple.

All the same, changes and improvements are constantly made.
During 1953 in London—to take but one example—various country
services were pruned, ten new routes were introduced (six of them
to meet new housing and industrial requirements) and seventeen
existing services were extended. Four of the new services connected
densely populated areas with hospitals lying well away from the main
routes.

This is typical of the work that is being done by every undertaking year by year, and although the economic aspect has been
stressed—no bus company could stay in business if it were not considered all the time—the fact remains that a large number of
services have to be run at a loss. Buses that should be full can run
empty week after week, and yet the service must not be abandoned.

What is more, the number of passengers wanting a service
changes very quickly and unpredictably. A route that has seemed
satisfactory in one year may be all but deserted in the next, or else
overworked by the opening of a new school or factory, by some shift
in the population, or by something as unpredictable as a vogue for
autocycles.

V

The chief traffic problem for all undertakings that work in or
near towns comes from the peak-periods in the morning and evening

and, to a smaller degree, at mid-day. A good example in a large city is provided by Manchester. Between seven and nine o'clock in the morning, and between five and seven o'clock in the evening, three to four times as many vehicles may be required as at any other time of the day. Not only are these additional crews and vehicles likely to be idle during the greater part of the day, but some may only be required for one or two journeys at the peak-periods. What is more, if they have to run to housing estates on the perimeter of the city, they are likely to be almost empty on the way out in the morning and running home to their depots at night.

So it happens that, although peak-periods are the busiest time for urban transport, the revenue from many vehicles may be less than at other periods of the day; while the volume of traffic makes running times slower, and costs proportionately higher. For these reasons 'split duties', as they are called, are a problem for all urban operators, whether municipal or independent; and there is no short cut to solving it.

Apart from the problem of finding suitable work for the surplus crews during the greater part of the day—some undertakings employ them in coach-building, vehicle maintenance, and general building work—there is the simple fact that vehicles standing idle represent capital depreciation and increase the overhead cost of workshops, licences, lighting, and garage staff. If, during any period, licensed vehicles and paid crews are not carrying passengers on the road, the efficiency of the unit is to that extent reduced. This applies not only to the question of 'split duties', but also to all periods of waiting at the terminal points on every route.

Unimportant though this may sound to anyone outside the industry, these waiting periods on a hundred routes or so can represent a considerable loss in the course of a week. It is therefore the aim of the Traffic Manager to have the highest possible number of vehicles working on the road at all times. Because of working-hours, vehicle maintenance, and the factors already mentioned, this may be possible only for a short part of the day. Nevertheless, it is every Traffic Manager's aim.

'Split duties', concession fares for workmen, and 'extra' services of all kinds, plus the ever increasing cost of wages, fuel, insurance, and equipment, make every undertaking's overheads mount up. Once takings and numbers of passengers have been calculated by the Finance Section on a battery of adding-machines, the basic cost of running one vehicle for one mile must be worked out. This 'cost per car mile' when compared with the receipts per car mile' indicates, obviously enough, the amount of revenue for which the undertaking is working. It is, and always has been, the basic calculation in all road transport work, for it indicates not only what everyone wants to know, but the economic efficiency of the company.

Influenced as it has been by wage increases, fuel costs, traffic congestion, and numerous other factors, the operating cost of all vehicles in London 'per car mile' is over two shillings. If therefore the casual passenger supposes that his sixpenny ticket represents a profit of threepence, he imagines a vain thing. A bus that earns twopence profit in the course of a mile is doing well.

VI

The supervision of services and the distribution of crews and vehicles are not the end of the Traffic Manager's work. He is responsible for the smooth working of the agreements and joint services with other undertakings. That many companies and local authorities have dozens of these working agreements has already been stressed. Thames Valley and Aldershot companies run a joint service between Reading and Aldershot. Time-tables are issued on certain routes connecting with plane services at London Airport, and other buses pick up and set down employees of B.O.A.C. and B.E.A.

The high degree of inter-relationship with the railways further complicates the work of the Traffic Manager. It is no use having road and rail connections at key points, with inter-available return tickets and season tickets in conjunction with the railways, or such innovations as the combined road and rail travel bureau at Maidenhead which Thames Valley opened in 1953, unless buses are at hand to carry out the companies' promises and run to time.

For each of the various working agreements between undertakings there is some agreed method of pooling the receipts. The Manchester area offers an excellent example of the kind of agreement that has grown up in the course of time between local authorities and other companies. The through-route between Rochdale and Bury, covered by the transport of these Corporations, has 2·16 miles in Rochdale, 3·47 miles in the town of Heywood—which thus has the use of the service—and 1·39 miles in Bury. The eightpenny fare is therefore divided between the three authorities in the proportions twopence-halfpenny, fourpence, and three-halfpence respectively. Before paying Heywood's portion, Bury and Rochdale deduct their running expenses.

This arrangement naturally belongs to Finance, but one can easily infer from it the interdependence of the three branches in any one company, and it once more underlines the responsibility of the man who had to translate the agreement into actual buses, running and ready to run.

VII

It follows, too, that a Traffic Manager is not concerned exclusively with the operation of his own services. Liaison and co-operation with other operators are just as important.

According to the type of undertaking he works for, the Traffic Manager usually has a Booking and Charting section. This deals with the summer Touring and Excursion services, and the Contract or private hire work, all of which have to be planned and costed no less carefully. Through his Inspectors and supervisors he is also responsible for the training and discipline of all drivers and conductors. From the moment the latter take up their position on the platform of a public bus, he is as sharply concerned with their courtesy and efficiency as he is with the accuracy of their waybills and their skill with a ticket machine.

Linked with the Finance or Secretarial section, there is usually a head store-keeper to control the company's garage and uniform stores, and a Claims officer who investigates and deals—for instance —with the type of accident which arises when, as passengers so often allege, a bus in a busy street moves off before someone is firmly aboard. To a company proud of its prestige and anxious to maintain friendly relations with its public, the tactful handling of such matters is no less important than the efficient treatment of lost property. This branch of the work, all other considerations apart, is an important factor in public relations, for the passenger who recovers a lost glove or umbrella is usually grateful to the organisation that returns it. And here—once again—though there are various members of the organisation who are concerned with the complaints of a critical public, it is the Traffic Manager who, more often than not, is the ultimate target.

He bears the blame, not only when there is a serious breakdown in a service, but when route numbers on vehicles are incorrect, when 'Duplicate' buses do not proclaim upon their blinds where they are going, and when, after a succession of traffic jams, a number of buses arrive at a stop in convoy. (This phenomenon can have other causes, but none exonerates him.)

He bears the blame when one vehicle out of a hundred keeps passengers waiting in the wind, or when a time-table fails to show some recent amendment to a service. He bears the blame, too, when some busy conductor fails to be the walking encyclopædia that passengers expect him to be. Though discourtesy and unhelpfulness are the last things that any Traffic Manager is going to excuse, it is well to remember that it is not a simple matter to find men of the calibre he would like to employ. In short, although the greater part of an undertaking's achievement may stand to his credit, a Traffic Manager's back has to be very, very broad.

CHAPTER XXVII

Engineering

'What happens to a bus when it's ill?'
QUERY BY A SIX YEAR OLD BOY.

A TECHNICAL account of motor transport engineering would be out of place in a book of this kind; but the human aspect of it, the way in which changing conditions affect the daily lives of the people who get their living in the industry, must always interest any normal reader. He likes to know what has been done to make the men's work easier since the days when the pioneers had to lie in grease and mud in order to remove bearings, fiddle with leaky radiators, and wrestle, cursing hopefully, with solid tyres. In recent decades both the design of the buses and methods of maintaining them have been drastically improved, and it will be worth our while to see in brief what is involved in the day-to-day running of a modern passenger road transport undertaking.

In the later 'twenties, the pneumatic tyre and the forward driver's cab, improvements in which Scotland had given an early lead, came slowly into general use. After 1930, when the Road Traffic Act made a Certificate of Fitness imperative for every public service vehicle, further improvements quickly followed. Diesel engines were developed about this time. More robust and reliable, and having a longer life than any petrol engine, they brought about fundamental changes in motor-bus engineering. Even though, during the years of the Second World War, standards of vehicle maintenance were relaxed, important facts were discovered. Circumstances often made it essential for vehicles to be overloaded to a fantastic extent, and the engines, through sheer necessity, showed what they would stand. From the wartime performances of their tired vehicles engineers learned a great deal.

Today, as has been shown, most undertakings are equipped with vehicles which have engines and bodies of the latest design. Internal heaters, where the conditions call for them, better ventilation and improved seating aim at the greatest possible comfort of the passenger. Since the war, many companies have been able to design and introduce vehicles especially suited to their needs. All have been able to equip their garages with the latest types of plant which, through its efficiency in saving time, helps to keep labour costs to a minimum.

The details of the work carried out must naturally vary from one garage to another, since each has to cater for a fleet of a certain size which operates in special conditions. Two concerns may be close neighbours and yet have very different engineering problems. Nevertheless, all motor-bus maintenance involves the same basic needs: (*a*) daily, or nightly, inspection and cleaning, (*b*) weekly or fortnightly inspections, (*c*) minor docks, (*d*) major docks, and (*e*) some form of complete overhaul.

The Road Traffic Act of 1930 laid down in unmistakable terms that the principal responsibility of an undertaking was to provide the public with vehicles which are safe and give the performance expected of them. In order to fulfil this requirement with fleets that have expanded so rapidly in the last twenty-five years, it has become the practice to inspect vehicles at regular intervals. The frequency of the inspection is dictated by experience; vehicles always have to satisfy the requirements of Ministry of Transport inspectors.

To save fuel and time, buses undergo their routine inspections and light overhauls at their running garage. They need only be brought into the company's main works for major overhauls. It is true that a few companies with compact areas of operation prefer the greater part of their maintenance work to be done in the main works, but this is a matter of convenience: it happens to suit the organisations that use it. Corporations, for instance, usually have a central garage where the greater part of their routine work is done. In the case of undertakings whose work is spread over a wide area, it is clearly better for the vehicles to be maintained where they are housed.

Because of the varying conditions of operation there cannot be any standard procedure or any remote agreement upon the frequency of overhaul. It is of interest to note that the modern diesel engine can cover from two hundred thousand to two hundred and fifty thousand miles before it needs to be overhauled, and that the life of a well maintained bus can be as high as one million miles. Some undertakings think it economic to repair or change engines and major units in the course of routine overhauls in main workshops. Others prefer to change engines, gear-boxes, and rear-axles at the garages whenever this becomes necessary.

In either case, a modern bus is likely to have had at least four different engines before it is scrapped.

II

Though details in procedure must vary, all vehicles, when they are brought into their depot garages in the evening, are signed off by their drivers, who report any known fault. The vehicles are then fuelled, oil levels checked, superficially examined, and finally cleaned both outside and in. For this branch of the work women are often employed. At frequent intervals also, brakes and any of the other controls are tested. In some undertakings every driver has a routine inspection to make before the vehicle is taken out on the road. This inspection includes the more obvious points in daily maintenance, from tyres and fuel to the tightness of wheel-nuts and the correct operation of the horn. By the rules of these undertakings, the driver must be satisfied that he is taking into service a completely reliable vehicle, and he is obliged to sign to this effect.

In some of the latest garages the routine daily cleaning has been mechanised to a high level of efficiency. Brooms and pails of water have been replaced by vacuum cleaners and frames of rotating brushes. Nevertheless, although in certain undertakings split-shifts allow some of this work to be done during the day, the arrival of fifty dirty buses late in the evening involves a considerable amount of night work, and it is not hard to imagine the refuse that many of them collect.

Every two or three weeks, the interval varying from one under-taking to another, it is the practice to give each vehicle a thorough check-over and, when it has been completely cleaned, to inspect it in detail. This examination includes the steering, brakes, chassis bolts, wheel-nuts, electrical equipment—everything, in fact, upon which the safety and comfort of the passengers depend.

III

So much for the cleaning and inspection which is a matter of routine week by week. On the question of complete overhauls, it is impossible to outline any uniform procedure, because methods vary so greatly. Granted that a pre-war vehicle needed overhaul after a hundred and twenty thousand miles, some engineers would argue that this figure can nowadays be doubled. And, of course, the stress and strain on buses vary with the work they have to do. Coaches running in comparatively easy conditions can do three hundred miles a day. Double-deckers, travelling seven hundred miles a week in the rigours of city traffic, suffer much greater wear and tear. This comes from the continual stopping and starting, which imposes a severe strain on all parts of the vehicle but particularly on the brakes, the engine, and the transmission. In dense traffic, when pedestrian crossings, lights, and other vehicles make it necessary for a bus to stop ten or more times in every mile, the engine revolutions are much higher than those of a country bus which is making perhaps one or two stops to its mile.

Furthermore, the four hundred thousand or so passengers who are likely to have used a city bus in the course of a year produce a deal of wear, not only to engine and chassis, but to body, springing, floors, and furnishings. Strongly built though they are, buses are subject to hard usage, and all these factors affect the frequency and extent of the overhauls that they require.

In undertakings that use the Light and Heavy docking system, it is roughly true to say that the first Light dock becomes necessary at about thirty thousand to forty thousand miles. Some undertakings give their vehicles a Heavy dock at eighty thousand to a hundred thousand miles; and, bearing in mind what has been said regarding conditions of service, this may well include the fitting of a reconditioned engine.

IV

What is important in the present context is the amount of time and labour which has to be spent to ensure that every vehicle is mechanically sound and fit for the road. Incidentally, it is by no means simple to take vehicles off the road for routine maintenance work in their correct rotation and without upsetting normal services. The amount of labour demanded by all these considerations makes it more and more important to obtain the greatest efficiency from the system adopted, and in this respect the unit-exchange system used by London Transport and many other undertakings is worth remark.

In the London Transport system, the fleet of over eight thousand buses and coaches is distributed over four Central and two Country Divisions. Each Division comprises a number of Districts, and each District contains Parent and subsidiary garages. Certain units, such as engines, fuel injection pumps, and gear-boxes, are changed at the

London—Paris coach-air link operated by East Kent
Road Car Company seen at Lympne

Omnibus Station, Folkestone—East Kent Road Car Company

'Smiling in the Snow'—three conductresses employed by the Yorkshire
Traction Company

What next!

garages whenever their condition requires it. The units removed are then returned to the Central Unit Overhaul works at Chiswick for reconditioning and re-issue. (There is also a fleet of nearly one thousand eight hundred trolley-buses which are dealt with at their own running depots.)

The subsidiary garages see to the daily maintenance and a short mileage rota inspection, which is carried out every three weeks. They also see to some medium mileage inspections at intervals of nine weeks in the Central Area, or twelve weeks in Country Divisions. The rest of the medium mileage inspections are undertaken at Parent garages. Every eighteen weeks, or in Country Divisions every twenty-four weeks, vehicles are brought to their Parent garage for a much more extensive cleaning and examination which includes the relining of the brakes and a number of other important mechanical adjustments.

Thus, with technical variations to suit their particular needs, the country's many undertakings keep their vehicles in sound working order for four or five years. Then, after it has run some two hundred thousand miles, every vehicle undergoes a complete stripping-down in the company's main workshops. Once again, the details of the work carried out may vary from place to place, though all leading undertakings have self-contained works and body-building shops fitted with the most modern equipment and plant. In addition to the fitters and machine hands who deal with mechanical parts and units, there are numerous welders, blacksmiths, and sheet metal workers, as well as trimmers, electricians, and painters who work on the bodies.

To the casual observer, such workshops are hives of activity whose cells are strangely isolated and varied. Whether it is done in the elaborate garages owned by Corporations and large undertakings, or in some of the smaller works of the independent operators, modern methods of taking a bus to pieces and putting it together again are impressive enough. There are all manner of operations to delight the schoolboy and fascinate the spectator with a taste for engineering. To us at the moment, the details of the work are less important than the fact that a certain proportion of every fleet is continually being renewed. What goes on in London Transport's new works at Aldenham can illustrate this more dramatically than the procedure in most other works.

When a vehicle is to be overhauled, the body is examined to ascertain the repairs which it will need. After it has been lifted from the chassis, the body is placed in a C-shaped cradle called an 'inverter' which turns it on its side, so that the underside can be cleaned by high pressure hot water and get attention for repairs. In this works the system of moving bus bodies about on trucks has been superseded by the use of overhead travelling cranes. These carry the bodies, passing one over another if necessary, from one position to the next.

From the inverter a body is transferred to a working bay, where it is placed on stilts surrounded by gantries, so that all repair work, both inside and out, can be conveniently carried out. After the necessary structural work has been finished, the body is placed on another inverter, and a coat of bitumastic paint is put upon the underside to protect it against the effects of water and mud. The renovated body is now ready for its chassis.

Meanwhile, any body parts which have been removed and can be made to work again are transferred to the reconditioning shops. From there they pass to Stores, and are held in readiness for issue to the body repair assembly line.

Next comes the chassis. This is first washed by high pressure hot water in a special cubicle. Then it is placed on a conveyer which runs parallel to the Body Repair Shop and is stripped of its unit and components. The units which have been removed are returned to the Chiswick Works for reconditioning, while any necessary repairs to the chassis frame itself are done in a shop alongside the conveyer. The chassis is then rebuilt on another conveyer, placed end-on to the stripping conveyer, with reconditioned units from the Stores. It is then sprayed with paint, and brought to a mounting point which connects with the body repair line. Here, body and chassis are fitted together.

After the rebuilt vehicle has been examined and tested and any necessary correction made, it is ready for the finishing work that gives a London bus its distinctive appearance. One or two things are necessary as a preliminary to painting; the windows and openings are masked, and the vehicle is placed on a further conveyer which takes it through the paint and varnish booths, moving it from one spraying or drying process to another at intervals of about an hour. Then, after a certain amount of hand work in the finishing line, the vehicle is ready for a final inspection, and for the further examination by the officers of the Licensing Authority, who carry this out on the·premises. Thus, in the course of a circular tour taking them through all the operations described above, the buses are completely rebuilt and returned to service at the rate of eight a day.

V

Similar, if less elaborate works are to be found in many parts of the country. All have—indeed, must have—the technical proficiency characteristic of the modern bus industry, but each has its specialities and techniques. For example, spray painting is not the practice at all of them, because the colour schemes of many undertakings make it impracticable.

Many other examples could be given. The point that matters is that in the engineering field, as in everything else, each undertaking has methods that suit its needs.

Maintenance and overhauls, however, are not the end of the engineer's problems. Economy in running costs is constantly forced upon his attention, and he is continually experimenting with means to reduce them, such as the use of plastic reinforced with fibre glass, a comparatively new development which is cheaper than metal panelling and which helps to reduce the weight of a vehicle. A lighter vehicle with a lower fuel consumption is the aim in modern bus design. Many engineers have experimented with aluminium alloy and other all-metal bodies, as well as with vehicles of integral construction. This development work has resulted in a number of successful lightweight vehicles, both single- and double-deck, which give increased comfort to passengers, and considerable economy in running.

VI

The performance of modern vehicles and the fatigue-saving controls with which they are often fitted bring attention to the driver, upon whom, to some extent, the life of the vehicle depends. It is only right and proper that this mechanical chapter should conclude with a few remarks about the driver's work.

Naturally, the man upon whom so many lives depend is carefully chosen. Some companies like him to have had considerable experience with heavy vehicles before he starts to drive a bus. By law he is compelled to pass the most exacting tests before his Public Service Vehicle Drivers' licence is granted. Not only has he to be physically fit before he can take these tests, but he has to remain fit, and, after the age of sixty-five, he usually has to pass regular medical examinations.

The public may wonder why this is not a universal rule. It is certainly a reasonable one. Although the Road Traffic Act has long since put an end to the very long hours that drivers sometimes had to work, their duties both on long-distance driving and in the traffic of a modern city are arduous enough. Though bus schedules naturally take account of traffic difficulties, no foresight can prevent the weather and fluctuations on day-to-day traffic from upsetting the time-table to which a driver is working. Moreover, be his driving conditions easy or difficult, the passengers behind him are, understandably, his severest critics, even when they themselves could not drive a small car with the same degree of safety. Every driver well knows that any complaint will be thoroughly investigated by his superiors, and that every error in judgment is likely to involve a large number of people. Indeed, the efficiency of the industry is as dependent as it ever was upon the skill of its best drivers. This is often confirmed in private contract work, when an able driver is asked for by name.

The reader may wonder what a driver who thirty years ago drove a solid-tyred vehicle over cobblestones thinks about his modern bus. Surely the warmth and protection of a driving-cab and the efficiency of the latest type of controls make his job much easier?

Of the many answers to that question, most boil down to the fact that, though vehicles are now much easier to handle and have improved mechanically out of all recognition, traffic conditions have got so much worse that the balance comes out about even. The modern bus is designed to make its journey as smoothly as possible, but everything else on the road seems intent on getting in its way. Today, therefore, a driver does as hard a day's work as he ever did, and, with his partner on the platform behind him, he is often working when everyone else is on holiday. Nevertheless, he no longer has any cause to doubt the skill of the men who design his vehicle and keep it in condition.

CHAPTER XXVIII

The Bus Crew

'The bus business has always attracted people who enjoy the personal responsibility of being on the road in charge of a vehicle and passengers. . . .'

CHAIRMAN OF A YORKSHIRE BUS COMPANY.

AT this point in the story it might be well to glance at the human side of an industry which for its wellbeing depends, even more than most, upon successful and harmonious human relationships. Where stress so often falls on the operational side of the bus industry, the problems of time-tables, maintenance, and traffic control, we do well to remind ourselves of Rudyard Kipling's dictum that things are done by means of people. Human problems come first.

Break them down, get to bed rock, and what on the surface appear to be problems in economics prove very often to be problems in human relationships. A strike is hardly ever rooted in the incident or the hardship that occasions it. The occasion is seized on as a pretext for expressing violently what has been a long time simmering in the strikers' minds. Plain human dissatisfaction can wreck a commercial enterprise as surely as satisfaction with treatment and working conditions can make it prosper. Judged on these principles, the bus industry has deserved its prosperity: for, as we shall see, it has known few strikes, and most of those belonged to its early years.

First of all, let us glance at the numbers engaged in the industry. For these we are indebted to the Ministry of Labour. No systematic records were kept before 1901, and the figures for that year and for 1911, though based on the best information available to the Ministry, are estimates only: but the numbers are as follows:

1901	..	..	..	35,000
1911	..	..	..	67,000
1921	..	..	..	119,000
1931	..	..	..	215,000
1951	..	..	..	288,000

These figures in each instance represent the entire labour force of the industry, employers, workers, and unemployed. They include every type of occupation which the industry provides, but, of course, by far the greater number are drivers and conductors. The figures cover all undertakings which run buses, trams, and trolley-buses, and all motor-coach services which work to regular schedules.

For two years only, 1931 and 1951, the total number can be broken up into details. The number of employees for the first year was two hundred thousand, as against two hundred and eighty-four thousand for the second, and the unemployed dropped steeply from eleven thousand in 1931—a year of slump—to three thousand in 1951.

II

It would be inappropriate, besides being impracticable, in this book, to attempt to deal in any detail with the economic position of employees in the industry and their relationship with the employers, whether they be the British Transport Commission, London Transport Executive, the Municipalities or private companies. It is a subject that deserves a book to itself, but no history of the industry would be complete without some reference to the immense progress that has been made during the last century in the terms and conditions of employment of the workers. It is obviously impossible to examine the records of every undertaking in the country. We have therefore taken the London Transport Executive and a typical provincial municipal undertaking, that run by the Eastbourne Corporation, who have courteously allowed us access to their books and to their records.

The capital city naturally comes first, so let us begin with the L.G.O.C. From 1856 to 1891, the normal working day for driver and conductor lasted from fifteen to seventeen hours. After 1891, when there was a strike, it was reduced to an average of twelve hours, arrived at by a rotation of fifteen and nine hour days. Relief men worked two shifts of six hours each, taking over from the nine hour men.

From 1891 to 1911 a seventy-two hour week was worked. In 1911 the figure dropped to sixty, and in 1919 to forty-eight. Since 1947 the men have worked a forty-four hour week plus considerable overtime; and a new agreement coming into force during 1956 has as its basis an eleven day fortnight, with a standard day of seven hours and forty minutes.

Wages were not fixed definitely until 1859, when for his day of fifteen to seventeen hours a driver received six shillings and a conductor four. These rates remained in force until 1891, but the men became slightly better off, since prices were falling steadily throughout this period. The strike of 1891 raised the rates to seven and sixpence a day for drivers and six shillings for conductors, and, as we have seen, it achieved a twelve hour day.

After February 1911 wage payments were based on mileage. With a rough average of four hundred and eighty miles a week, by the outbreak of war in 1914 a driver was earning three pounds, and a conductor two pounds five shillings and sixpence.

By November 1918 these rates had risen to four pounds nine and sixpence and three pounds fifteen shillings respectively.

After April 1919 the former time basis was restored, so that by May 1920 a driver was getting a basic five pounds for his week of forty-eight hours, and the conductor four pounds seven shillings.

By 1935 the gap between the two was narrowed to six shillings. In 1941 wages rose again, and by 1946 the conductor was only four shillings behind his colleague.

III

In the last century the L.G.O.C. shared the customary conservative opposition to trade unions. Traces of what it termed 'combination' can be found in 1851, but here the men were banding together not so much against the companies as against various petty exactions. A union was formed in the early seventies, probably on the inspiration of a successful union among the Liverpool busmen, but it had no effect in London; the L.G.O.C. would accept no representations from any union until compelled to do so by the strike of 1891.

This was the first general strike of employees against the L.G.O.C. Horse keepers, whose earnings were limited to a guinea a week plus unofficial 'yard fees', had struck in 1857 and 1866, but they received no support from other workers. In 1874, when a number of drivers went home because of a heavy fall of snow, the company dismissed them, and a strike followed; but it collapsed.

The 1891 strike was a classical instance of the occasion being a pretext only and masking the real cause. The cause given by the men was the introduction of the roll ticket system, but the real cause was their long dissatisfaction about wages and hours of work. This strike succeeded, and made a real turning point in the history of the relationship between employers and employees. It established basic principles of work which were in keeping with the general industrial progress of the country, and it paved the way for the relationship between employer and employee that we accept as normal in the twentieth century.

IV

Welfare work existed in the industry as early as 1849, in the shape of the Omnibus Servants' Provident Society. The L.G.O.C. proposed the establishment of a provident fund as early as 1857, but it was abandoned because there seemed to be no call for it. Accident funds in each district were started in 1858, and annual bean-feasts, financed by the company and by subscriptions collected from the passengers, in 1856.

Uniforms were not issued to L.G.O.C. crews until the era of the motor-bus. The driver of the horse-bus was given an apron, but had to provide his own clothing, and took a pride in it. As soon as the motor-bus came in, the L.G.O.C. gave the driver his uniform cap and coat, but he had to find his own suit—a state of things which lasted until after the Second World War.

V

The Eastbourne Corporation's bus service was first fully organised in 1905. This enables an interesting comparison to be made between the position then and fifty years later in 1955. On the opposite page is an extract from a Wages Sheet in November, 1905, and it shows the earnings and hours worked of drivers and conductors. The total wages of these ten men came to the modest sum of £11 9s. 10d., and it will be seen that some were not in regular daily employment, a fact which suggests they were taken on as necessity required.

In a week in November, 1955, that is fifty years later, the average wage of 12 drivers, taken at random for a 44-hour week, plus overtime, was £9 9s. 8d. The average wage for a similar number of conductors, taken at random from a wage sheet, was £9 8s.

The differences in other directions are equally striking. Whilst

Week Ending Nov. 30/05

	Fri	Sat	Mon.	Tues	Wed	Thurs	Total	Rate	£	s.	d
F Cook.	9^3	7^3	5^3	9^1	6^2	9^2	48^2	$4\frac{1}{2}$		18	2
Hoad	10^2					10^1	20^3	4		6	11
Price		5^2	6^2	9^2	$12.$	8	41^2	4		13	10
Bradford					7^2	4^2	12^2	4		4	0
Cobb.	10.	9^2	9^1	6^3	9^1	5^3	50^2	$4\frac{1}{2}$		18	11
Smith	9^2	9^2	10	8^3	10^1	9^1	57^1	5	1	5	0
Hepburn	8^1	9^2	9^1	10^1	9^1	10.	56^2	"	1	5	0
Piper	9^2	12^2	10^2	9^1	10.	9	60^3	"	1	5	0
Hoare	7^1	10.	$6\frac{1}{4}$	9^2	5^3	9^1	48	$4\frac{1}{2}$		18	0
Bartholemew		9^3	9^2	7.	9^1	6^1	41^3	5	1	5	0
Shoesmith	7^1	8	9^1	10.	8^3	10.	53^1	"	1	5	0
Pjodger.	10.	9^2	10.	10	10	10	59^2	"	1	5	0
									11	9	10
	87	91^2	86^1	90^1	98^2	101^3	550^1				

Eastbourne Corporation Transport Department. Extract from Conductors' Wages Book, 30th November, 1905

there is no specific reference in the Minutes of the Corporation's Committee dealing with Transport which covers the issue of uniforms, the figures in the Annual Accounts suggest that uniforms were in fact supplied annually. Today they cost the Corporation between thirteen and fourteen hundred pounds a year.

Welfare work has progressed steadily. The first records show that the staff received a day and a half's pay for working on bank holidays, had Christmas Day off, and three days' holiday each year. Today, they are entitled to twelve days annual holiday, plus six days national and bank holidays.

The following excerpt from the minutes of the Eastbourne Corporation Electric Lighting Committee, dated June 28th, 1904, though not strictly relevant, is worth quoting because it shows so clearly the *ad hoc* way in which early bus services developed, and also explains the fluctuations in wages of some of the employees. Now and then, there are records of small sums being paid, apparently as extras, to drivers. The explanation seems to be that these were in the form of compensation to a man whose bus had broken down when there was no other bus available to replace it, in order to compensate him for not having driven the regular number of hours needed to make up his weekly wage.

The extract from the Minutes is as follows:

'Meads 'bus—I am informed that Mr. Gowring, of St. Bede's School, is inconvenienced by reason of this 'bus not starting before 9.30 a.m., as he has six boys who would patronise the 'bus every morning if it started at 9 a.m. Resolved; That subject to Mr. Gowring guaranteeing the use of the 'bus every morning by six of his pupils, the same start at 9 a.m.—A letter was read from the Rev. E. L. Browne offering to exhibit a notice on his premises should this 'bus be off service at any time. Resolved; That the offer be accepted with thanks.'

In 1904 the cost of one of the Corporation's Milnes-Daimler buses was seven hundred and fifty pounds. The cost of the latest double-deck buses being delivered to the Corporation works out at approximately four thousand eight hundred and seventy-seven pounds inclusive of tyres.

Whilst there has been this striking increase in costs, the fares seem to have been in no way correspondingly increased. For example, in July, 1903, in what was the first time-table issued by a municipal undertaking in this country, possibly in the world, the following fare was advertised 'Archery to Cemetary—3*d*.' Fifty years later, in November, 1953, the charge was only 4*d*., but the destination board now reads 'Archery to Ocklynge Hill'. Such is progress.

At the beginning of the century there were, as there still are, critics who were prepared to write to the Editor of their favourite paper to show what was wrong and how it could be put right. I have before me a press cutting showing a letter dated May 18th, 1903, signed 'Cosmopolitan', objecting to the charge of 1*d*. for one half of a distance and 2*d*. for the other. This, 'Cosmopolitan' describes as 'absurd' and goes on to say:

'If the journey is up-hill in one direction it must be remembered it is down-hill the reverse way, and the question is whether it pays best to run the 'bus well filled at 1*d*. each or often nearly empty at 2*d*.'

vi

'The bus business has always attracted people who enjoy the personal responsibility of being on the road in charge of a vehicle and passengers—people who like doing a public service, and who prefer work without constant supervision. They are less concerned with regularity of hours than with the interesting nature of the occupation.'

These remarks were made in February, 1956, by the Chairman of a Yorkshire bus company at a dinner given to some hundred and sixty veteran employees of the Company. The occasion was the annual 'Twenty-five years service' dinner, for which twenty-five drivers and other employees had qualified during the year, and received the certificates and medals acknowledging their services.

One driver, who had been forty years with the Company, had driven one million two hundred thousand miles, a distance equivalent to forty-eight circuits of the world, had carried ten million passengers, never been involved in even the most trivial accident, and had an entirely clean driving licence.

Of five hundred and four men who were working for the Company in 1930, close on forty per cent were still on its pay roll in 1956—a fact which suggests that, despite its exacting nature, the job has its attractions.

It is this human element, this immediate responsibility for the welfare of others, and the continual warmth of human contacts, that make the job so popular and so well worthwhile. No one who knows bus crews and their conditions of work will idealise it, but the predominantly genial give-and-take, the good-humoured back-chat between conductor and passengers, the solidarity between driver and conductor, and their solicitude for the people they carry, are sufficient witness to the fact that, by and large, the job is satisfactorily done.

This aspect of the work was well summed up by Mr. R. M. Robbins, Secretary of the London Transport Executive, in an address to the Institute of Transport, stressing the human aspect of the bus industry.

'On the railway there is no place for the individualist, but on the road it is different. True, busmen work as units in a larger team, there is a schedule, and there are supervisors, but essentially it is their bus, and the passengers are in their sole charge.

'The goodwill of the undertaking depends on the way they drive and conduct. Personality counts, and that is why, whatever attractions other jobs may offer, the busman's job always attracts a certain kind of man who has a feeling of personal, individual responsibility, and likes to see life going on busily around him.

'That is why the bus in London has always had at front and back a certain London type of man (and, lately, woman): lively, confident, sometimes a bit cheeky, independent in thought, who comes out best when conditions are difficult and does all manner of things the book doesn't provide for to get the passengers home and the bus back to the garage.'

This general spirit of goodwill is the rule between bus crews and their passengers, whether on the little village bus which is a kind of travelling club where almost every passenger is known by name to Fred who drives and Joe who takes the tickets, or on the city bus where the multitude of passengers are changing and anonymous. When tempers sharpen, it is almost always because driver or conductor are blamed, as the nearest objects to hand, for shortcomings of the service which are not in their control.

"Where have all the Number Nines got to, eh?"

"I been 'ere close on 'arf an hour, and now yer won't let me get on."

But, by and large, a little backchat eases the tension, and good humour and goodwill prevail.

CHAPTER XXIX

Coaching Today

'Peregrinations charm our senses with such unspeakable and
sweet variety that some count him unhappy who has never travelled.'

BURTON.

ROAD travel is an important branch of social history. The ugly,
box-like char-à-bancs of the early 'twenties, with their solid tyres
and poor weather protection, served a useful purpose in giving the
first taste of freedom to townsfolk who could not afford a car; but
their life was short. Their success made it so. So many people seized
the chances they offered that they had to improve, and improve
quickly. The popularity of touring and of long-distance coach runs
compelled the swift development both of time-tables and vehicles.

Soon, therefore, well-sprung, softly upholstered coaches with
balloon tyres and big windows appeared in large numbers, and a
new chapter in road travel had begun. Not only were these services
cheaper than those of the railways, but they brought their passenger
closer to the life of the towns and villages than the train. They offered
him almost as much as the motor-car, at a price within the reach of
all but the poorest. It will be worth our while to glance at the way
in which this form of travel grew and what it brought to the country.

Once again, we need not study in detail the methods by which
most of the leading undertakings extended their long-distance services and improved their coaches. The contrast between an old
coach and a new makes the superficial changes clear enough, and a
look at a coach time-table shows the comprehensive service which
the modern industry has to offer. Much of this development was
achieved by voluntary agreements between the various undertakings, who set up bodies charged with making them and giving
them effect. Associations within the various bus Groups, on the lines
of Associated Motorways, which has its headquarters at Cheltenham, steadily improved the co-ordination of coach services.

This particular body, started in 1934, was a major 'pooling'
scheme in which the original partners were Red and White Services,
Midland Red, Black and White Motorways, Greyhound Motors,
and the United Counties Omnibus Company. As a result of its
meetings, the competitive services worked by seven or eight operators on some of the longer runs were reduced to a number of

co-ordinated journeys covered by a single Road Service licence: a network of long-distance routes from Torquay and Portsmouth in the south to Blackpool and Nottingham in the north were worked at the minimum cost.

The other Groups made similar plans. The 'thirties had brought in the day of fast, comfortable, cheap road travel, and the undertakings had to give the public what it wanted.

At first, many of the travel agencies mistrusted motor-coaches, and did not like the idea of working against the railways. These difficulties were overcome as soon as everyone could see that the motor-coach was safe and reliable, and booking offices were opened in all parts of the country. In the south, control centres and coach stations were developed at Gloucester, London, Birmingham, Oxford, and Bournemouth, and refreshment-rooms were opened at main terminals and at convenient stopping-places along each route. Today, when relatively low fares are making coaches more popular than ever, it is possible to be picked up by an express service at numerous stopping-points along its route and to travel, by one service or another, to almost any town in the country. Even on stage-carriage routes Day Tickets enable a passenger for a fixed sum to travel as far as he can between morning and night. Through Tickets make a cross-country journey by a series of coaches as simple as is geographically and physically possible.

All this, before the Second World War, had raised the work of the industry to a level that could be seriously compared with that of the railways.

II

No account of long-distance travel would be adequate without a description of the organisation of one of the leading coach stations. The work of London Coastal Coaches Limited, the private company which owns Victoria Coach Station, provides an excellent example, for it handles the greater part of the long-distance traffic from London. In some respects its organisation is unique, and the story that lies behind it deserves attention, since the service this Company has for so long offered the public explains in part how the motor-coach came to hold its own with the railways.

The story began soon after the First World War, when Pickfords and one or two other London firms started to run vehicles from London to a number of coastal resorts. Thomas Tilling soon joined the enterprise, and, in spite of the fact that people had to pay a guinea for a not too comfortable ride to Brighton and back, these long-distance runs soon became popular.

After a time, Pickfords withdrew their vehicles, and, as other operators became interested, it was decided that a central booking organisation should be set up. With an office in Lower Belgrave Street, London Coastal Coaches Limited was incorporated in 1925 with a capital of a thousand pounds, and its receipts were shared among the various companies which had a hand in it.

The amount of parking and picking up, which then had to be done in the street, soon proved a nuisance to all concerned, and in 1928 a site for the first coach station was obtained in Lupus Street. Though the rent was high, and the railways at that time were likely to become serious competitors in the operation of road transport, the coach station was a success from the start. During its first Easter week-end, some twelve hundred laden vehicles set off to various parts of the country. Primitive as they were when measured by modern standards, the most up-to-date vehicles of that day could leave London at nine in the morning and arrive at Ilfracombe in time to see the sun go down. Operators and public were delighted. Not only had coaching regained the status it had lost a century earlier; it was cheaper, more efficient, more enjoyable than ever before. From that time forwards the new coach station set itself to provide services throughout the year.

The layout of a motor-coach station was a new problem, offering its owners and architects more difficulties than any railway station. In those days the vehicles of some twenty different companies could cause hopeless congestion in Lupus Street, for the entrance was also the exit, and there was no means of arranging one-way traffic. How were the authorities to design a building that could cope with an ever-increasing number of vehicles, allowing each to drop or pick up passengers with the least delay? What unforeseen developments would they have to meet? Suppose the rapid growth did not go on?

To the company's credit, it decided against the cautious policy of advancing by degrees. Chancing their arm, the directors went forward boldly. They raised the necessary money, and prepared plans for an unheard-of terminal which would be the last word in coach stations for years to come.

III

The Victoria Coach Station, standing at the junction of Buckingham Palace Road and Elizabeth Street, was opened in

1932. Today, nearly a quarter of a century later, it still provides one of the most remarkable services in passenger transport.

At first its work was concentrated mainly in the summer months, but the popularity of coach travel, encouraged by fares that have always compared favourably with those of the railways, has gradually brought about a large number of services on every day of the year. What is more, for services running through London from north to south and east to west, the station is more convenient than any of the main-line railway terminals. A passenger has only to step from one coach to another.

Since normal operations were resumed at the end of the Second World War, the number of coaches leaving the station has increased. More than sixty routes are served regularly in winter, more than ninety in summer. Throughout the year an average number of over four hundred coaches leaves the station daily, the number rising to fifteen hundred per day at peak periods during the summer. The total number of departures is a hundred and fifty thousand a year, which means that some seven million passengers have passed through the station. It is therefore not surprising that a building which was so much ahead of its time twenty-five years ago, is now hard put to it to deal with the volume of traffic.

It is impressive and fascinating to watch the even flow of one-way traffic through the station hour by hour, as the coaches pull into their appropriate lanes and load or unload their passengers. The parking and refuelling problems for such a large number of visiting vehicles are as hard to imagine in detail as the catering arrangements for this unceasing flow of passengers. Naturally the organisation behind the scenes is complex; far more complex than the ordinary traveller would suppose. Not the least complex is the Traffic Staff, which deals with the bookings and the services for the thirty or more companies making use of the station.

The pivot of this work is the Chart Room. This, a much larger version of the section which comes under the control of most Traffic Managers, is sub-divided into the geographical areas which the various companies cover. Here the bookings for numerous agencies in all parts of the country are received, and individual instructions are prepared for every vehicle scheduled to leave the station. When it leaves, each has full details of where its various passengers wish to get out, and where others have to be picked up. With dozens of reservations arriving every few minutes, the greatest care and accuracy must be used to ensure that no vehicle is over-booked. If over-booking seems likely on some particular route, extra vehicles have to be arranged with the company concerned, or provided from some other source, until every passenger has a seat.

Elaborate as any booking system may seem which has to deal with so much at such a speed, it is the ceaseless hum of activity which impresses an observer. After a day-staff has been bombarded by hundreds of telephone calls from all parts of the country, a night staff deals with postal reservations, so that there will be no delay next morning in dealing with the fresh rush of bookings. The telephone system with over a hundred lines makes it possible to apportion calls from the various agents, so that the whole network does not become overloaded with demands for the services of one particular company; and a control board makes it possible for the supervisor in the Chart Room to see whether any section is being overtaxed.

The postal section for general enquiries deals with up to five hundred letters a day, and every enquirer is given full instructions for the journey he wants to make. A separate department deals with the booking of Inclusive Tours in Britain and the Continent, and makes arrangements with Continental services for passengers to travel to many European countries. Of all the work that these various bookings throw upon the Accountancy section, the most fascinating feature for the outsider is the punch-card system, which records the details of every ticket issued in such a way that monthly summaries can be prepared quickly and sent off to every company concerned.

Thus, in brief, London Coastal Coaches helps to co-ordinate the long-distance work of these many undertakings, and make it possible for thousands to travel to all parts of the country in comfort and confidence. And when the problems that can be thrown up by congested roads, bad weather, and even a few breakdowns are kept in mind, the co-ordinated movement of so many individual coaches is seen as an extraordinary achievement. There are, of course, other coach stations that do comparable work, but London Coastal Coaches was the first and remains the greatest of them all.

IV

Developed and extended as it has been by all the leading undertakings, the motor-coach tour has done much to reawaken the life of the road. During the 'twenties and 'thirties, the hotels and inns which had once been built to cater for parties of tired travellers awoke to the new trade which the coaches were bringing to their

P

doors. In the areas most suitable for touring, new hotels sprang up. In quiet market towns where, for years, only the local trade had been thought of, old inns were rejuvenated. Chromium plate and ill-cooked food too often squandered the tradition of inns whose hospitality the 'stage' once made famous, but at worst they began once more to cater for the needs of genuine travellers and to offer, as every tradesman must, what their patrons wanted. Even the least attractive of the cafés and snack-bars that line the modern highway are an attempt, however ignorant and jejune, to answer the needs of the new coaching age.

Gradually the local tours and the day-excursions to London or to seaside towns increased and extended. Every operator who ran them knew the needs of his particular public, and developed, licence by licence, the kind of excursion that would appeal to them. Trips lasting three to sixteen days were already popular in the 'thirties. Today, such holiday tours can cover a remarkable amount of the country in a week or two, or, taking some town as a centre, can offer various shorter runs to places of interest near it.

The ticket for all such tours, both at home and abroad, covers the cost of hotel accommodation, so that the passenger has no worries about incidental expenses for meals and tips. Once he has paid for his ticket and taken his seat, he has a programme that needs no thought on his part for as long as the tour lasts.

To those independent spirits whose idea of a holiday is to cycle and camp and go great distances on their own, coach tours seem to pander to the lazy and the unadventurous. These individualists are in the minority. The coaches belong to our age. They have carried millions of people into country and amongst people they would not otherwise have seen. They are what millions of holiday-makers want, and the coach operators lay them on. Meals, accommodation, guides, schedules, maps, periods of free time, all are provided. Even a customs official can sometimes be pacified on a passenger's behalf.

All this from time to time has led enthusiastic journalists to claim that the gallant days of stage and mail have been restored. Obviously, nothing can revive that supremacy of the road, even for the sentimentalist who forgets the hardships that belonged with it. Still, the motor-coach has revived certain attributes of travel which the train had banished.

What it cannot do is provide the fast, direct journey of the train which, on account of its speed alone, turns the passing town or village into a blur of rooftops or the rattling outlines of a railway station. The coach, slowed down by traffic, lets one observe the contrast between country and town. It offers its passengers the interest of roadside incident, and, at stopping-places, the simple pleasures of getting out to stretch the legs, admire the view, or pop into the nearest pub. If the railway journey is, as often as not, mechanically precise, the road has still a wealth of spectacle, traffic, incident, activity. The train insulates us from all life but its own. In the coach we still have a chance to share in the life of each place we come to.

And there is another quality of travel by coach. Apart from all that can be seen in this part of the country or that, the passengers in a coach have—for good or ill—a certain unity imposed upon them by the fact that they are all travelling in one vehicle, and not in a series of separate compartments. They are all members of a single party going somewhere together. They are all linked, too, by the fact that, unlike travellers by train, they can see their driver getting them where they want to go. They can see the obstacles that delay him, the lorries, the drove of cattle, the foolish pedestrians, and share the joy of watching him surmount them. And when the coach stops for a time, they can meet each other, and talk, and amuse themselves in a way more reminiscent of the coaching days than of anything offered by the train.

Its opponents claim that coach travel is slower and more monotonous than travel by train. It is slower, certainly. But when all its advantages have been reckoned, cheapness, interest, friendliness, variety, we can understand its steadily growing popularity. A great many people are beginning to realise that speed is not everything.

CHAPTER XXX

The Road Today

'With roads of good, hard, smooth surfaces . . . there would be
less necessity for light railways and tramways, which render the
roads less commodious and useful for ordinary traffic. Motor-
omnibuses would take their place as means of communication
between town and country, and would be much more effective,
inasmuch as they can go to the very doors of the people.'
ALFRED T. DAVIS, in his presidential address to the
Institute of Municipal and County Engineers, 1904.

IN the stage at which road-engineering was last mentioned, in
Chapter VIII, methods had only just been found for laying the
dust-clouds raised by the early motor-cars. In 1910, eleven years
after Lord Montagu of Beaulieu was prevented from driving a
motor-car through the sacred approaches of Parliament, the newest
technique was to coat the surface of the road with tar. And although
the rapid evolution of the motor-car gave urgent impetus to road-
engineering in all parts of Britain, a great deal had to happen before
the highways began to be adequate for the industry.

Historically, 1909 is an important year, not only because the
central Government took responsibility for the roads, but because
in so doing it put an end to centuries of *laissez-faire* in the matter of
road maintenance. This happy change we owe to the motor-car. In
that year, largely through the work of Lloyd George, who was then
Chancellor of the Exchequer, a central Road Board was empowered
to make grants to local authorities. Funds for this purpose were
raised from taxes on vehicle licences and petrol, and, in 1909, the
first road engineers to become civil servants set to work.

In order to widen roads, level them, and make their curves less
dangerous for cars, the Road Board had authority to purchase
narrow strips of land on either side of the highway. In 1913 it was
given the duty of classifying roads. Its work here recalls the system
used by the Romans, for the first two classes of road were to receive
substantial grants towards the cost of maintenance. If, in its purchase of land, the Board had been able to go further, it might have
been able to prevent the ribbon-development which followed the
First World War, from which the country still suffers.

Nevertheless, though only a major prophet could have forecast the growth of the motoring age for which these roads were being developed, the Board made great advances. The ancient Fosse Way between Leicester and Newark was opened up, and many famous coaching routes were turned into sixty-foot highways. During the war of 1914–18, when motor transport became essential to the country's life, the need for better roads was evident. In these years, too, a material called concrete showed roadmakers what it might be able to offer them presently.

II

After the war, the need for a better national transport organisation was obvious, and the Ministry of Transport, established in 1919 (see Chapter XIX), took over the Road Board. From that time, the work of classifying roads was given to the Minister, whom the Act charged with the duty of 'dealing in the ordinary course of departmental business with road construction, improvement, maintenance and development'. The road development plans which the Ministry prepared (and which helped to relieve post-war unemployment) needed considerably more money than the old Road Improvements Fund could provide. To meet this need, the Roads Act of 1920 introduced a new system of licensing, the proceeds of which were to go into a new Road Fund and be used for grants to local authorities, half the cost of maintenance and of minor improvements of first-class roads, and a quarter of the cost of similar work on second-class roads. Additional sums were provided for major improvements.

These contributions were later increased to seventy-five per cent in the case of Class I roads (which came to include most main highways and what were later known as Trunk Roads) and sixty per cent in the case of Class II roads (which, for the most part, are the links between Class I roads, and between the smaller towns). A third classification was introduced in 1946, and fifty per cent of the upkeep of Class III is now paid for by the State.

It would be disingenuous to hide the fact that the passenger road transport industry, as a very considerable user, is critical of the niggardly sums of money spent by the Government on the nation's roads, particularly when compared with the enormous levies of fuel tax, purchase tax, and licence duty from road users. Thus, while the Government took £443,180,000 in tax and duty in the year ended March 31st, 1955, and about £494,000,000 in the following year, the amounts spent on the roads were £38,500,000 and £47,000,000 respectively, i.e., less than ten per cent in each case. This disparity is all the more resented by the industry because of its rooted dislike of the tax on bus fuel oil, which it looks on as unjust.

III

The coming of the mass-produced motor car and the rapid expansion of the whole transport industry required a more thorough overhaul of the country's road system than might have been expected in 1919. In view of this, critics feared that the grants local authorities were to expect from the Exchequer would make them compete with one another in a way that must prevent any national policy from developing. This did not happen. Since the Roads Act arranged for major constructional work to be dealt with separately, and the Minister's Divisional Engineers, working in liaison with County Councils, impartially considered the proposals submitted to them, roads which were judged essential to public safety, to industrial development, or to town planning were given priority, and the Minister, in fact, was able to co-ordinate the various local plans.

But the Roads Act of 1920 was not enough in itself. For when the Local Government Act of 1929 made County Boroughs responsible for all public roads within their boundaries, Urban Districts responsible for all unclassified roads in theirs, and the County Councils responsible for all others, the repair of principal highways like the Great West Road was left a patchwork operation, shared by a number of local authorities. Each County had its own Surveyor, whose ideas about road widening, bridges, surfacing, etc., did not necessarily agree with those of his neighbour. Such lack of system could never have produced highways capable of dealing with the ever-increasing volume of traffic which, in the 'thirties, was surprising everyone.

The Trunk Roads Act of 1936 therefore put four thousand five hundred miles of these main highways under the complete control of the Minister; and he, using the County Councils as his agent for the work involved, became responsible for their total upkeep. Since then the Ministry of Transport has had a department which deals exclusively with Trunk roads and works in close connection with the Town and Country Planning authorities.

Needless to say, miles and miles of constructional work did not go forward as smoothly as this legislation intended. Like Telford and McAdam before them, road engineers in the new motoring age had their experiments to make and their problems to overcome. Soon after the First World War, when ex-Army 'jitneys' and char-à-bancs were chasing one another in competitive confusion, it was clear that nearly every road was going to need something more than a patchwork dressing of tar. As solid-tyred vehicles continued to tear the roads to pieces, experiments with different types of surface went forward; and when the pneumatic tyre was established at the end of the decade, tarmacadam seemed the most successful. Since then, bitumen has become an important road material. Today, with the latest equipment, this type of road can be laid surprisingly fast, and its dustless, waterproof surface gives tyres a firmer grip than tar.

A further device is the building of by-pass roads to keep through-traffic away from the centre of busy towns. It is an irony of history that towns where the councils were once indignant because the Turnpike roads passed them by are now only too anxious to have circular routes which keep through-traffic from their already overcrowded streets.

At the time of writing, Oxford is a staring example of the many cities with narrow, hopelessly overcrowded streets, that cannot devise alternative routes unless they pierce the surrounding countryside with yet another concrete highway, and encourage the red-roofed villages to which such roads give rise. Thus, since the cure for overcrowded streets can be almost as bad as the disease, the ancient city of Oxford has an almost insoluble traffic problem.

IV

The truth is that modern highways are less easily decided and brought into being than most people would suppose. They are intended to serve the community, but the men who consider them on the community's behalf often prefer the evil they know to the uncertain results of another highway. If this over-populated island is not to be broken into tiny fragments by multitudinous roads until a man may have to travel ten miles from a city before he can lose the noise of traffic, the modern highway needs to be something more than a strip of concrete measuring the shortest distance between two points. And if it cannot always curve gracefully, taking in suitable places and avoiding those in which it is not wanted, at least it can be something more than one of the utilitarian bare white scars in the chalk hills of southern England, meanly lined with cafés, villas, shacks, and petrol stations.

On the other hand beautiful, tree-lined roads cannot be made easily in Britain. Land is precious; the acreages which are necessary for the magnificent dual-carriageways of New England, Canada, or Germany can here be achieved only at the expense of agriculture. A few of our latest highways may have reached comparable standards, but only a few. And although our road engineers may want the roads of Britain to be as efficient and pleasant as any in the world, their correct setting will cost time and money. Trees take years to grow, and a road of this kind can cost a hundred thousand pounds a mile.

Still, this is a poor answer to the motorist who, tired of congested roads, proclaims the need of new ones. Even if it were possible to meet his demand, the transport industry is growing at such speed that the leisureliness the roads had once can never be regained. A realistic view was emphasised by Mr. Thomas Sharp in his book *Town and Countryside*, as early as the 'twenties.

> Even if we opened up a multitude of new roads, still we would not get the ancient quietness and calm back again. We should only invade still further the sweet peace of the countryside; a double loss. We must now acknowledge that the measure of the road's success is its ability to provide for travel with reasonable speed, safety and comfort. Pleasantness may perhaps be retained: everything that can be done to retain it must be done. But safe, swift movement must be the first consideration. We must make the principal roads suitable for hurrying traffic; we may even have to limit certain types of traffic to them, such as charabanc and lorry traffic—and, perhaps, by so doing, by concentrating noise and speed where it already is, we may still retain some peace and pleasure on the by-roads.

Many a modern highway has obliterated the original road on which the Roman legions marched and along which 'stage' and 'mail' capered and flew towards London. But each road and its users played their part, and helped to make the road what it is. Today, when we look forward, it is hard to be certain of anything. Yet we may feel reasonably sure that, as long as there are men to travel, they will need a road.

CHAPTER XXXI

The Road Ahead

'Transport is a social function, its objective the improvement of
the standard of life of a population.'
C. E. R. SHERRINGTON: *A Hundred Years of Inland Transport.*

THE intention of this book has been to take the history of the
industry up to 1948, the year when the Transport Act of the
previous year came into force. This Act declared its intention of
providing 'an efficient, adequate, economical and properly inte-
grated system of public inland transport and port facilities within
Great Britain for passengers and goods. . . .' Later, the Act was
modified so far as road transport was concerned by the Transport
Act of 1953. As I said in the Foreword, it is no part of a work such
as this to take sides on the respective advantages or disadvantages
of nationalisation. Even so, a word must be said on the special
position of road passenger transport as the result of the two Acts
in question.

Under the 1947 Act the buses in the Greater London area and
those outside it were ultimately to be brought under the control
of the Commission. The London Passenger Transport Board was
disbanded, and the undertaking transferred to the London Transport Executive, a 'limb' of the British Transport Commission.
This entailed no very drastic revolution, for the L.P.T.B. was
already a public board, as its name implied. The effect of the Act
was to bring London Transport into a public national system (that
is to say, under the same ownership as the railways) in place of a
public London system, which had a pooling scheme with the
railway companies. That position the 1953 Act left virtually
unaltered.

Outside London, the 1947 Act contemplated, but only
'permissively', 'area schemes' of nationalisation, by which the
buses would be brought under the control of Regional Boards
responsible to the British Transport Commission. The one scheme
submitted for approval, however, met with such determined opposition that it was never approved by the Minister, and the machinery
for the schemes was abolished by the Act of 1953. In the result, the
vast majority of provincial services remained under the banners of
municipal or private enterprise, as they are today.

The Commission, however, acquired all the shares in the Scottish Motor Traction, Thomas Tilling, and 'Red and White' Groups. With regard to the first two Groups, the Commission, as successors to the former railway companies, already had very large interests, amounting to some forty-five per cent, in the companies concerned; and when Thomas Tilling Ltd., under the Chairmanship of Sir Frederick Heaton, agreed to sell their holdings to the B.T.C., the latter, through the machinery of the Companies Acts, were able to obtain control of all the shares in these companies. They were also able to buy all the shares in the Red and White Group, where the railways had not been concerned.

As a result, the Commission are today the sole owners of shares in a number of companies, operating about fourteen thousand vehicles, roughly one-fifth of the whole, if London is excluded. The company structure has been left intact, and, with some exceptions, names remain unchanged.

Under the Act of 1953 there is power for the Minister of Transport to require the Commission to relinquish control in these companies; but at the time of going to Press this power has not been exercised.

II

As must be clear by now, bus services should be essentially local affairs. They have been built up by men who understand the needs of their public and the best way to meet them. As long as Company and Municipal Undertaking managers and their local staffs are able to keep their services flexible and to adapt them freely to the needs of the public which they alone understand, this fundamental requirement is met.

On the other hand, centralisation in any industry always runs the risk of building up a top-heavy administration which, for road transport particularly, could have a devastating effect on the men who have to provide services in this place or that, miles away from the administrators. In a country which is in danger of becoming more and more bureaucratic, this tendency is well understood.

Still, whatever the future brings, and no matter what controversies are aroused, we come back to solid, four-wheeled fact. Let Governments decide what they may, buses must go on running. Services started to meet local needs have grown into a transport system on which all Britain depends. No one can dispute the achievement, or fail to pay it tribute. Many services today are owned jointly by independent companies, and by publicly-owned bus undertakings; many, as we have seen, are operated jointly with the transport authorities of the various municipalities. This proves at least that these joint ownerships and working agreements are effective. Politics do not upset them. Such shared services have been brought about by men who understand their advantages; and members of the public do not often care who happens to own the buses they ride in, as long as those buses run punctually, are comfortable, and charge reasonable fares.

By and large these demands are met. The range is wide. From the urban services on which industry and commerce depend, to the rural services which take children to school, deliver newspapers, bring villagers to the town and townsmen to the country, the list of services which the modern industry offers is all but endless. Most people take for granted the transport on which they rely for their holidays, to reach their entertainments, to visit their friends, and to return home at the day's end. On their journeys to church, to the theatre, to shop, to play football, few, unless something goes wrong, stop to consider the vehicle that carries them, the organisation that lies behind it, still less the story that has brought both of them into being. The bus is there. All you have to do is to get on board and pay the fare.

III

I said a moment ago that the public takes the services for granted until something goes wrong. Not every branch of the industry pays enough attention to the vital question of public relations. Now and then, the primary object of serving the public has been allowed to come second to the convenience of the men who run the buses. With the long-distance coaches the relationship of the public is satisfactory, though one must note that most travel agencies state that they will accept no responsibility if a passenger by coach who has booked his seat finds no seat waiting for him.

On the whole, too, the country services satisfy and please their users. Where they do not—where buses drive away from stations when a train has just come in and passengers are running towards them—the fault is not always with the schedules. A bus which waits for a train at one end of its run may thereby miss one at the other. Very many undertakings have to decide which of two stations their buses will connect with. In nineteen cases out of twenty, the grievance of the bus that just fails to connect with the train can be justified, even to the bitterest complainant, by showing him the detailed interlocking schedule which would be thrown out of gear by the change he clamours for. (In a really well-run undertaking, which understands public relations work, a representative will call on him at his home and tell him the whole story.)

Still, there are grievances. Of these, the worst is the crawling bus in the cities. This the public looks on as a breach of faith. Though buses cannot run to time as trains are supposed to, a man who knows that a bus normally takes ten minutes between A and B is justly angry if, unhampered by traffic, it deliberately takes fifteen or twenty and makes him miss his train.

Whenever this practice of deliberate dawdling has been attacked in Parliament, the official answer has always been that it is necessary for the preservation of schedules. The bus must not reach its terminus too soon. The general public is not satisfied with this argument. Neither am I—although I have heard many other arguments in support of it.

Schedule tyranny is also responsible for the bus that races past the request stop, its driver stonily unseeing of the uplifted hands, and the conductor who yells 'Full up' when there are empty seats on top. The public can be maddening, heaven knows, and conductors and drivers have every excuse for the impatience they sometimes show, but the organisation itself should not add to their burdens.

In the long run, anything that annoys the customer is bad for the business.

IV

Passenger road transport is a great industry. Bus and coach have changed the outlook of our people. They are the people's carriages, as Train called his tram: they take us wherever we want to go. To the men who have made the industry what it is we owe a very great debt. Yet what they have done is only the most recent chapter in a long, long story that began before history was written or schedules dreamed of, in the England of the Greenways.

Thus, at last, we regain our theme, the road. For many chapters now we have all but lost sight of it beneath a crowd of buses—as one all but loses sight of the surface of Oxford Street on a busy day, getting at best a glimpse of the smooth dark surface here and there, in the gaps between vehicles. And, once again, we come up against the paradox that, while the road makes the vehicles, the vehicles make the road. The road makes the vehicles, in the sense that a new vehicle cannot be tested, much less used, until there is a road fit for it. On the other hand, just as the first crude carrying device, too primitive even to be called a wagon, made a track in the grass over which it was dragged, the coach of today creates the road which can safety bear it.

We see this even more clearly in America, where the needs of fast traffic have called into being noble systems of roads to carry it, and on the Continent, in the Autobahnen and the wide straight roads of France. We are beginning to see it in Ireland, where miles of flat country favour the building of immensely wide, straight, level road-ways. Short of some geological upheaval, or the most drastic and uncharacteristic levelling, our British roads will always roll.

But, wherever the example, the basic truth is clear. Our great roads, west and north, are the direct offspring of the Roman roads, and, before them, the Greenways. The need of man to travel and transport his merchandise has found its satisfaction in the making of roads which represent his best endeavour.

It is unlikely, now, that anything less than the total collapse of a civilisation will allow Britain's roads to fall into the neglect they suffered for so many hundred years; since on the roads civilisation itself depends.

Today, we are working to develop them. 1948 is the limit of our survey, a fact which excludes some notable recent feats of road-making: but, even within our limit, we have abundant grounds for saying that passenger transport by road awaits immense develop-ments in which the roads perforce must share.

'Keep right on to the end of the road,' sang the great Harry Lauder, and the metaphor proclaimed full trust in a literal truth. There would always be a road, and it would be so made and so maintained that one could, keep right on to its end.

Bibliography

ALLAN, R., *The Royal Road* (Pitman and Sons, 1946).

ANDERSON, R. M. C., *The Roads of England* (Benn, 1932).

BARR, ROBERT, *I Travel the Road* (Quality Press Ltd., 1945).

BOULTON, W. H., *The Pageant of Transport Through the Ages* (Sampson Low, Marston and Co., 1931).

BURKE, THOMAS, *Travel in England* (Batsford, 1942).

CROSLAND-TAYLOR, W. J., *Crosville The Sowing and the Harvest* (Littlebury Bros. Ltd., 1948).

———— *State Owned without Tears*, 1948–53 (Littlebury Bros. Ltd., 1954).

DEFOE, DANIEL, *A Tour through England and Wales* (1724–6).

DOWDING, W., *Thirty Years of Progress in Passenger Road Transport* (A History of the Red and White Group of Omnibus Companies, 1950).

FIENNES, CELIA, *Diary* (c. 1697).

FULFORD, ROGER, *Five Decades of B.E.T.* (Argus Press, 1946).

GILBEY, SIR WALTER, *Early Carriages and Roads* (Vinton & Co., 1903).

HARPER, C. G., *Stage Coach and Mail in Days of Yore* (Chapman and Hall, 1903).

HIPPISLEY-COX, R., *The Green Roads of England* (Methuen, 1914).

INSTITUTE OF TRANSPORT. *Proceedings*.

McCAUSLAND, HUGH, *The English Carriage* (Batchworth Press, 1948).

MARGARY, IVAN D., *Roman Roads in Britain: I* (Phoenix House, 1955).

MOORE, HENRY CHARLES, *Omnibuses and Cabs* (Chapman and Hall, 1902).

OLIVER, JANE, *The Ancient Roads of England* (Cassell & Co., 1949).

PILCHER, R. STUART, *Road Transport Operation—Passenger* (Pitman and Sons, 1930).

————*Road Passenger Transport* (Pitman and Sons, 1937).

PUBLIC TRANSPORT ASSOCIATION. *Conference Reports*.

REYNARDSON, BIRCH, *Down the Road*.

SCOTT-GILES, C. W., *The Road Goes On* (Epworth Press, 1946).

SEKON, G. A., *Locomotion in Victorian London* (Oxford University Press, 1938).

Shakespeare's England, Vol. I.

SHERRINGTON, C. E. R., *A Hundred Years of Inland Transport*, 1830–1933 (Duckworth, 1934.)

SOMERFIELD, VERNON, *London Buses* (St. Catherine's Press, 1933).

—————— *London Transport* (L.P.T.B. Publication, 1934).

STRAUSS, RALPH, *Carriages and Coaches* (Martin Secker, 1912).

WRIGHT, W. H. K., *Locomotion: Past and Present.* (Transactions of the Plymouth Institution and Devon and Cornwall Natural History Society, 1897–98).

INDEX